the histor
BRITISH BUS
SERVICES

John Hibbs

David & Charles

A DAVID & CHARLES BOOK

David & Charles is a subsidiary of F&W (UK) Ltd.,
an F&W Publications Inc. company

First published in the UK in 1968
Second revised edition 1989
First paperback edition 2004

A catalogue record for this book is available from the British Library.

ISBN 0 7153 8962 9 hardback
ISBN 0 7153 1938 8 paperback

Printed in Great Britain by CPI Bath Press
for David & Charles
Brunel House   Newton Abbot   Devon

Visit our website at www.davidandcharles.co.uk

David & Charles books are available from all good bookshops; alterna-
tively you can contact our Orderline on (0)1626 334555 or write to us
at FREEPOST EX2 110, David & Charles Direct, Newton Abbot,
TQ12 4ZZ (no stamp required UK mainland).

CONTENTS

Foreword by Professor T. C. Barker

CONTENTS

FOREWORD
by Professor T. C. Barker, London School of Economics

When this book was first published, in 1968, it was the only introduction to the subject. It still is. It has been out of print for some time and its reappearance is warmly to be welcomed, especially as it now includes an additional chapter, bringing the story up to date.

The motor car, and to some extent the motor bicycle, have been given more than their fair share of attention by those who write about road passenger transport; the pedal cycle and the motor bus not enough. (In Britain the tramcar and the trolley bus, though important in their relatively short day, seem to have been a passing phase.) Only the fortunate minority could afford cars or motor bicycles before the Second World War, and even today about forty per cent of households do not have the use of a car. It is the motor bus which, taking the twentieth century as a whole, has brought the social benefits of the internal combustion engine to most people. It has been an essential part of all our lives, even those of car owners, especially when we were younger; and it has been of particular importance to country dwellers, as those who have suffered from declining rural bus services are realising to their cost. This readable, evocatively illustrated book is to be commended to all those who are interested in discovering when and how these valuable, if unglamorous, and often criticised bus services, recalled for the arresting colour of the vehicles if for nothing else, came to be developed, and the reasons for their present difficulties.

Professor Hibbs is not only a well-known transport specialist. He has himself worked in the bus industry, and writes from practical experience.

Theo Barker
1989

CHAPTER ONE

WHAT IT'S ABOUT

LIKE many other good things, the omnibus came from France, where it was invented by the philosopher, mathematician and scientist, Blaise Pascal. It has never been so much a special type of vehicle as a special principle of public transport operation. It was a Frenchman, too, who invented the name for this vehicle that carries anyone and goes everywhere, though the English abbreviation has spread throughout the world. Americans may call a coach a bus, and a trolleybus a trolley-coach, but the British can take pride in the history of their plebeian word which has found its way onto bus-stop signs in most unlikely places.

We tend to think of the bus as being peculiarly British, and many foreigners do no doubt believe that, in Britain, everyone rides in red double-deckers, so different from their own sleek and pastel-coloured saloons. It would be amusing to attempt to relate national characteristics to favoured types of buses and coaches— clearly, Paris is distinguished by its buses from anywhere else in France, and even within the British Isles there are subtle differences, each city having its own flavour and the remoter country districts recalling memories of earlier days.

Few countries outside Britain have carried the development of bus services to the same length, perhaps because so many states limited the growth of the industry in the interest of their railways. In Britain, the industry remained unregulated until steps were taken to protect the railway companies in the late 'twenties, but by then bus and coach operation had become established on so broad a base that its growth continued. Bus services have been shared out among operators, giving each a virtual monopoly on his route or, at most, sharing it with a few others. But while a part of the industry is owned by the State, a large part is not, and much of the enterprise shown in the transport of private parties may be due to the competition in this field between the big companies and the multitude of small businesses, some of them one-man-one-bus-concerns.

The bus in Britain has become, on the whole, a lower-middle and working-class means of transport, in contrast to Pascal's buses in Paris in 1662, which were forbidden by royal letters patent to carry peasants or soldiers. This has not always been true, for at least until the end of the nineteenth century the tram was the lower class vehicle, and when tramways were first built in London, Train's line by Pimlico was charging a penny against the fourpence charged for a similar journey by bus. The *Railway Times* observed in 1897 that the bus 'was not a working-class conveyance'.

Although circumstances have changed, and buses have acquired a different image, there are still exceptions to the general rule, such as the express coaches which (outside the summer weekend peaks) carry a somewhat select clientele made up of those who can afford to spend time more readily than money; frequently students and retired people. For many, however, a bus is something frequently seen but never ridden in. How many people after all can report accurately upon the colour of their local buses? Even so percipient an author as Glyn Daniel slipped up on this when, in *The Cambridge Murders*, he sent a red bus up a road where only green or navy blue ones were to be seen.

Throughout the history of transport in modern times, the public service vehicle has played its varying part, constantly adjusting itself to changing demand. At one time supreme (in the shape of the mail coach), it still flourished in the humbler form of the omnibus and the carrier's cart when the railways took the front of the stage. When the electric motor and the internal-combustion engine changed the balance of power, the motor coach and omnibus—with, for a while, the trolleybus and tramcar—caused a social revolution as marked as that which accompanied the railway age. And now that the private car has become commonplace and generally available, the public road transport industry has once again had to adapt itself to changed conditions.

Socially, the motor bus has never been quite sure of its place in the order of things, and operators still tend to wince when people refer to modern motor coaches as 'charas', with the strong flavour of pub outings in the 'twenties. The tramcar, on the other hand, was throughout its days a proletarian vehicle, which is perhaps why it became rather unfashionable in its later years. But the bus was welcomed in many places as an alternative to the undesirable tram, and because of its lower capital cost was able to serve less crowded routes. This meant that it could provide public transport for the wealthier suburbs, which neither wanted nor could justify a tramway. Nevertheless, although Oxford accepted motor buses as preferable to electric trams in 1913, A. C. Godley expressed a deeply-felt reservation in his famous lines beginning :

> What is this that roareth thus?
> Can it be a motor bus?

Buses in general, however, do not figure prominently in contemporary literature, though in *The George and the Crown* Sheila Kaye Smith gave a good account of the life of a conductor in what is manifestly Southdown Motor Services, and one or two more recent novels have described the same sort of work today. Richard Hoggart, in *The Uses of Literacy*, also has an extensive passage on the place of the coach outing in the working class community of a northern city (pages 146-148 of the Pelican edition). There is a descriptive passage about Nottingham trolleybuses in Alan Sillitoe's *Saturday Night and Sunday Morning* and Philip Larkin evokes the flavour of buses in a Midland city in *A Girl in Winter*. One aspect of the recent tendency for novelists to concern themselves with life outside the middle and upper classes—the so-called 'kitchen sink' literature— has been for commonplace things like bus journeys to become more acceptable in fiction.

Poets in the 'thirties paid special attention to urban and industrial landscapes, and Louis MacNeice in *An Eclogue for*

Christmas (1934) paints this picture of a city street at dusk in a passage which comes at the turning point of the poem :

> But yet there is beauty narcotic and deciduous
> In this vast organism grown out of us,
> On all the traffic-islands stand white globes like moons
> The city's haze is clouded amber that purrs and croons,
> And tilting by the noble curve bus after tall bus comes
> With an osculation of yellow light, with a glory like
>   Chrysanthemums.

Perhaps unfortunately, the motor bus seems to be post-Betjeman, whose evocations of the tram :

> Thunder under, rumble over
> Train and tram alternate go

and :

> O the after-tram-ride quiet

are memorable. But Larkin, in bringing Hull to life in 'Here' (*The Whitsun Weddings*, 1964) very properly includes the trolleybus :

> And residents from raw estates brought down
> The dead straight miles by stealing flat-faced trolleys,
> Push through plate-glass swing doors to their desires.

Perhaps one of the most effective references to buses in recent literature is to be found in one of John Wyndham's short stories, 'Random Quest', where he gives point to his 'twist in time' theme by making his hero see the word 'General' in gold letters on the scarlet side of a London bus in 1953. Although he has to explain in a digression that this has not been possible since the formation of the London Passenger Transport Board in 1933, he seems to make a sharper impact in this way than if he had used the horse-bus to establish his point.

*   *   *

What then is the linking theme in a story that stretches from the appearance of the hackney in the early seventeenth century down to the motorway coach of today? What were the roots of the motor bus industry of Great Britain? They are to be found in the story of the stage coaches, the carriers' carts, the horse-drawn omnibuses and trams, through the beginnings of mechanisation with steam and electric tramways and early motor vehicles, and through the pioneering days when the industry was created upon all these older foundations. The buses owe their existence to men of vision : engineers, businessmen, railway officers and the humbler 'pirates' and owner-drivers; to the ability of busmen to discover and serve the needs of the public. They owe not a little to their competitors, the railways, and still more to the financiers who created the great combines. Perhaps they owe most of all to the men 'on the back', the conductors and drivers, fitters, regulators and all the individuals for whom they have been a way of life.

This book will try to tell their story, and to trace the continuing thread that runs through it, as well as to show where it fits into the wider history of its period. It is written from no particular viewpoint, but will try to balance the contributions of all the different interests that make up the motor bus industry today. It is not meant to be a scholarly history—that has still to be written—so much as a story that should be told all of a piece, so that those who want to know more can see where all the pieces fit in.

This history of the industry falls into four parts, to each of which a chapter has been devoted. First comes the background story, from the early days up to the appearance of the motor vehicle. Then follows the period of experiment, by the end of which the motor bus had established itself in both the mechanical and the commercial senses. This lasted from 1895 to 1919, and during these years certain decisions were reached that were to influence the subsequent history of the industry. During the post-war years, the phenomenal expansion of the industry was matched by its technical advance, and by its impact upon railway traffics. This was the period of the so-called 'pirates', remembered with affection or acrimony according to the experience of those who knew them. Towards its end, the Royal Commission on Transport of 1929 expressed the official attitude to the industry as it then was, when it recommended a new system of licensing that would encourage 'rationalisation as a prelude to nationalisation'. At this time also a major clash between the motor bus combine and the railways (armed with power to run their own buses) was avoided by a series of negotiations which included a take-over bid and consequent battle for control reminiscent of more recent commercial history.

The next period opens with the new system of licensing coming into effect under the Road Traffic Act of 1930, whose passage forms one of the most important landmarks in the story. Because of its effect upon the industry, a chapter is devoted to describing the Act and its impact, while another describes the growth and importance of the express coach services and tours which today represent the most prosperous sector of the trade. The main narrative is continued with the story of the industry under statutory control, the hardship and heroism of the war years, leading on to the division of the combine in 1942, which is seen to have foreshadowed the different attitudes towards nationalisation shown by H. C. Drayton and Sir J. Frederick Heaton six years later.

The next period commences with the formation of the British Transport Commission in 1948 and some of the more important developments since then are recorded in the hope that they may be more easily understood in the light of what has gone before. The problems of today are never the same as those of yesterday, but they are related and this must be the justification for going back to the start of the story. Road passenger transport has a long and distinguished tradition, and for our purpose we must trace it from a very early stage in its development, 270 years before the motor bus appeared.

It was with the formation of the Commission in 1948 that the book originally ended, but now it is becoming plain that a new period of change was even then being born, and for this edition there is a further chapter, bringing the story up to the threshold of what promises to be perhaps the most challenging time since the motor bus first emerged. But the past can often illuminate the present, and maybe the story we have to tell will help us to understand the British bus industry as it faces the future.

CHAPTER TWO

BACKGROUND AND ORIGINS:
1625-1895

ONLY an arbitrary date can be chosen for the beginning of a story such as this. When the first motor car was imported from France there were men who saw its commercial possibilities, and these were the pioneers. But to understand how the motor wagonettes of the 'nineties became the motorbuses and touring coaches of today, we must first look at their ancestors, and at the foundations of the industry in the previous 300 years.

THE PRINCIPLES

As prosperity and settlement grew during the seventeenth century, public passenger transport emerged in response to a growing demand for a means of travel cheaper than the private coach. The hackney carriage, which appeared about 1625, embodies the principle of *plying for hire*, a means by which travel could be cheapened by spreading the cost of keeping a carriage over a greater number of passengers. The number, however, depended upon the cab-driver's success in finding his customers, and this was largely a matter of chance; if he merely waited for them to come to him, many of them might prefer to walk to their destination. Today's cruising taxi is faced with precisely the same problem.

The answer was found in a second principle, at first applied independently. This was *scheduled operation*, which is itself very much older than modern transport but found a new form with the development of the stage coach. By prior advertisement of a regular timetable for a service over a defined route, passengers could be brought together, or even persuaded to go out of their way, in order to use a public vehicle. It thus became possible to provide more seats, spreading the costs over a still greater number of customers and so cheapening travel still more. The omnibus combines both of these principles, which is why it is cheaper to use a bus than a taxi.

But the omnibus appeared some 200 years after the hackney. In the meantime, the principle of scheduled operation had been taken up by the stage coaches, and subsequently by the railways, although neither could truly be said to be plying for hire. Stage coaches flourished in England from about the middle of the seventeenth century, linking London with the larger provincial cities and extending into Scotland. Travel at first was rough and slow, but it was an improvement over the stage wagon, which remained the cheapest form of transport, and it offered a means of making longer journeys than were possible by carrier's cart. It also had the advantage of enabling passengers to travel in company, which was some protection against footpads, as well as offering the assurance of a driver who knew the way.

By the end of the eighteenth century, public transport had become a well-established industry providing various levels of comfort and convenience and a widespread network of services. John Palmer's mail coaches, the first of which began to run between London, Bath and Bristol on 2 August 1784, offered a superior class of travel, while the 'flying wagons' of Pickford and other carriers offered an intermediate stage. The improvement of the roads under the influence of Telford and Macadam, and of the vehicles themselves as the result of better springing, made travel more comfortable, while the increased carrying-capacity of the coaches allowed fares to be progressively reduced. The industry was highly competitive, with numerous owners putting vehicles on the more popular routes and cutting times and fares to attract traffic. The less profitable routes had the consolation of offering a monopoly to the operator prepared to serve them, and therefore less incentive to cheapen the cost of travel.

By the end of the coaching age the industry had attracted a

sizeable investment. When the Pickford partnership was re-organised in 1817, the firm's assets were valued at £48,000. The London coaching trade was then largely in the hands of five operators, the most substantial one being W. J. Chaplin who, in 1838, owned sixty-eight coaches. The others were Benjamin Horne, Edward Sherman, Mrs Mountain and Mrs Nelson. Sherman, an aggressive character, was responsible for a number of improvements in the standards of operation. He brought to coaching a flair for organisation rather than any great technical ability (he was not a 'horsey' man and was never seen to drive a coach), and his main contribution was to arrange for the horsing of his coaches in shorter stages, so that greater distances could be covered by daylight. In the face of his competition, the 'Beehive' coach to Manchester was equipped by its owners with numbered, spring-cushion seats and an interior lamp for its overnight journey. Sherman himself, competing with Chaplin's 'Defiance' on this route, had his coach, the 'Telegraph', designed with flattened springs to give a low centre of gravity.

But while stage coach services were developing to an extent comparable with the express coach industry of today, and carriers were laying the foundations of today's country bus services, most towns were still too small to encourage any growth of urban public transport, except in the form of the hackney. London was a different matter and its size accounts for the establishment there of short-stage coach services, running from the City or the West End to the suburbs, surrounding towns such as Croydon, and to country districts. These included routes like Paddington to the Bank, which were purely urban, as well as commuters' services and others reminiscent of the present-day function of the Green Line. They were not bus services as we know them, because of their high fares and the assumption that seats would be booked in advance (though casual passengers were not refused). They paid a tax based on mileage, but varying with seating capacity and as, even with four horses, they were restricted to eighteen passengers, there was little scope for lowering fares by spreading costs over a bigger load. Moreover, to protect the hackney cabs whose monopoly had been established in an attempt to reduce

B

congestion, they were forbidden to carry passengers on journeys wholly within central London.

There is little evidence of similar development outside London, although the distinction between long- and short-stage coaches was not exact and circumstances varied in different places. Coaches began to operate over the twelve miles between Rochdale and Manchester in 1790, with fares of 2s 6d inside and 1s 6d out, and these were certainly more closely related to the inter-urban buses of today than to the express motor coach. Districts like the Black Country offered sufficient concentration of population for public transport to develop and by 1835 (when omnibuses had only just started running in Birmingham), West Bromwich had, among other longer routes, coaches to Birmingham every hour, to Wolverhampton eight times a day, to Dudley five times, to Wednesbury twice and to Walsall once. An exception to the general rule was the city of Edinburgh, scene of a number of pioneering developments, which had a service to and from Leith in about 1610. But over most of Great Britain at the close of the coaching age, urban services were rare and inter-urban services between neighbouring towns were generally provided by long-distance coaches passing through.

THE COMING OF THE RAILWAY

The story of the collapse of the stage coach industry with the coming of the railway has been frequently told. The railway offered a cheaper form of travel because it could carry far more pasengers for each unit of motive power, and it was so much faster that, even at a higher charge, it would still have been more attractive to passengers. The small and slow road vehicles could not compete on either score.

From the outset, the railway developed the principle of scheduled operation; the philosophy of railway building, with its proliferation of branch lines and intermediate stations, was that every community other than the smallest should be accessible by rail from all others; and that every journey, long or short, should be catered for. The extent to which this became a practical possibility has lead to the misconception that the road transport industry counted for little during the railway age.

The mechanisation of public transport spread over a period of about 100 years. Almost by chance, the railways obtained an advantage over the coaches that enabled them to dominate the market for most of the time. Nevertheless, road passenger transport remained a live industry and the traditions of the coaching age were not entirely lost. Michael Robbins defines the railway age as lasting from 1830 to 1914; an age which, he very rightly says, 'left its mark on the physical landscape, on social organisation, on political groupings, and on the map of the world'. He would surely agree that the railway age saw equally substantial achievements in road passenger transport.

It was by no means a foregone conclusion that the mechanisation of transport should have been so closely bound up with the railways. A model vehicle had been powered by steam before 1687, and the idea of using steam for traction continued to fascinate engineers until, in 1769, Joseph Cugnot built in France a full-sized vehicle which was capable of a speed of two and a quarter miles an hour. A second machine built by Cugnot may be seen in Paris today. Various experiments in France, England and America followed, until in 1801 Richard Trevithick, a Cornishman, put the first really successful steam carriage on the road. There was then a pause, until the years between 1820 and 1840 saw rapid progress with the advent of the steam railway engine, the emergence of the steamboat, and the development of road steamers. This was a period when British engineering was at its height and its contribution to world transportation by rail and sea was of revolutionary importance. Why, in view of such success, was steam-driven road transport almost entirely a failure?

Certainly it was not for want of trying. Coach building had become a highly specialised trade, and improved suspension as well as better roads made possible reasonably comfortable vehicles. Other important developments dating from this period included both shaft and chain drives, the idea of change-speed gears and the Ackerman principle of steering. The fundamental invention needed for a mechanical drive—the differential—was patented in France and England by separate inventors almost simultaneously. Nor was the steam engine exclusive to private carriages; amongst the most successful vehicles were the steam coaches with which various services were operated. On 21 February 1831, Sir Charles Dance started to run a service between Gloucester and Cheltenham three times a day, using vehicles built by Sir Goldsworthy Gurney. The overall average speed for the nine miles was between ten and twelve miles an hour, and as this was little better than the stage coaches, their strong opposition soon forced the service off the road. Walter Hancock was more successful in London, both mechanically and commercially. In that same month he started what seems to have been a demonstration service from his works at Stratford into London, and by 1833 had found enough support to give hopes of development. The London & Paddington Steam Carriage Company formed in that year actually ran one of Hancock's vehicles, the *Enterprise*, as an omnibus along what later became Shillibeer's original route, but there were misgivings amongst those who were financing the project and, after a fortnight, Hancock took the vehicle back. He continued to operate it himself, along with another vehicle, the *Autopsy* (the origin of some of Hancock's names is obscure), throughout that and the following summer. In 1835, he demonstrated the *Erin* (previously the *Era*) in Dublin, Birmingham and elsewhere, and in the summer of 1836 he ran several services in London. One vehicle he introduced that year, the *Automaton*, seated twenty-two pasengers and reached speeds aproaching 20 mph. But success evaded Hancock and his services were withdrawn after 1840 as a commercial if not a mechanical failure.

In 1834, John Scott Russell ran six vehicles, built by the Steam Carriage Company of Scotland, between Glasgow and Paisley. The running time was about forty minutes and the coaches ran at hourly intervals. This was undoubtedly a success, but after a fatal accident due to sabotage the service had to be abandoned. Macerone and Squire ran a satisfactory vehicle between Paddington and Edgware for some weeks in 1833, and even greater possibilities were foreshadowed by the twelve-seater coach built in 1839-40 by Frank Hills of Deptford, which travelled to Windsor and Brighton and made the return journey to Hastings in one day. The Science Museum's *History of Steam Road Vehicles* comments: 'His long experience proved that passengers could be conveyed by steam vehicles at half the expense and twice the speed of the stage coach'.

These innovations constituted a frontal attack upon the coaching trade, and attracted violent opposition, while at the same time the invention of the steam train was meeting with a success proportionate to its scale. Many of the early railway engineers were men of vision, with heavier responsibilities and greater opportunities than those who tried to run steam engines on the public roads. The railways were civil engineering as well as mechanical undertakings, and represented business on a bigger scale than the nation had ever known. When once they were under way, they had to succeed. The only hint of an alternative was the formation, in January 1834, of the London, Holyhead & Liverpool Steam Coach & Road Company, with Telford and Stephenson as its engineers. It was to provide a stone pavement alongside the existing road, upon which it would operate its own vehicles, as well as charging tolls for private traffic. Had it succeeded, we might have had a very different transport industry today, but the company failed to carry out its intentions.

The opposition of vested interests to the mechanisation of road transport was fierce and effective, supplemented, of course, by the same widespread prejudice that the railway promoters had to overcome. The Turnpike Trusts, which had given the country a network of roads quite capable of carrying steam carriages, discriminated strongly against them, even though the House of Commons Select Committee of 1831 had found that the wheels of horse-drawn vehicles were more likely to damage the roads than those of steamers. The following examples of tolls illustrate the extent of discrimination in 1831:

	Horse Coach	Steam Carriage
Liverpool—Prescott	4s	48s
Ashburton—Totnes	5s	27s
Teignmouth—Dawlish	2s	12s

But the most important factor in the success of steam haulage on rails and its failure on the road was the nation's adoption of the railway as its symbol of progress, and the resultant attraction of investment to the railway companies. By 1840, the development of steam-hauled road vehicles had lost impetus, the decline of the roads had set in, and inventive talent was limited to the development of steam traction engines for short-haul and agricultural work. In 1861 (the year of the first tramway in London), Parliament laid down restrictive conditions and speed limits which the Locomotive Act of 1865 (the 'Red Flag' Act) re-inforced. Steam traction never again came really close to being the means of mechanising road transport.

THE TRAIN, THE COACH AND THE OMNIBUS

It is not necessary to dwell upon the sudden and complete loss of traffic the coaches experienced as each extension of the railway network took place. What is less generally realised is the extent to which the coaches went on providing an essential part of the passenger transport of the railway age. There is little direct evidence of a transfer of capital from coach operation to the expanding omnibus trade, but the link between the decline of one and the growth of the other is too obvious to leave room for doubt.

While Chaplin and Horne came to terms with the railways (Chaplin eventually became chairman of the London & South Western), Sherman opposed and obstructed them and finally passed from the transport scene. As the main lines were built the coach routes were cut back to the advancing railhead, until in time the railway replaced them entirely. William White's gazetteers provide examples of this, and Map 1 illustrates the state of affairs in Essex in 1848. White's Suffolk gazetteer of 1855 lists the various coaches running from Saxmundham and Woodbridge to Ipswich 'to meet the Railway Trains and Steamers from London, &c'. One of these was 'The Railway Co's. 'Bus to Yoxford, via Woodbridge, Melton, Wickham Market and Saxmundham, every Tuesday and Thursday evening at 5, and on

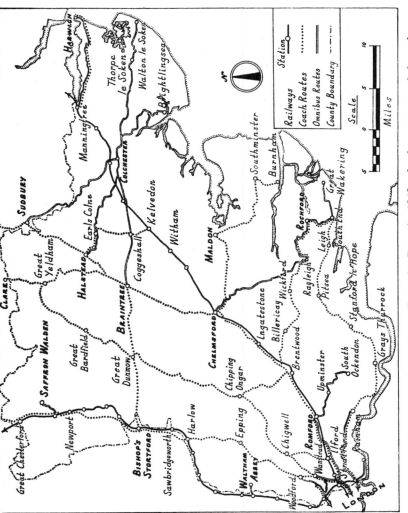

MAP 1. Railways, coaches and omnibuses in Essex in 1848: the horse retreats before the advancing train

Sundays, at 10½ morning, from the Crown & Anchor and Chaise & Pair Inns'. These would, in their turn, have disappeared with the opening of the East Suffolk line in 1859, but although this was the first direct rail connection between Ipswich and Lowestoft, the coaches had already been displaced from through running by the alternative rail route via Norwich.

Similar stories could be told of other parts of the country as the railways expanded. It was, of course, the cream of the industry that was first and hardest hit, and the peculiar glamour of stage-coach travel was quickly lost. However, in many parts of the country stage-coach services survived, supplementing the railways or maintaining the old tradition. The service from Wendover to London ceased operation only in 1892, when the Metropolitan Railway reached the town, while places like Shaftesbury, which lay some distance from the nearest station, had to depend upon horse-drawn connections. On the other hand, there were some parts of the country that suffered at least a temporary worsening of service because of the spread of railways. Michael Robbins, writing in the *Journal of Transport History*, quotes from the diary of R. B. Dockray, an engineer of the LNWR, in 1850:

> (The Buckinghamshire Railway) will make quite a social revo-
> lution in the district which until the opening of this line may
> be said to have been almost cut off from the (? outside,
> entire) world. The opening of the railway in the eastern, western
> and central parts (of England) having diverted from it all the
> old stage coaches which used formerly to afford the means of
> communication; so that unless by the expensive means of posting
> it was no easy matter to move about among the little towns of
> Buckinghamshire.

The stage-coach proprietors, their employees, and the catering industry were not the only people financially interested in horse-drawn transport. The provision of horses and fodder, the construction of vehicles, the disposal of the by-products, all involved interests which had no wish to see road transport die or become mechanised. Alternative employment was required for the assets displaced from stage-coaching, and this was found in the same circumstances that encouraged the growth of the railways. Until the early part of the nineteenth century, towns were hardly large enough to support local services plying for hire on a scheduled basis. The mathematician Pascal and a group of friends had tried to provide such a service in Paris in 1662. It was an initial success (perhaps because of its novelty), but ended with Pascal's death, and urban transport in France as in Britain remained the preserve of the hackney carriage for another century and a half.

The growth of towns that accompanied the expansion of the railways created a demand for a new form of urban passenger transport. Something very like an omnibus was introduced in 1824 between Manchester and Pendleton by a man called John Greenwood, and there were similar developments in France, in the provincial city of Nantes. The success of the French experiments, the invention of the word 'omnibus' and the eventual introduction of the idea to London by George Shillibeer have become familiar, but John Greenwood's Salford vehicle should not be forgotteen.

Whether the Nantes vehicles were consciously modelled on Pascal's invention seems as uncertain as the story that the name came from the slogan of a M. Omnes, a Nantois whose shop was labelled 'Omnes Omnibus'. But the name was certainly inspired and has joined the distinguished company of inter-lingual words like 'bar' and 'post'. The man who brought the idea from Nantes to Paris was Stanislaus Baudry, when in 1828 he put 100 omnibuses on the road, serving ten distinct routes. Success was immediate. Twenty other operators appeared on the scene almost at once, and Shillibeer, a London carriage builder who had interests in Paris and wanted to break into the London hackney monopoly, saw his opportunity. He moved quickly, sending to the Treasury as early as July 1828 a memorial which sought permission to provide a service in London at less than threepence a mile. He proposed the 'more English' name of 'Economist', and said his object was 'to give the public a safe and comfortable conveyance over the London stones at one-fourth the price of the present hackney carriages'.

The Treasury refused Shillibeer's application, but with a foretaste of that ingenuity which was to be shown by bus operators in London nearly a hundred years later, he set about finding a route free of restriction. The monopoly of the hackneys extended to the limits of seventeenth-century London, but the growth of the city had lead to the creation of large housing areas outside 'the stones' that marked that boundary, and through these ran the 'new road'—now Marylebone Road and Euston

OMNIBUS.

G. SHILLIBEER, induced by the universal admiration the above Vehicles called forth at Paris, has commenced running one upon the Parisian mode, from **PADDINGTON to the BANK.**

The superiority of this Carriage over the ordinary Stage Coaches, for comfort and safety, must be obvious, all the Passengers being Inside, and the Fare charged from Paddington to the Bank being One Shilling, and from Islington to the Bank or Paddington, only Sixpence.

The Proprietor begs to add, that a person of great respectability attends his Vehicle as Conductor; and every possible attention will be paid to the accommodation of Ladies and Children.

Hours of Starting :—From Paddington Green to the Bank, at 9, 12, 3, 6, and 8 o'clock ; from the Bank to Paddington, at 10, 1, 4, 7, and 9 o'clock.

FIG. 1.   *The original omnibus*

Road—along which many of the short-stage coaches reached the City. On 4 July 1829, Shillibeer began to run his 'Omnibus' (he had dropped the idea of calling it 'Economist') over this route between Paddington Green and the Bank. Scheduled operation to a timetable and the principle of plying for hire at low fares combined to make it a success, although we must not underrate the effect of Shillibeer's advertisement, which said : 'a person of great respectability attends (the) vehicle as conductor'.

T. C. Barker, in the *History of London Transport*, gives a clear definition of the economics of the new type of service. 'The success of the omnibus', he says, 'clearly depended not upon its size but upon its loading. The operator had to fill a higher proportion of seats than was usual on the short stages, partly by attracting a succession of short-distance passengers'. Shillibeer set out to achieve this by plain good management : his respectable conductors made it easy to use his vehicles because the passenger paid the low fare on the spot and, as the omnibuses would stop anywhere, it was easy to join and leave them. But above all, speed and punctuality were the ruling principles, and here the omnibus was an immediate improvement over the short-stage coaches. There seems no evidence to show why the new vehicle adopted the American term 'conductor' in place of the traditional 'guard' (which, incidentally, is still heard in Manchester today, although a female guard there was called a conductress).

Success attracted obstruction, and within a week of opening the service Shillibeer was charged with permitting a vehicle to wait longer than was permissable in the City. However, the Lord Mayor dismissed the case, observing that the omnibus had 'advantages of a very high order'. But success also attracted emulation and a number of new routes were opened both by Shillibeer and his rivals until, by May 1830, there were thirty-nine omnibuses running in London. In 1832, the Stage Carriage Act legalised plying for hire and permitted passengers to be carried within the hackneys' old monopoly area in London. Though the short-stage coaches did not entirely disappear, the omnibuses flourished, but Shillibeer himself failed to achieve any lasting success. Insolvent at least from 1831, and not always on the right side of the law, he seems after 1840 to have left the omnibus business and made a living as an undertaker, patenting a new type of hearse which for many years bore his name. He was sixty-nine when he died in 1866, and he is buried in the churchyard at Chigwell, where a memorial was erected in 1929.

The development of the omnibus in the provinces lacks the documentation available for London. As early as February 1831, the timetable of the Liverpool & Manchester Railway referred to omnibuses owned by the company and meeting its trains, but it is not clear whether they followed regular routes, or were nearer to the 'hotel omnibus' of later days. In Birmingham, a certain John Smith began to run between Snow Hill and the Bristol Road tollgate in 1834, an example copied by other operators, just as Greenwood's service in Salford had been. The Birmingham operators soon extended their services throughout the Black Country and were joined by others in the towns they served, so that by 1841 there was an hourly service between Birmingham and West Bromwich. Birmingham also saw investment in omnibuses on a large scale in a period when it was usual for such enterprise to be of a personal character. The Birmingham Omnibus Conveyance Company was floated in January 1836 with a capital of £5,000, and was followed in August of that year by the Midland Omnibus Company, whose sponsors aimed to raise £15,000. Both companies established themselves, the Midland buying up some of the private operators, but the Conveyance Company seems to have gone out of business in 1837, and the Midland by 1843. Services were continued by various individuals and it was another thirty years before company operation reappeared.

Clearly, the short-stage coaches had little chance of survival in competition with the railways. When the Manchester & Leeds Railway reached Littleborough in 1839, some of the coaches between Manchester and Rochdale tried to compete by charging lower fares, but with the full opening of the line in 1841 they were withdrawn. The railway's advantage in speed and comfort was enough to make the train 'cheaper' than the coach, even at a higher fare. The omnibus was the road industry's reply and, ceasing to cater for inter-urban traffic, it exploited instead the growth of the suburbs and the appearance of the commuter. Thus, on Merseyside, the omnibuses that started running in Birkenhead in the 'forties connected with the boats to and from Liverpool, for the convenience of business people. At first, the round trip each weekday was sufficient, but later there were Sunday journeys and then regular services throughout the day.

Buses in Liverpool are described in the diary of R. B. Dockray. Writing in 1853, he says:

We returned (to Aigburth) in an omnibus. These vehicles are much superior to those in London, or indeed anywhere else, that I have seen; they are so broad that the conductor can walk between people's knees without inconveniencing the passengers; it is possible that this width would be inconvenient in the narrow crowded streets of London. They use glass for the whole length. During summer, the doors are removed, which admits of the best ventilation. The centre part, longitudinally, is raised to give more head room, and has a brass rod on each side for persons to hold in walking along; this head room forms the seat for the outside passengers. Altogether they are a very comfortable and conveniently arranged vehicle, and as a consequence they are used by the upper ranks of society and by ladies unaccompanied by male attendants—a practice quite unknown in London.

Shillibeer's omnibus of 1829, which the *Morning Post* described as being 'in the shape of a van, with windows on each side, and one at the end', was itself a departure from stage-coach tradition. Its imitators produced lighter and less revolutionary vehicles, using two horses instead of three, but retaining the fundamental distinction of the rear entrance, on the step of which stood the conductor. The idea of carrying passengers 'outside' seems to have grown up quite casually; at first a few passengers were carried next to the driver, who sat at roof level; later, a second row was arranged behind him. The Economic Conveyance Company introduced a vehicle in 1847 with a roof seat lengthwise on the clerestory, but it was another ten years before the arrangement was widely copied. The vehicle was heavier and more expensive, but the outside passengers paid roughly half the fare charged inside the bus.

Charles E. Lee has described the development of the omnibus, and points out that it was not the form but the use of the vehicle that was revolutionary. With the attention of historians concentrated upon the railway age, it is easy to see how the parallel achievement of the road industry came to be forgotten; yet the rapid establishment of the omnibus as a commonplace form of urban passenger transport clearly demonstrates both the versatility and the tenacity of the industry. Railway and omnibus services alike grew up in response to the increased population and prosperity of the nineteenth century, and each took advantage of the growing demand for transport over well-defined routes, either national or local. Only the railway made use of mechanical traction, for mechanisation was expensive and the cheaper omnibus could and did fill the gaps the railways had to leave in their system.

THE OMNIBUS TAKES TO RAILS

During its first thirty years, the omnibus established itself wherever there was enough urban development to justify a service. More a trade than an industry, the operation of horse buses did not at first attract investment other than on a personal scale, and the ease with which new competition could appear discouraged the growth of large undertakings. It was not until the second half of the nineteenth century that there began the change which was to continue through mechanisation to form the motor bus industry as we know it today.

In London, the Great Exhibition of 1851 caused a boom in the horse-bus trade and many newcomers entered the market. It was followed by a corresponding slump which soon led to a lowering of standards. It was at this stage that the first attempt was made to introduce large-scale ownership to the trade, and the fleet name 'General'—still associated with bus company titles—appeared on the side of a bus for the first time. Amongst other things the slump had given rise to a movement towards combination among some of the omnibus proprietors, reinforced by a rise in the price of fodder following the outbreak of the Crimean War in 1854. In 1855, developments in London were once again foreshadowed in Paris when the eleven firms operating there merged into one, the Compagnie Générale des Omnibus, with monopoly rights for thirty years. A French businessman, Léopold Foucaud, who had been associated with the new company and had seen the profits open to it, began to negotiate a similar merger in London, on a voluntary basis. In collaboration with Joseph Orsi, a fellow-countryman in business in London, and with the blessing of the reformer Edwin Chadwick, he approached some of the London proprietors in October 1855.

Orsi and Foucaud met with some opposition, but by mid-November three of the largest proprietors, McNamara, Willing and John Wilson, had accepted their proposals. Even so, they accounted for only one-tenth of the vehicles on the road, and not for the last time leaders of the trade were accused of selling their small competitors down the river. Undeterred, the promoters proceeded to raise capital (in France) on false statements, such as that six hundred omnibuses had already been purchased. The Compagnie Générale des Omnibus de Londres was formed in Paris in December 1855, with an address in London and an office staff of three, all of whom had left the Eastern Counties Railway under a cloud. In January 1856, the new company began to buy up existing businesses, offering £510 in cash for each omnibus, or the alternative of ruthless competition. Not surprisingly, in face of these terms, the opposition rapidly disappeared and many of the proprietors took posts with the new company, bringing with them those who shared the routes they ran on. By December 1856, the 'General' owned 600 of the 810 omnibuses that had been working in London the previous year, and although some independents remained, it was now easily the largest omnibus undertaking in the world.

Though quick to introduce efficient management control, the company was slow to make improvements, and suffered from the first from the doubtful activities of some of its promoters. It also found itself in some financial difficulty, and by 1858 rising costs and the pressure of competition upon revenue had cut drastically into its profits. There was opposition, too, to the idea of a French 'monopoly' in London, and so, on 1 January 1859, the company was naturalised, becoming the London General Omnibus Company Ltd, registered in England. In the meantime, however, it had become involved in an attempt to introduce London's first street tramway.

While the omnibus was imported from France to England,

the tramway was an American invention, although it, too, was first imported into France. The tramway took a further step towards cheapening the cost of travel, because steel wheels running on steel rails allowed the tramcar to run more easily than the horse bus on the roads of the time, so enabling more passengers to be carried (forty-six on a tramcar compared with twenty-six on a horse bus). Hence the fixed costs of the undertaking, even after providing the track, could be spread over a greater number of passengers and fares could be lower (or profits greater at the same fare).

Public passenger services in New York had been pioneered by Abraham Bower who, in 1830, introduced an 'omnibus' that was an exact copy of Shillibeer's, both in construction and operation. The atrocious state of the streets and suburban roads gave the idea of the tramway to a young man called John Stephenson, a coach builder familiar with the newly developing railroads at home and in England. In 1831, he and two fellow Irishmen formed the New York & Harlaem Railroad Company and commenced running in November 1832 between the Bowery and Fourteenth Street on Fourth Avenue. At first horse-drawn, the cars were being steam-hauled (quite illegally) as early as 1833, although this was a short-lived experiment. Various other cities in the United States copied the idea, and between 1840 and 1842 some sort of a horse-drawn tramway existed in Vienna, though the tramway did not really appear in Europe until 1852. In that year, Alphonse Loubat was granted authority to build a line in Paris, which he opened in 1853 and sold to the CGOP in 1855. The line ran from Place de la Concorde to Pont de Sèvres, and to reach the Louvre the vehicles worked as buses, with their wheels suitably adjusted. An Englishman, William Joseph Curtis, visited Paris in 1855 and was much impressed by Loubat's system. He adapted and improved the idea, and for nine months in 1859 he (and others who copied him) ran a service over the goods tramway of the Mersey Docks & Harbour Board in Liverpool.

Meanwhile, the directors of the CGOL were under pressure to introduce the *Chemin de fer Américain* to London, and on

13 October 1857 a London Omnibus Tramway Company Ltd was incorporated to seek Parliamentary powers to build and work tramways within a radius of twenty miles of the General Post Office. Its Bill failed to obtain a second reading, largely owing to opposition from municipal interests and from the Chief Commissioner of Public Works, Sir Benjamin Hall, MP. The company was liquidated, but a successor was kept alive by the LGOC until 1882. The General's active interest in tramways, however, was confined to contracting for the provision of horses.

The man who really achieved fame as the introducer of tramways in Europe, despite the earlier enterprises of Loubat and Curtis, was George Francis Train. An American who embodied traditional Yankee exuberance to an almost laughable degree, he chose to ignore his predecessors and called his line in Birkenhead 'the first street railway in Europe'. It was opened on 30 August 1860, and ran for a mile and a quarter between Birkenhead Park and Woodside Ferry. All the crowned heads of Europe, except the King of Naples, were invited to the opening, and though none of them came the line was off to a flamboyant start. It was successful at once, and met with the same sort of opposition as tramways have attracted ever since. In fact, it had one major disadvantage; its rails were not laid flush with the street but projected to form a sort of canal which filled with water and added to the hazard the rails presented to other traffic. James McHenry, one of Train's local backers, raised the capital necessary to replace them with a type of rail that lay flush with the road surface and, despite further opposition, the line continued to flourish.

Train next turned his attention to London, where Curtis had been having no success in his attempt to introduce tramways. Train quickly achieved results. A line from Marble Arch along Bayswater Road to Porchester Terrace was licensed by the local authority and opened with a great flourish on 23 March 1861. Another, in Victoria Street, followed on 15 April, while a third, between Westminster Bridge and Kennington Gate, started on

c

15 August. But Train's choice of route and rail in London proved far less happy than on Merseyside. The residents of the Bayswater Road were 'carriage folk', not the commuters of Birkenhead, and despite the numbers of passengers carried, the unreformed local authorities set their faces against the tramways, and Train was forced to remove them. He ran into the same difficulties in Darlington, and only in the Potteries did a line of his achieve the success he had won at Birkenhead. The tramway from Hanley to Burslem was opened on 13 January 1862, but here again the track had been relaid flush with the roadway by the end of 1864. Disillusioned, Train left the country in 1862, and it cannot be said that his activities did more than provide publicity (much of it adverse) for the idea of the tramway. In most cases, he seems to have found local finance, but in London he was backed by Kinnairds of the Consolidated Bank and supported by the Ebbw Vale Company, who provided the rails.

While Train was active, another project which deserves mention was being developed. In 1861, John Greenwood of Pendleton, by now an established bus proprietor in Salford, was authorised to build a three-rail line from Pendleton to Albert Bridge on 'John Haworth's Patent Perambulating Principle'. While the outer rails were flat and level with the street, the centre one was grooved to take a guide wheel, or 'perambulator', which kept the wheels of the vehicle running on the outer plateways. When required, the guide wheel could be lifted and the car could then travel freely on the road. The compromise was successful and Greenwood's line lasted at least until 1866.

Apart from one or two lines that were railways on streets rather than buses on rails, the next development was the formation of the Liverpool Tramways Company in 1865. This was notable for having parliamentary authority (which Curtis, Train and Greenwood had all lacked) and the company's first lines were built to Walton and to Dingle, and in the form of an inner circle route. Cars began to run on 1 November 1869 on this first British street tramway to be built under full powers but within a few years the company found itself in financial trouble and was merged in 1876 with one of its chief competitors, the Liverpool Road & Railway Omnibus Company Ltd, the largest horse-bus operator in the city. By this time the tram had re-appeared in London where, in 1869, no less than three companies obtained parliamentary powers. The advantages of the tramway had now been generally accepted, and with the passing of the Tramways Act of 1870 the procedure for obtaining powers became simpler.

This Act was to have a considerable influence upon the motor bus industry half a century later. The clauses requiring tramway undertakings to pave the street between the rails and for eighteen inches outside them, and giving powers of veto and compulsory purchase to local authorities, will be described in a later chapter; for the moment, it is sufficient to mention the ease with which tramways could now be laid down. Supervisory powers were given to the Board of Trade, and the procedure for obtaining authority became that of the Provisional Order, confirmed by Act. Local authorities acquired the right to own tramways but not to operate them.

Street tramways became commonplace during the remainder of the nineteenth century and both steam and cable traction were used on them. Steam was unpopular in the south but more acceptable in the industrial areas, while cable haulage was confined to two steep lines in London and a more level one in Birmingham, except for the complex and extensive network of services in Edinburgh. (The tram escaped the limitations imposed by the Locomotives on Highways Acts, which had put an end to the development of steam cars and buses). Invariably, the use of steam meant that the tramcar was hauled by a locomotive, itself sometimes disguised as a tram. An Act of 1879 for the Use of Mechanical Power on Tramways laid down the conditions under which steam could be used: speed was to be mechanically limited to ten miles an hour, silence and safety were to be assured and no smoke or steam was to be allowed to escape. There were, by then, some fifty undertakings in the British Isles employing steam traction, and provided always that there was sufficient traffic to justify the heavy capital investment, the high-capacity vehicles were capable of very economical operation. In practice, steam tramway engines usually hauled cars that were more like an electric tramcar than one of the contemporary horse cars; bogies and enclosed upper decks were not unknown.

The steam tramway, like many full-sized railways, was an example of the tenacity with which certain transport undertakings continue to trade when the prospects that called them into being had long since faded. One of the largest promoters of steam tramways, Henry Osborne O'Hagan, showed very little return upon the capital put into his schemes, and, according to the *Railway Times*, 75 per cent of the capital put into lines built by his City of London Contract Corporation had been lost. But once a line was running, the fact that it was earning no interest was no bar to its continuance until renewal of track or equipment became due, and the unfortunate investors could do nothing but regret their mistaken judgment.

THE END OF THE CENTURY

Over most of the British Isles, however, mechanical traction was reserved to the railways. In the more inaccessible parts of the country the horse coaches lingered on, and in the Lake District, Scotland, Devon and Cornwall there were extensive networks that outlasted the first world war, many of them running in connection with train services. The GWR timetable in 1902 listed some fifty 'conveyances' running 'to and from the company's stations', which are clearly regular feeder services to the trains. There were also numerous others that seem to have been more like market-day omnibuses, or which ran in the summer only for sightseers. Another seventy-three places were listed at which omnibuses ran to and from the station for local traffic; 'cars and conveyances' could be hired at many of these and from numerous others that appeared in yet another list. The GWR also provided for passengers to hire omnibuses through the company, provided adequate notice was given, for journeys in London between Paddington and their 'Residences or Hotel'.

Everywhere the horse continued to be the normal motive power for rural transport in the absence of a branch railway line, while in the towns the horse bus similarly filled the gaps left by the tramways. In London, by 1870, the tramway companies had been amalgamated into three, the North Metropolitan, the London Tramways and the London Street Tramways companies, together accounting for a capital investment of over a million pounds. Their failure to obtain power to cross the centre of London benefited the buses but, where they were in direct competition, the buses could not compete with the tramway fares. By 1875, the three companies were carrying almost as many passengers as the LGOC, over half of them on the North Metropolitan system. Fares were well under a penny a mile, yet the North Metropolitan was able to pay a dividend of $8\frac{1}{4}$ per cent. Throughout the remainder of the century their operation remained profitable, largely because of falling prices for fodder. Between 1875 and 1880 the LGOC paid a dividend of about 12 per cent, and although after 1878, when it ceased to provide tramway horses, its revenue fell back slightly, it soon returned to previous levels.

Characteristic of the history of public transport is a tendency for competing operators to enter into some more or less explicit agreement aimed at regulating the trade and discouraging the entry of newcomers. In London, the LGOC sought to protect itself from the start by using the system of 'associations' which it found already in existence. The earliest of these associations originated from Shillibeer's success on the Paddington route in the early days of the London omnibus. By 1831, competition had become severe and the Stage Carriage Act had yet to be passed. The proprietors met on 10 September, and Shillibeer, despite his bankruptcy, was elected to the chair. In his speech, he attacked the violent activities of the crews on the road and advocated the restraint of competition. This was brought about by an agreement which reduced the number of vehicles on the route and put their operation on a systematic basis. A regular service every three minutes was introduced, inspectors were appointed to enforce the schedules and a committee representing the proprietors was formed to control the system.

Other associations were formed in the course of the next six years but they do not appear to have stopped price competition, though after a spell during which a penny fare appeared on one route, the usual minimum seems to have settled at three pence. During 1851 fares generally rose, but in the years immediately following the Great Exhibition the inflated level of supply led to a period of cut-throat competition and, even before the LGOC appeared on the scene, there was once more a movement towards combination. The LGOC bought shares in the various associations along with the businesses it acquired, and as it dominated the trade in London, so it dominated the association system.

Twenty years after its formation in 1856, the LGOC had become a profitable but rather unprogressive concern. Apart from Thomas Tilling, who had entered the trade in 1851 and remained an independent power operating in and from his south London fortress, all its competitors were fairly small. But in 1881 the London Road Car Company Ltd came on the scene with the avowed intention of cutting into the General's profits by providing better vehicles. These soon brought about a substantial change in design, for other operators were quick to copy them. They introduced the idea of a platform, copied from the tramcars, with a staircase instead of a ladder to the top deck, where the 'knifeboard' was replaced by the 'garden seat'. This twenty-six-seater (twelve inside, fourteen outside) remained standard until the disappearance of the horse bus from the London streets.

The LRCC also tried to make capital out of the 'French' associations of the LGOC, and all its buses flew a small Union Jack. Financially shaky and inefficiently managed, it got away to a poor start, but turned the corner with a profit in 1884 and went on to become a considerable success. The new competition soon led to cheaper fares and better services from the LGOC and its associates. By 1889 the penny fare stage had become common, but three years later, in 1891, forty per cent of the LGOC's vehicles were still of an obsolete design and stated to be too old to be adapted; a fair comment on the condition of the fleet before the LRCC appeared. The two underground railways— the Metropolitan and the Metropolitan District—and the tramway companies were, by then, also running buses in connection with their trains and a number of other newcomers had appeared. Rivalry between the General and the Road Car was brisk, and Compton Mackenzie has recalled that small boys supported one or other as fervently as they did Oxford or Cambridge in the boat race. The LGOC was not at first affected financially by the new competition, but by 1890 it had become a poor investment and out of 50,000 £4 shares offered at £7 each in that year, only 17,000 were subscribed. The weakness was largely in the management, and A. G. Church, who had been secretary from the beginning of the company as well as its manager from 1867 until he retired in 1891, seems to have been a classic example of an able man who stayed on too long and allowed matters to get beyond his control.

Church had been opposed to the introduction of tickets, which the LRCC had used from the start. Directly he had retired, his successor, R. G. Hall, under pressure from the board, arranged for tickets to be supplied by the Bell Punch Company and on 31 May 1891, the ticket system was introduced on all buses of the LGOC and its associates. Wages, incidentally, received little more than a token increase to compensate the crews for their loss of illicit revenue. The LGOC had tried without success to introduce a sort of ticket system in the 1850s and there can be little doubt that the practice of the conductor retaining part of the revenue, which he shared with the driver and horsekeeper, had the tacit approval of the company's management in its earlier days. It may well have started before the formation of the LGOC, when smaller proprietors dominated the trade, many of them working on their own buses and keeping accountancy to a minimum. Even the tramway companies, which had used tickets from the beginning, tolerated a fair amount of misuse of the system, but the LGOC now made it clear that their ticket system would be strictly enforced, and in due course the increase in its annual revenue reflected the amount of money which had been involved.

The men's opposition to the new system was led by Thomas Sutherst who, in 1889, had founded a trade union for tramway and omnibus men which had had some success in improving working conditions on the trams. A strike was called at a midnight meeting on Saturday, 6 June 1891, and while it did not bring about a total stoppage, it greatly reduced the number of buses on the streets. Men from the LRCC and other undertakings came out in sympathy, although Tillings conceded Sutherst's terms and continued to run. Ostensibly, the strike was for a shorter working day, which was generally attractive as the men were working between fifteen and sixteen hours seven days a week. The LGOC management offered a twelve-hour day with a slight increase in wages (tacit recognition of the real cause of the strike), and after a week Sutherst accepted this offer and the strike ended. The other companies also introduced the twelve-hour day, but by the middle of the 1890s fifteen hours was at least as common as before. The union does not seem to have lasted very long, although its short life was a useful one and it was responsible for considerable improvements in working conditions of bus and tram crews between 1885 and 1895.

In the matter of fare collection, however, the LGOC had achieved its aim and, following shortly on the issue of tickets, the bell punch was introduced in 1892. In 1891, the LGOC's dividend had to be paid out of reserves, the company having lost over £23,000, but by the following year income had risen to £805,000, as against £696,000 in 1890. Even so, expenses also went up sharply, £13,000 more than the increase in revenue over the same two years. The dividend was whittled down to 5 per cent, which led to the dismissal of Hall and to a period which the historians of London transport describe as one of 'peaceful co-existence'. After the storms of its competitive days, the LGOC came now to prefer agreement to confrontation, and this policy, which later developed into more of a principle, was to influence the development of the transport industry in the twentieth century throughout Great Britain. Henry Hicks, who became vice-chairman of the LGOC in 1891, was largely responsible for the subsequent history of the company during its independent days, as well as for bringing into road passenger transport his son, the redoubtable 'Jix'.

CHAPTER THREE

GETTING STARTED : 1895-1920

T HE early motorists were not only men of persistence and ingenuity, but also of influence; while openly flouting the 'Red Flag' Act, they were also instrumental in securing its prompt amendment. Thus 1896 was a notable year for road transport; it saw the passing of the Locomotives on Highways Act, whose emancipation of the motor car is still celebrated annually by the veteran cars' run to Brighton; it saw the introduction of the Light Railways Act, which assisted the growth of the electric tramway and, significantly for the future of the motor bus industry, it also saw the registration of the British Electric Traction Company.

THE PIONEERS

Numerous experiments were made before the introduction of regular public services by motor buses, but the first true motor-bus service can be dated with considerable certainty. Both E. S. Shrapnell-Smith and Charles E. Lee record its start in Edinburgh on 19 May 1898, only eighteen months after the passing of the emancipating Act. It was operated with 'small Daimler and MMC petrol wagonettes', and ran along Princes Street from the GPO to Haymarket Station, a mile and a half of level road. John Love of Kirkaldy, supported by Norman D. MacDonald and T. Rowland Outhwaite, formed the Edinburgh Autocar Company Ltd to run the motor buses, and Shrapnell-Smith quotes Outhwaite as saying that as many as 5,000 fares were taken in a single day. Unfortunately, it was not a financial success and, after experimenting with a Lifu steam bus, the company ceased to function in 1901, having lost £14,000. Elsewhere in 1898, other services were started at Falkirk, Mansfield, Llandudno, Mablethorpe, Torquay and Clacton. The first rural bus service was also opened in December of that year when, according to Shrapnell-Smith, 'Dr E. H. Hailey . . . in conjunction with Mr W. Carlisle, MP . . . in order to aid local people, started a service of vehicles each carrying from eight to twelve passengers between Newport Pagnell and Olney'.

The petrol engine was not the only form of mechanical traction to be tried out in the early years of mechanisation. The Dover & East Kent Motor Bus Company Ltd, formed on 9 March 1899, operated three Lifu steam buses between Dover and Deal, but the high cost of maintenance is said by Lee to have been the main cause of the company's failure in 1901. Far more successful, both as inventor and operator, was Thomas Clarkson, whose activities will be described later. Yet while Clarkson's were the only steamers to achieve widespread use, those of Sidney Straker had the odd distinction of being associated with the first petrol bus service to operate in London. With the backing of Harry John Lawson, who had been instrumental in introducing the motor car into this country, Straker and E. H. Bayley formed the London Steam Omnibus Company Ltd on 30 June 1898, whose prospectus spoke of running twice a day between London and Brighton, as well as services to Kingston, Barnet, Windsor and elsewhere. No steam-bus service was ever run and in 1899 the company changed its name to the Motor Traction Company Ltd and started the first London motor-bus service on 9 October 1899. The chassis of the company's two vehicles were built to Straker's design and fitted with Cannstätt-Daimler petrol engines, and they ran at first between Kennington Park and Victoria Station, via Westminster Bridge. In the following year the route was altered to Kennington-Oxford Circus, but the service ceased in December 1900.

The early years of the twentieth century were marked by the increasing success of the motor bus as a reliable commercial vehicle. The period was noted for men of great foresight working individually in various parts of the country towards a future that only they could envisage. The engineers are best remembered, but credit must also go to those who shared their confidence in the industry, who supported them financially, or who managed the operation of the vehicles in commercial service. Amongst the earliest of these pioneers, almost against his will, was Emile Garcke, founder and later chairman of the British Electric Traction Company Ltd.

BET represents an element in road transport history which both in scale and concept is different from all others. From the beginning, main-line railway organisation was taken as the model, even down to gold passes for directors and senior officers (these were the days when Clifton Robinson, manager of London United Tramways, had a private siding in his own front garden and the general manager of Birmingham Corporation Tramways travelled to his office daily in a special tramcar). The country was divided into districts, each headed by a superintendent with senior rank in the company, and the aim was to develop mechanical traction on roads and light railways throughout the British Isles.

The early years of BET were marked by political conflict over the question of municipal trading, and the company, referred to as 'the Octopus', became a by-word in left-wing circles. The *Daily News* and *Daily Chronicle* carried on what now appears to have been an absurd vendetta against it, while the company was itself associated with the extreme right-wing Industrial Freedom League. In fact, as George Bernard Shaw pointed out at the time, it was the consumer who suffered, and while the conflict ended in compromise, it cannot be said that it made for the happiest of marriages between private and public enterprise. But perhaps this was inevitable, given the strength of character that made Garcke and Shaw the men they were.

Much has been made of the irony whereby BET was both the pioneer of electric tramways and the patron of the motor buses that replaced them. The irony lies not in the logical reaction of the company to the circumstances of public service operation, but in the changing and often irrational pressures of legislation and public opinion that brought those circumstances about. BET was from the first an industrial company aiming to make its living out of the exploitation of technical developments, and it had as its originator an exceptional man whose reputation rested equally upon his technical and his financial abilities. BET was 'his' company, both as an electrical engineer and as a business man, and it has retained not a little of his influence to this day.

Electric traction quickly proved more successful than steam in the mechanisation of tramways. Dr Werner von Siemens built a demonstration line for an exhibition in Berlin in 1879, and this was followed by the first electric street tramway, opened at Anhalt on 12 May 1881. On 4 August 1883, Magnus Volk started the electric railway along the beach at Brighton that is still known by his name. The first true street tramway in Great Britain to be worked electrically was opened in Blackpool on 29 September 1885, taking its current from a conductor rail carried in a slot between the running rails, known as a conduit. The overhead wire conductor was developed in the United States and first appeared in this country in Leeds in 1891.

The construction of an electric tramway was an expensive business, even when compared with the cost of providing steam locomotives for traction, and the Tramways Act of 1870 contained provisions which made investment on this scale unattractive. It gave local authorities power to own but not to operate tramways and the right to veto the construction of a tramway on their streets. And once an approved tramway had been constructed, the Act also gave them the right of compulsory purchase after twenty-one years, virtually at scrap prices. Many lines were later electrified by municipalities which obtained operating powers, but towards the end of the nineteenth century very few of the lessee companies could hope to regain the cost of electrification within the time remaining to them.

The Light Railways Act of 1896 offered greater security of tenure and it was no coincidence that Emile Garcke was a member of the conference at the Board of Trade which preceded the Act. After its passage, electrification went ahead faster, and while BET was responsible for a good deal of it, other financial interests also took part. The aim of these companies was the same as that of many local authorities who built their own electric tramways : the production of electric power both for traction and for sale. In the absence of any great industrial use, the heaviest demand for power came during the hours of darkness, and traction provided an off-peak load. Where generating plant was in the same ownership, an accountancy transaction enabled current to be supplied at low rates to the tramway undertaking, so enabling passengers to be carried at extremely low fares. This, together with the economy resulting from the use of still larger vehicles, made the electric tramcar the progress symbol of the Edwardian age, just as the steam train had been seventy years earlier.

The tramway industry's contribution to the history of the motor bus will be discussed later, but in the case of BET, the bus came to supplant the tram, although the BET bus interests are almost as old as the company itself. As early as 1899, a district superintendent was sent to inspect the Olney-Newport Pagnell service, and his report, quoted in Roger Fulford's history of the company, is a good example of the mixture of caution and foresight which marked the company's approach to the motor bus. Satisfied with the mechanical aspect, the superintendent at once spotted the weakness that had ended so many similar experiments : the high cost of maintenance. If this could be reduced, he thought the motor bus would 'compete with other means of locomotion on fairly good roads'. The company did not disagree with his finding that this time had not yet come, but in the following year they bought two Straker steam buses which, in April 1901, started work for the Potteries Electric Traction Company Ltd. They were built at the Vulcan Ironworks at Fishponds, Bristol, had a pinion drive which proved noisy and unsatisfactory, and were fitted with double-deck bodies having glass windscreens to protect the upper-deck passengers. The tramway company used them to provide feeder services through the outlying districts, but the steep hills in the Potteries proved too much for them and by March 1902 they had been sold. In that year, however, the board of BET appointed an automobile committee which included, beside Emile Garcke himself, J. S. Critchley, a former manager of the Daimler Motor Company. Construction as well as operation of motor buses was at first envisaged, but building was later left to the Brush Manufacturing Company Ltd, a BET associate. Garcke for long remained convinced that the motor bus should be regarded as an auxiliary to the electric tram, and there was some friction between him and his son, Sidney, who had a much clearer vision of the future of motor bus transport in its own right.

Before congested urban areas could be served at fares cheap enough to be competitive with trams and horse buses, something more robust was needed, and it is not surprising to find towns like Tunbridge Wells and Folkestone supporting motor buses before they started to run in London. In Eastbourne, for instance, the corporation had resisted construction of tramways in 1885, and again in 1899, when BET had put forward a scheme, but in 1902 they secured an Act giving them authority to 'provide and run motor omnibuses within and for a distance of one mile beyond the borough'. These were the first motor-bus powers to be given to a local authority (Southampton Corporation had run an unauthorised service for a few months in 1901), and on 12 April 1903 Eastbourne's municipal bus service commenced. Milnes-Daimler single-deckers, recognisably omnibuses rather than wagonettes, were used, and in the following year double-deck buses from the same manufacturer were added to the fleet. Operation has continued without a break ever since.

BET, however, was by no means the only major concern to be interested in exploiting the possibilities of the motor bus, and after the Great Western Railway had taken note of what was going on in various parts of the country, the chairman, addressing the shareholders' half-yearly meeting in August 1903, referred to 'motor cars', which, he said, 'outside persons were successfully operating'. The sequel was that the GWR itself decided to acquire a fleet of motor buses, to be used in areas of thin population as an alternative to extending the railway line. Five Milnes-Daimler open, single-deck vehicles were obtained, looking much more like wagonettes than those used at Eastbourne, and a service from Helston to the Lizard was started on 17 August 1903. (Two of these buses had already been in use, having been bought from

Sir George Newnes, who had run them in connection with the Lynton & Barnstaple Railway.) A fully enclosed vehicle went into service in October 1903.

The GWR service was suspended between October 1904 and April 1905 owing to a dispute with the local authority which was settled when the railway agreed to loan the council a steam-roller, said to have been the first in Cornwall. Services at Penzance and around Plymouth followed, and by the end of 1906 the GWR owned a fleet of eighty vehicles. Another railway, however—the North Eastern—also has a strong claim to be regarded as the pioneer of railway bus services, for on 7 September 1903 it began to run between Beverley and Beeford, and this service, unlike the GWR's Helston-Lizard service, continued without interruption. A link with the early days was the sign still to be seen in 1966 at Penzance railway station : 'To the motor cars for Land's End' (more effectively sited than the posters directing passengers to the heliport).

Within a few years, railway buses were running in many other parts of Great Britain. The Great Eastern obtained powers in its Act of 1904, and started a service on 18 July between Lowestoft and Southwold. It then built a fleet of twelve petrol double-deckers in its locomotive works at Stratford, and with these and others opened services at Clacton, Ipswich, Norwich, Chelmsford and Bury St Edmunds. In Scotland, the Great North of Scotland Railway opened a number of routes in Aberdeenshire, the first of which, between Ballater and Braemar, began on 2 May 1904. The London & South Western started running petrol buses between Exeter and Chagford on 1 June 1904, but suspended the service for the winter, later re-opening it with steam buses built by Thomas Clarkson. The GWR used similar vehicles when it started its Wolverhampton-Bridgnorth route on 7 November 1904. Other railways to run their own bus services were the Cambrian (Pwllheli-Nevin, commenced 1906), the Midland, the London & North Western (which had a number of services scattered at different points in its area), and the Lancashire & Yorkshire.

Most of the successful services opened during the earliest

years of the twentieth century were in country areas or small towns where traffic conditions were easy. Even so, they had their difficulties, often because of poor road surfaces, and the entire GER fleet had to be withdrawn for three months in 1906. It is not surprising that the development of the motor bus in the more congested areas took longer, and that the larger urban transport undertakings were cautious in their approach to the new vehicle. In London, various operators experimented with electric, steam and petrol buses. Some were newcomers to the trade, others long-established horse-bus operators, such as Tillings and Birch Brothers.

After the failure of the first petrol buses in London, the tendency was to experiment with much smaller vehicles, basically ordinary motor cars fitted with wagonette bodies, as had been used initially in Edinburgh. Walter Flexman French, one of the greatest of the pioneers, formed the South Western Motor Car Company Ltd, which opened such a service between Streatham and Clapham Junction on 1 April 1901. His example was soon followed by F. J. Bell, who began running between Putney and Piccadilly Circus on 18 September. C. E. Lee speaks of a 'moderate success', which attracted Edwin James Harrison of Kilburn, a partner in the firm of Harrison & Dudden. In 1902 a service was opened between Cricklewood and Marble Arch, a route that had been served slightly earlier by the Middlesex Motor Carriage Company Ltd. Harrison & Dudden carried eight or nine passengers on their vehicles, while the Middlesex company had a 6 hp Daimler licensed to carry only three. The wagonettes were too light to stand up to conditions that had driven bigger vehicles off the road, and their function disappeared with the successful development of larger buses. On 26 November 1902 the London Motor Omnibus Syndicate put a 12 hp Scott-Stirling twelve-seater on the Edgware Road route and mechanisation of the London bus trade had really begun.

There were a number of other London pioneers, prominent among them being Thomas Tilling. His father had moved from Gloucestershire to Middlesex early in the nineteenth century, and he himself came to London in 1847 and set up as a 'jobmaster',

D

LONDON AND SOUTH WESTERN RAILWAY.

ROAD MOTOR SERVICE

BETWEEN

FARNHAM & HASLEMERE

(Via FRENSHAM POND, CHURT POST OFFICE, BEACON HOTEL & HINDHEAD),

In connection with Trains from and to

LONDON AND OTHER PLACES.

ON MONDAY, 3rd JUNE, 1912.

And EVERY WEEK-DAY thereafter until further notice,

THE SERVICE WILL BE AS UNDER:

TIMES OF DEPARTURE FROM FARNHAM (BUSH HOTEL).				TIMES OF DEPARTURE FROM HASLEMERE STATION.			
	a.m.	a.m.	a.m.		a.m.	p.m.	p.m.
FARNHAM (Bush Hotel) ... depart	8 30	10 50	4 38'	HASLEMERE STATION depart	10 20	12 55	4 26
FARNHAM STATION ... ,,	8 33	10 53	4 41	NUTCOMBE LANE ...	10 29	1	4 37
BOURNE (Post Office) ... ,,	8 43	11 3	51	HINDHEAD (Huts Hotel)	10 43	1 18	4 51
MILLBRIDGE, Frensham ... ,,	8 51	11 13	5	HINDHEAD GOLF CLUB ...	10 53	1 28	5 1
FRENSHAM (Schools) ... ,,	8 57	11 17	5	CHURT (Post Office) ...	11 3	1 36	5 11
FRENSHAM (Pond) ... ,,	4 11	24 3	12	FRENSHAM (Pond) ...	11 11	1 46	5 19
CHURT (Post Office) ... ,,	9 11	23 3	17	FRENSHAM (Schools) ...	11 15	1 53	5 26
HINDHEAD GOLF CLUB ... ,,	9 17	11 47	35	MILLBRIDGE, Frensham ...	11 22	1 57	5 30
HINDHEAD (Huts Hotel) ... ,,	9 41	1 3	49	BOURNE (Post Office) ...	11 33	2 10	5 43
NUTCOMBE LANE ... ,,	9 51	1 13	59	FARNHAM STATION arrive	11 44	2 19	5 58
HASLEMERE STATION arrive	10 0	1 20	4 8	FARNHAM (Bush Hotel) ... ,,	11 47	2 22	5 55

SINGLE JOURNEY FARES FOR PASSENGERS.

FROM	FARNHAM BUSH HOTEL.	FARNHAM STATION.	BOURNE (Post Office.)	MILL BRIDGE, FRENSHAM or FRENSHAM SCHOOLS.	FRENSHAM POND.	CHURT, (Post Office.)	HINDHEAD GOLF CLUB.	HINDHEAD BEACON HOTEL or HUTS HOTEL.	NUT-COMBE LANE.	HASLE-MERE STATION.
FARNHAM (Bush Hotel)...	—	3d.	3d.	6d.	9d.	1/-	1/3	1/6	1/9	2/-
FARNHAM (Station) ...	3d.	—	3d.	6d.	9d.	1/-	1/3	1/6	1/9	2/-
BOURNE (Post Office) ...	3d.	3d.	—	3d.	6d.	9d.	1/-	1/3	1/6	1/9
MILLBRIDGE, Frensham or FRENSHAM SCHOOLS	6d.	6d.	3d.	—	3d.	6d.	9d.	1/-	1/3	1/6
FRENSHAM (Pond) ...	9d.	9d.	6d.	3d.	—	3d.	6d.	9d,	1/-	1/3
CHURT (Post Office) ...	1/-	1/-	9d.	6d.	3d.·	—	3d.	6d.	9d,	1/-
HINDHEAD GOLF CLUB	1/3	1/3	1/-	9d.	6d.	3d.	—	3d.	6d	9d.
HINDHEAD (BEACON HOTEL)	1/6	1/6	1/3	1/-	9d.	6d.	3d.	—	3d.	6d.
NUTCOMBE LANE ...	1/9	1/9	1/6	1/3	1/-	9d.	6d	3d.	—	3d.
HASLEMERE STATION ...	2/-	2/-	1/9	1/6	1/3	1/-	9d.	6d.	3d.	—

CHARGES FOR LUGGAGE ACCOMPANYING PASSENGERS :
Small Articles 2d. per package ; Large or Bulky Articles 4d. per package.

DOGS.—Dogs are not conveyed.

BICYCLES, MAIL CARTS and PERAMBULATORS.—A charge of 6d. each will be made for Bicycles, Mail Carts and Perambulators, and they will only be carried if accommodation permits and subject to the Company's Risk.

STOPPING PLACES.—The Vehicle will stop if required at any point on the journey other than the booked places. Passengers joining the Vehicle at any intermediate point must pay the fare from the previous booked stopping place.

TICKETS.—Tickets will be issued by the Conductor, and must be held till the end of the journey.

RECEIPTS.—Passengers should be careful to obtain printed Receipts for all amounts paid for Luggage, &c. and all traffic is accepted subject to the conditions appearing on the Company's receipts.

N.B.—The Time Table shows the time at which the Vehicle may be expected to start and arrive, but the Company do not undertake that the Vehicle will start or arrive at such times, and the Company reserve the right to alter or suspend the running of the Vehicle without notice. Connection with the Trains is not guaranteed, and the Company will not be responsible for any loss, inconvenience, or injury to Passengers or their property, resulting from delay or detention however caused.

H. A. WALKER, General Manager

FIG. 2.   *Farnham & Haslemere timetable*

owning to begin with a grey mare, 'Kitty', and a carriage which cost him £30. Ten years later he owned seventy horses (still mostly greys) and, while still undertaking any kind of carriage work, had established himself as a bus proprietor. In December 1849 he entered into an agreement with W. Stevens for the purchase of a horse bus, and this was concluded in January 1850; with it he acquired the right to run four journeys a day between Peckham and the 'Green Man and Still', in Oxford Street.

Tilling's sound business sense enabled him to survive the recession that followed the year of the Great Exhibition; his buses were fast and punctual, and would not lag behind if they were not full. By 1856 he was working jointly with the LGOC, and he was a member of the Atlas and Waterloo and of the King's Cross and Barnsbury Associations, but he developed a business on a larger scale than most of his contemporaries. In due course 'Tilling' became as much a household word in south London as 'General' was elsewhere, and even achieved the distinction of a *Punch* cartoon, Tillings' quarter-hourly service to the City being described by a conductor as 'A quarter arter, 'arf arter, quarter to, and at'.

In 1897, under the direction of Tilling's two sons, Richard and Edward, and his son-in-law, Walter Wolsey, the company became a public one with an issued capital of £400,000, and a stable of about 4,000 horses. Tillings still remained jobmasters, providing all kinds of horse-drawn transport for private individuals, the Post Office, the War Office, the London Fire Brigade and others, as well as operating buses and cabs on their own account. In 1901, they were running 220 horse buses but, recognising the necessity for mechanisation, their first motor bus was put to work on 30 September 1904. There followed the inevitable financial problems, but Tillings persevered successfully, helped by the broad base of their activities and the fact that the demand for horses continued after the horse bus had all but disappeared.

The story of Birch Brothers also starts in the West Country, where William Birch was running stage and mail coaches between Plymouth and Exeter at the end of the eighteenth century. His son came to London and in 1832 started operating cabs from premises in the Horseferry Road. He died after an accident in 1846, but his widow continued the business and was associated with the opening of a new bus route between Pimlico and Mansion House in 1847. In the Exhibition year she put four buses of her own in service, later becoming owner of half the shares in the Westminster Association. When the LGOC was formed, it bought the remaining shares and Birches stayed inside the association system, on a pooling basis with the General, so long as the horse-bus industry in London lasted. Mrs Birch died in 1874 and after 1878 her two sons traded separately until, in November 1899, they joined forces and Birch Brothers became a limited liability company. The brothers had been prominent in the affairs of the associations and had engaged in vigorous competition, especially with the London Road Car Company. The LGOC appears to have been a reluctant ally and the associations had largely to fight their own battles. On 11 October 1904, realising that the end of the horse-bus age was in sight, Birch Brothers put two Milnes-Daimlers to work, but in the words of J. M. Birch, 'The roads were very bad, the machines very unreliable, the drivers very inexperienced and the maintenance staff very ignorant'. By 24 October 1907, having run at a heavy loss, all the Birch motor buses had been withdrawn and sold at a further loss. In 1912, Birch Brothers gave up horse buses, too, and concentrated on other activities until after the first world war.

Between 1904 and 1908, thirty-three operators ran motor buses in London, but only three of them—the Road Car Company, the LGOC and Tillings—continued through the whole of that period. The Great Eastern London Motor Omnibus Company Ltd ran continuously from 1905, as did the London Motor Omnibus Company Ltd (which in 1907 adopted the fleet name 'Vanguard'), but most of the others survived for only about two years, usually 1905 and 1906. In 1904, London saw its first Milnes-Daimler, and in 1905 the contract price for solid rubber tyres capable of carrying a double-decker came down to around twopence a mile. This was the signal for London bus operation really to begin. The Milnes-Daimler originated from an agreement between the German manufacturer and the British firm of G. F. Milnes & Company Ltd (better known as builders of tramcars) by which Daimlers were to be made under licence in England. It was the most successful of the early motors, and in May 1906 there were 175 of them in London, compared with 101 Straker-Squires, 52 de Dions, 27 Dürkopps, 14 Stirlings, 13 Brilliés, 12 Leylands, 7 Orions and 11 Clarkson steamers. The Straker-Squire used an engine built under licence from the German firm of Büssing.

The London Motor Omnibus Company was one of the first operators to start as a motor-bus company without previous horse-bus tradition. It obtained priority in the delivery of the Milnes-Daimler and by 1908 was running 386 vehicles in the largest motor-bus fleet in London. The Road Car Company experimented with various makes, including the Clarkson steam bus, of which it had seventy in 1906, but its petrol fleet consisted mainly of Straker-Squire-Büssings. The most numerous make of vehicle in the General fleet at this time was the de Dion. Other operators used petrol-electric and battery vehicles, and one, the Metropolitan Steam Omnibus Company Ltd, ran Darracq-Serpollet steamers from 1907 to 1912.

To run motor buses under city conditions in those days was an expensive and risky business. By 1908, only eleven operators remained in London, yet it was clear mechanisation had gone so far that, for those still involved, there could be no turning back. The London bus trade had never been fully competitive, the voluntary associations having protected their members from each other and from outsiders, but from time to time, especially with the appearance of the LRCC, the Star Omnibus Company and others, the horse-bus operators (including the General) had had to face enough new competition to prevent them becoming complacent. The coming of the motor bus changed all this, and with it, too, came the need for much larger capital investment. After most of the smaller operators had given up the struggle, those with most to lose came to the conclusion that their only future lay in outright amalgamation. The critical year was 1907,

when Tillings' profit fell from £28,000 to £3,000, to rise again
to £19,500 in 1908 (the average profit for 1900-5 had been
approaching £36,000). The directors of the LGOC, the Road
Car and the Vanguard companies reached agreement and on
1 July 1908 the three were merged, retaining the title of London
General Omnibus Company Ltd. Collectively, they had been
losing £250,000 a year.

This was the first move towards combination, a process which
has dominated the history of the industry ever since. From the
merger, the expanded LGOC acquired a total of 994 vehicles,
making it by far the largest motor-bus concern in the country.
It found itself also with two men whose qualities enabled it to
survive the difficult days to come: G. S. Dicks and Frank Searle.
Dicks had been traffic manager of Vanguard, where he made his
position one of real influence. Realising that the greater speed
of the motor bus made the route information traditionally shown
on the side of omnibuses illegible, he introduced the modern
concepts of a fleet name and of numbered routes.

Searle, on the other hand, was an engineer who had at one
time been on the staff of the Arrow fleet, the London & District
Motorbus Company Ltd, which was in the same group as
Vanguard. On 14 February 1907 he had been appointed a depot
manager, and on 16 May 1907, chief motor engineer of the
LGOC. He now became chief engineer of the combined undertaking and his influence extended over an even wider field.
Dicks remained in the industry, although he played no further
notable part and in later years ran excursions from Brighton
with the fleet name 'Vanguard'. He died in about 1924.

Searle, however, remained to play an important part in the
events leading to a settlement between the London Electric
Railway and British Electric Traction groups, which will be
described later in this chapter. Trained as a locomotive engineer,
he set up in 1905 as a consultant specialising in motor-bus
engineering. He served in the Tank Corps during the first world
war, gaining the DSO and CBE, and thereafter remained with the
BSA-Daimler group, but had no further connection with the
motor-bus industry. He died on 4 April 1948.

THE GROWTH OF THE LONDON COMBINE

While the motor bus was in its experimental stage in London, other forms of transport were also being developed. The idea of a tube railway had been proved feasible as early as 1870, with the opening of Greathead and Barlow's Tower Subway, and in 1884 Greathead himself obtained powers to build the City & South London Railway, which was opened on 18 December 1890. The next three years saw four more tube railways incorporated, and two others followed in 1897 and 1899. But the c&slr was no great financial success, since road competition kept fares low, and the experience of the Central London Railway, although happier, did not encourage investors. Money could not readily be obtained for the various schemes, and it is questionable whether any further progress would have been made had it not been for the introduction of capital from the United States.

Charles Tyson Yerkes came to London in 1900 and bought the parliamentary powers for the Charing Cross, Euston & Hampstead Railway, incorporated in 1893, for £100,000. The following year he founded the Metropolitan District Electric Traction Company Ltd with American money, through which he controlled both the Hampstead tube and the District Railway, which he had also acquired that year. He used his trans-Atlantic resources to electrify the latter, extending his tube empire at the same time. The two companies making up the Piccadilly line were bought in 1901 and merged in 1902, when he also purchased the powers for the Bakerloo. In the same year he renamed his holding company the Underground Electric Railways Company of London Ltd, and acquired the London United Tramways, whose manager, J. Clifton Robinson, a devoted tramway man, had been Train's office boy. Its lines from Shepherd's Bush westward were electrified in stages, beginning on 4 April 1901.

But in spite of the confidence of Yerkes and his backers, the tubes were not an outstanding financial success. Yerkes died in 1905 and was succeeded as chairman of the holding company by Edgar Speyer of the New York firm of Speyer Brothers, while

Sir George Gibb, general manager of the North Eastern Railway, became deputy chairman and general manager, bringing with him as assistant a young man called Frank Pick. Gibb, who after experience in the States had re-organised the NER, could foresee reduced prospects for the group, in view of the success being achieved by both the motor bus and the electric tram. As a railwayman, his mind turned readily to the advantages of combination, especially in a field where increased costs were discouraging the entry of new competition. His attitude can be summed up in the words of the House of Commons Committee on Railways of 1853 : 'It is natural for traders to compete where the opportunity is unlimited for new rivals to enter the field. It is quite as natural for traders to combine so soon as the whole number of possible competitors may be ascertained and limited'.

Neither was Gibb any stranger to pooling agreements, the NER having been party as early as 1850 to the one that applied to the east coast route between London and Scotland. But pooling agreements hitherto had all been amongst railways, and Gibb's answer to the problem of the tubes was to bring surface transport into the combine with them, in order to recoup their losses from the profits of their competitors. As a result of his efforts, there met for the first time on 22 July 1907 the London Passenger Traffic Conference, consisting at that time of the Underground group companies, the Metropolitan Railway, the LGOC, LRCC, Vanguard, Tilling and a few other bus companies. Its immediate achievement was the co-ordination of fares amongst its members, the agreement coming into effect on 15 December 1907. Over the greater area of passenger transport in London, competition in charging had ceased to exist.

Gibb retired in 1910, the year in which the number of motor buses in London first exceeded that of horse buses. He was succeeded in office by a man who was to be prominently identified with the future development of passenger transport in London, Albert Stanley, later Lord Ashfield. Stanley started his transport career in the USA as office boy with the Detroit City Railway, where he rose to become general superintendent. In 1903 he became assistant general manager of the Public Service Corporation of New Jersey and was appointed general manager three months before he came to London. He it was who was responsible for the 'UndergrounD' device with which we are still familiar and which he introduced when he first took office. He was also responsible for the extension of Gibb's policies to their logical extent in London passenger transport and, as a consequence, for much that happened elsewhere in Great Britain. Stanley was born in England in 1874 of eastern European parents who were in the course of emigrating to Canada. At that time, it was common for the journey to be made in stages, emigrants arriving at Hull or some other east coast port, and then crossing England to reach the trans-Atlantic ship at Liverpool. It was also regarded as desirable for a child to be born on ship-board, so that the mother would be tended by a doctor from the first class, and perhaps attract the interest and financial help of other first-class passengers. The fact that Stanley took the title of Ashfield of Southwell may indicate the exact place of his birth, a subject on which he was always reticent.

Stanley found the motor bus an increasing success, and thus an increasing threat to the stability of his combine. After the merger of 1908, the LGOC had established itself, largely on the strength of Frank Searle's genius. His famous X-type double-decker was built by the company at the former Vanguard works at Walthamstow, being, according to Searle himself, an amalgamation of the successful features of the various buses the LGOC had tried out. It went into service on 16 December 1909 and was followed by the B-type on 7 October 1910. This was the famous 'Old Bill' of the first world war, of which some were still in service in 1926; it cost well under £300 a vehicle to produce, which was bringing motor-bus operation into the realms of solvency. Tillings' answer to the same problem was the development of the Tilling-Stevens petrol-electric bus, which originated from the work of Percy Frost Smith, their engineer, W. A. Stevens and Frank Brown, chairman of David Brown Ltd. With this vehicle, Tillings supplanted the mixed fleet that had established them as the principal operator in south London.

Tillings' position was secured in 1909 when a pooling agreement was reached with the LGOC. In the same year Thomas Clarkson began to operate. His steam buses had been tried out by various operators and rejected, his hopes being finally disappointed by the LGOC's sale of its thirteen steamers in October 1909. He had started to develop steam cars in 1894 and, after a spell in partnership with Capel at Dalston, had set up his own business at Chelmsford in 1903. The 'Chelmsford' chassis was bought by the LGOC and LRCC, and by two of the smaller London horse-bus operators, Burtwell Brothers of New Kent Road, and John Sharland & Sons. Early in 1907, there were forty-six Clarkson steamers in London, the LRCC fleet being the largest. Others worked at various times at Torquay, Oswestry, Worthing, Maidstone, Crewe and Harrogate.

Clarkson renamed his bus 'National' after demonstration vehicles from the Chelmsford works had taken part in the invasion tests of 1909. Keenly interested in the formation of the Territorials, he was associated with Colonel R. B. Colvin, chairman of the Essex County Territorial Association, and during manœuvres his buses travelled from Wickham Market to Sudbury and from Chelmsford to Folkestone and back with military baggage, and from Chelmsford to Colchester with personnel. These journeys, with the buses painted white and bearing the legends 'BE PREPARED' and 'WAKE UP ENGLAND' brought Clarkson considerable publicity and encouraged Colonel Colvin and others to support his next venture, which was to operate buses in London on his own account. This was the National Steam Car Company Ltd, founded on 19 June 1909 and destined later to play a notable part in the expansion of the motor-bus industry. The company's first buses ran between Westminster Bridge Road and Shepherds Bush on 2 November 1909, and by 1911 it was operating thirty-eight vehicles. They were paraffin fired and were popular for their smooth and silent running.

On 1 January 1911 the LGOC bought the Great Eastern company and became once more the undisputed leader in the London bus trade. On 15 May 1912 the pooling agreement with Tillings was converted into a closer association, and as this limited the Tilling London fleet to 150, it was not long before the Tilling directors were deciding to turn to the provinces for further expansion. In the meantime, having ridden the storm of mechanisation and seen their £100 stock rise in the market from £20 in 1909 to £190 in 1911, the directors of the LGOC sold their business to Albert Stanley's Underground group on 1 January 1912.

Frank Searle's successful development of a vehicle for the LGOC had affected the sales of Daimlers, and the Daimler/BSA group had made various attempts to re-enter this market. They also tried to obtain Searle himself, who eventually parted company with the General at a board meeting on 4 May 1911. The Premier Motorbus Company, which Daimler had hopefully formed, failed to get off the ground when the Tilling directors told the LGOC board at the same meeting that the 'KPL' (Knight/Pieper/Lanchester) petrol-electric vehicle it was intending to run infringed their patents.* Searle then joined Daimlers, where again he influenced bus history by designing a vehicle which sold for £825 and was an improvement on anything else then running, including his own B-type. The latter was by now the standard product of the Walthamstow works which, in 1912, the LGOC hived off as the Associated Equipment Company Ltd.

But Daimlers were not the only people watching the LGOC at the beginning of 1912 and waiting for Stanley to show his hand. There was also the British Electric Traction Company which, despite the legal difficulties in the way of company development of electric tramways, had greatly expanded its interests at home and abroad during the first fifteen years of its life, though with varying financial success. Emile Garcke was never blind to the potential of the motor bus, and in 1905 his automobile committee had blossomed into a new subsidiary, the British Automobile Development Company Ltd, which sponsored developments in

---

* It was from the contact established at this meeting that the LGOC-Tilling agreement of 1912 was to stem. The Premier Motorbus Company here must not be confused with W. P. Allen's company of the same name which introduced some de Dions in 1913 and was bought by the LGOC in 1916. The 'KPL' bus was based upon the petrol-electric system of Henri Pieper of Liege, which was to have been used by the Gearless Motor Omnibus Company Ltd, another Daimler-sponsored concern registered in 1906, which in fact ran normal Daimler vehicles as part of the LGOC pool.

various parts of the country and formed the Amalgamated Motor Bus Company Ltd in London in 1906. The original intention was to sponsor the mechanisation of various horse-bus undertakings within the associations, but this had failed to gain support and BAD had put a few Brush vehicles in service under Amalgamated management in February 1907. For a while, this was the only BET motor-bus interest in London, although their two tramway companies, Metropolitan Electric Tramways Ltd in the northern suburbs and the smaller South Metropolitan Electric Tramways & Lighting Company Ltd in the south, represented between them a considerable investment. As these tramways depended mainly upon local suburban traffic, any extension of the LGOC bus network to feed the tube railways would threaten this, as well as the limited amount of through traffic carried by the MET cars over LCC tramway lines.

Any such development, however, was precluded by the LGOC's articles of association, which limited it to a fifteen-mile radius from the GPO in St Martin's-le-Grand. Stanley's challenge to BET was the reconstruction of the company to abandon the limiting radius. The BET directors countered by forming the Tramways (MET) Omnibus Company Ltd, placing an order through Searle for 100 of the new Daimler buses, and negotiating a maintenance contract covering labour, materials, petrol and lubrication at a charge of 3½d a mile. Searle then called on Stanley and after telling him of the threat from BET, tried to sell him more Daimlers. Stanley was prepared to buy 250 vehicles, but only if Daimler undertook not to sell to any other London operator for five years. When Searle reported this to BET, they promptly increased their order to 350, and the maintenance charge was reduced to 3d a mile. The British Automobile Traction Company (BET's former BAD, now more happily named) also placed an order for Daimlers, so that a collision of interests seemed likely with all that that implied.

The dangers as well as the advantages of competition were fresh in the minds of Londoners. In a prosecution for dangerous driving in 1908, the magistrate had said that he was unable to understand the behaviour of the drivers concerned, one a

General and the other a Great Eastern man, until it was explained to him that 'Generals' were running in opposition to 'Great Easterns' along the Lea Bridge Road. Tactics that had been perfected in horse-bus days were still practised, and while the operators themselves were responsible for deliberately setting buses to 'nurse' their competitors, the men joined in the rivalry with enthusiasm and initiative. It seems likely that it was only the threat of new price competition that kept BET and LER interests from outright conflict and before the year was out a new settlement had been reached which was to have widespread effects. The LER agreed to limit the operating area of the LGOC, and BET, following Tillings' precedent, agreed upon a limit to their fleet in London. The Daimlers still went into service, becoming part of the LGOC pool, and such was the scope for expansion in London that before long they were all employed, whether as dark blue 'Metropolitans' or emerald green 'British'. This was a period in which many new services and extensions to the country surrounding London were being introduced.

Settlement of the tramway interests took rather longer, but on 20 November 1913 the London & Suburban Traction Company Ltd was formed, its capital being owned jointly by BET and the Underground group. It owned or controlled the three tramway companies, MET, LUT and Southmet, and the Tramways (MET) Omnibus Company. The Southern fleet of ten B-types were operated on behalf of the Southmet company by the LGOC, and an agreement with Daimlers allowed the Gearless company to operate a maximum of twenty vehicles as part of the pool, and gave the L&ST a minority interest in it. AEC and Daimler then became closely associated, Daimler engines being used in AEC chassis built at Walthamstow, but this link lasted only until 1914, when Daimlers repurchased the original 350 vehicles and sold them to the War Office.

The LGOC was now finally restricted to operation in London, its territory being limited to a thirty-mile radius, which, with various adjustments, has become the London Transport area of today. The development of bus services elsewhere in the British Isles was left to Tillings and BET and agreements to this effect were signed with each of the existing BET companies, wherever they were situated.

The settlement of 1912 left Albert Stanley the undisputed master of passenger transport over most of London, with only the Metropolitan and main-line railways, the LCC tramways, and the few remaining independents outside his sphere of influence. As to the latter, an agreement with Clarkson in December 1913 brought the National Steam Car Company into association with the Underground group and, in 1916, the LGOC bought the last remaining firms, W. P. Allen's Allen Omnibus Company Ltd and its associate, Premier. In 1915, the Common Fund Act had brought the suburban services of the main-line railways into the pool, so that when in the same year LER bought BET's share in the L&ST, Sir George Gibb's policy had been carried by his successor to what seemed to be its logical conclusion.

DEVELOPMENTS IN THE PROVINCES

The complexities of the London combine must not distract attention from the growth of the industry in the rest of the British Isles. The early railway bus services have already been described, and mention made of the importance of the Milnes-Daimler in providing a sturdy chassis capable of standing up to operating conditions. The technical breakthrough represented by the 2d a mile tyre contracts introduced in 1905 allowed provincial as well as metropolitan development to start in earnest, but, as in London, only an operator with ingenuity and perseverence, supported by adequate capital, could hope to set up a successful concern.

To begin with, initiative was individual and local, except for the activities of BET. Some of the pioneers were to become household names in the industry; J. B. Walford and the Ortona company at Cambridge; the Barton family at Long Eaton; Walter Flexman French, whose London activities of 1901 were followed by ventures in the south-east where he was instrumental in founding the East Kent, Maidstone & District and Southdown companies; and the Crosland-Taylors at Chester. E. B. Hutchinson took the whole east coast as his operating area when he formed United Automobile Services, starting almost simultaneously in Lowestoft and County Durham. But to concentrate upon these names alone would be unfair to many others who set their sights lower, and achieved proportionate success.

Amongst them was a man called Ezra Laycock. Laycock was the village postman at Cowlinge, between Keighley and Colne, and had to walk three miles to Cross Hills every morning to collect the mail. In about 1890 he decided to buy a horse and cart for the purpose; later on, he acquired a wagonette and began to carry passengers to Kildwick station, and occasionally to Colne or Keighley. When others followed his example, he decided, in 1905, to go one better and obtained a motor omnibus.

He was unable to find a vehicle in service in London, and so went to Brighton where, after seeing a Milnes-Daimler at work, he ordered a similar machine. The arrival of this bus in Yorkshire was something of an occasion, for Laycock took a party of twenty south with him, and they spent four days bringing the vehicle back. It has been said that this was the first motor bus (other than those of the NER and L&YR) to run in the north, although there seems to have been one working at Harrogate in 1903 or 1904. In any case, it was a success, and by the end of 1906 Laycocks were running three buses, one of which was a double-decker. Ezra Laycock died in 1933, having established himself at a time when others were failing; later, his sons ran the business, now transferred to Barnoldswick, from where they operated a service into Skipton.

The pioneers have left imprints upon the industry that are still recognisable today. C. E. Lee comments that the titles of many of the territorial companies clearly indicate whose was the initiative behind their formation. Thus W. F. French invariably used the term 'motor services', as in the case of Southdown, and Cannon and Mackenzie copied him in the other companies they were associated with. Ribble is another example, and Major Hickmott, who presided over its foundation, was an early associate of French. Sidney Garcke, on the other hand, tended to use the word 'traction' in the titles of the early BAT companies, such as Thames Valley, while Walter Wolsey used 'road car' in the case of West Yorkshire and other Tilling undertakings.

The first six years of the century saw development of bus services all over the country, with the railways taking the lead. Even so, the motor bus was still a rarity, and found more frequently in the remoter places than in the industrial areas and larger towns. By the end of 1906, there were buses running at Lands End and on the north coast of Scotland, and already the number of services was mounting into the hundreds. By the outbreak of war, most of the larger towns and cities had services of some kind, while a pattern of occupation had appeared over the remainder of the country. It is easier to define the areas *without* bus services in the summer of 1914 : except for south Devon and parts of Cornwall, they were rare in the West Country : they were uncommon in the south Midlands and East Anglia and absent in central Wales and in Lincolnshire; they were scattered widely throughout the north of England and Scotland, and virtually absent from Ireland. In areas of dense population the situation varied : there were many services in and around London but very few in the Welsh valleys; they were more common in the West Riding than in south Lancashire.

One of the reasons why the industry grew first in the smaller towns and rural areas was that the railway companies looked upon the motor bus mainly as a means of extending their services without going to the expense of building new lines. Another was the relative ease of running buses in the more leisurely conditions of the countryside, as compared with the wear and tear of operation on city streets. In Birmingham, for example, conditions were as arduous as they were in London, and so it is not surprising that the first experiment there was short lived. The Birmingham Motor Express Company Ltd was formed in 1903 and began running in October of that year between New Street and the 'Fountain', Hagley Road. The first three vehicles were built by Mulliners with Napier engines, and these were followed early in 1904 by six Milnes-Daimlers. In 1899 BET, which had been buying tramways in the Black Country and Birmingham with a view to electrification, found itself the owner of a number of horse buses, including some acquired when the Birmingham General Omnibus Company Ltd had failed that year. In 1902, the BGO buses were given to BET's City of Birmingham Tramways, and those of CBT were added to them in 1904.

The traffic manager of Birmingham Tramways at the time was O. C. Power, one of the most remarkable men the industry has known. An Irishman, born in 1880, he joined CBT in 1899, three years before BET acquired it and in the same year that R. J. Howley became BET's assistant permanent way engineer. He became traffic manager in 1900 and held the post (with Midland Red from 1905) until he died in office in 1943. At this time, however, Power lacked a colleague capable of giving him the technical support he needed to make motor buses a success. Nevertheless, in April 1905 the CBT Omnibus Department put four Dürkopp vehicles to work in competition with the Birmingham Motor Express, and when that company sought additional capital later in the year it was taken over by BET and renamed the Birmingham & Midland Motor Omnibus Company Ltd. As early as 1900, BET buses in Birmingham had been painted red, and thus the famous Midland Red was born. George Pollard, general manager of BME, became engineer to BMMO, but left in November 1905 to take up the post of second engineer with the London Motor Omnibus Company Ltd, and for the next two years BMMO were beset by difficulties beyond their mechanical ability. BET had acquired motor buses more or less by accident, for they had bought BME only to get rid of competition, and on 5 October 1907 the motor buses were withdrawn and BMMO reverted to horse buses for the next four and a half years.

One of the BET directors who had been working with BMMO during its first motorised years was Sidney Garcke, son of the chairman. At his suggestion, six Brush buses were driven down to Deal, where Garcke set up the Deal & District Motor Services in April 1908, the ownership of the fleet being transferred in 1910 to BAD. Thus for a time Midland Red buses were operating in Kent. For some years after this, Deal & District remained the only BET motor bus undertaking outside London until, in 1912,

E

the decision was taken to re-commence in Birmingham. The BMMO directors appointed as their chief engineer L. G. Wyndham Shire, who had been maintaining the fleet at Deal, and thirteen Tilling-Stevens petrol-electric vehicles went into service in May 1912.

In 1913, BAT seriously started to develop motor-bus operation, and it was not long before BET interest in the industry had become firmly established. In November 1913 a branch was opened at Macclesfield, and in July 1915 another was started in Reading. At about this time BAT also acquired interests in various established undertakings, including the Aldershot & District, Maidstone & District, and the Ortona and Trent companies. Additionally, it encouraged BET tramway subsidiaries to develop motor-bus services, and in some cases formed holding companies to provide local control of both the tramway and the motor-bus undertaking. Examples were the Scottish General Transport Company Ltd, the Northern General Transport Company Ltd, and the South Wales Transport Company Ltd.

The London settlements of 1912/13 which encouraged the provincial spread of BAT also drove Tillings to seek new fields for development. In April 1914 they formed the Folkestone District Road Car Company, and before long the two interests met in the difficult conditions of 1916. BAT had obtained control of two Thanet firms in which W. F. French had an interest, and these, along with the Deal & District undertaking and the Tilling branch, were merged in August 1916 to form the East Kent Road Car Company Ltd, with BAT and Tillings each holding an interest.

In 1915 Tillings started to operate in Hove, while BAT formed Southdown Motor Services Ltd by merging its London & Southern Counties Haulage Company with Worthing Motor Services Ltd, whose predecessor, the Sussex Motor Road Car Company, had started operating in 1904. Southdown also took over the country services of the Brighton, Hove & Preston United Omnibus Company Ltd which, in the following year, sold the rest of its business to Tillings. The BH&PU tours were then resold to Southdown, so that from 1917 Tillings had a share in a second BAT company. The National, limited in London by their agreement of

1913, also turned to provincial operation, and in July of that year took over the services radiating from Chelmsford which had been started by the Great Eastern Railway.

In October 1914, Birmingham Corporation (which had started running motor buses in 1913 to supplement its tramways) purchased the BMMO Tennant Street garage, together with thirty vehicles and all services running wholly within the city. The Birmingham settlement provided for the BMMO country services to carry traffic within the city, subject to protective fares, and this, in time, was to help make the company the largest of provincial operators. BMMO was also fortunate in that its petrol-electric buses were not favoured by the War Office, so that in October 1914 it was able to take over the services of BAT's Worcestershire Motor Transport Company Ltd, whose fleet of more orthodox vehicles had been commandeered. It also took over BAT's own services at Leamington and Warwick, established itself at Malvern and Shrewsbury and, in February 1918, acquired the share capital of the North Warwickshire Motor Omnibus & Traction Company Ltd, a substantial operator in the Tamworth and Nuneaton area.

Elsewhere, events up to 1919 moved at a similar pace, though many areas remained undeveloped until the post-war boom. In Scotland, the Scottish Motor Traction Company Ltd started its first service on 'Ne'er day' 1906, but its early Maudslays proved less than satisfactory, and Baillie William Thomson, the father of the company, designed the 'Lothian', with which SMT established itself rapidly after 1912. Apart from this, motor-bus services in Scotland before 1919 were limited to those of the GNSR on Deeside, various tramway companies in the Midlands (those of BET being combined into Scottish Transport and its subsidiaries), and a handful of independents. Few motor buses had yet appeared in Ireland, although the Belfast & Northern Counties Railway had started running some in 1902 between Whiteabbey and Greenisland. In England and Wales, the BAT companies had ear-marked large territorial areas and were starting to purchase competitors with a view to consolidation, with United and one or two other sizeable independents following suit. Railway bus operation was sporadic, the only systematic development being that of the GWR which, by 1908, owned over 100 vehicles, mainly in Wales and the West Country. Here and there municipal tramway departments were running a few motor buses.

Many petrol-engined vehicles had been requisitioned in 1914, and when, in 1916, development of new bus services was virtually prohibited, followed by fuel rationing in 1917, there was little the industry could do but await the future with the certain knowledge that it would offer unlimited scope for expansion.

CHAPTER FOUR

THE YEARS OF EXPANSION:
1920-1931

THE first world war proved to be one of the great turning points in the history of the motor-bus industry. In 1914 the horse bus still dominated the picture most people had of road transport, even though the motors had taken over in large areas of the country. The last London horse-bus service— run by Tillings between Peckham Rye and Honor Oak—had not been withdrawn until 4 August 1914, and the last London horse tram lingered on in the Rotherhithe Road until the following year. Wide areas of the provinces had never seen a motor bus, and in the industrial areas the electric tramway was still the symbol of a progressive municipal council. The last urban horse bus to disappear must have been the one that crossed the High Level Bridge at Newcastle-upon-Tyne until 13 June 1931; the toll was a halfpenny a wheel for vehicles and a halfpenny per foot passenger, and the bus was popular at a halfpenny single fare. In the country districts, the horse-drawn carriers' carts could not compete with motor buses and vans, but a Suffolk horse bus ran on market days from Wickhambrook to Newmarket until as late as 1932, when one of the horses died; though its survival was perhaps more a tribute to the tenacity of its owner rather than to the economic or social value of the service.

THE BASIS OF EXPANSION

All the same, by 1914 the pioneering days of the engineers were over and instead of the constant expense and discouragement of mechanical trouble, the industry had a fairly reliable and not unduly expensive tool to work with. The biggest problems—lubrication and tyre maintenance—had been solved, and in men like Dicks and Power there had appeared the managerial skill necessary to successful traffic organisation. The two main barriers to the growth of the industry were a relative shortage of capital and a much more serious shortage of mechanical skill, each of which were to disappear as the result of the war. It was not engineers who had been in short supply, so much as mechanics and drivers capable of maintaining the buses and handling them on the road, and this earlier shortage was ended by the return from war service of men who had learned mechanical trades. But while this enabled the industry to progress, it also introduced an entirely new factor. Many of these men were not anxious to work as fitters or drivers in the service of a company or municipal undertaking, but were looking forward to becoming their own masters. Some could turn to relatives willing to invest a few hundred pounds in what was generally thought to be a profitable enterprise; all of them had some form of gratuity. They were helped, too, by the sales of military vehicles, many of them suitable for commercial purposes, and they also had the support of the manufacturing industry, anxious to re-establish itself on a peacetime basis. Both British and foreign firms offered buses that were cheap to buy and deferred terms on which to buy them. The barriers that before the war had restricted bus operation to the larger operators were now down, but while the way was open for newcomers to the industry, it was equally easy for the established concerns to expand.

All this supply potential would have been useless without sufficient effective demand. Before the war, the industry had been largely engaged in providing a substitute for the horse bus in towns and cities, in very real competition with the electric tramway, while development of new services in country areas had been relatively slow and limited to a few of the more promising areas. The war, however, had built up a reserve of spending power and one of the few outlets available in the post-war world of shortages was in travel. So the new potential of the industry was matched by a corresponding demand for its services and the stage was set for expansion on the grand scale. By the end of the decade, the network of bus services that we have today had been established; the express coach services had appeared from nowhere and the whole economy of inland transport had been transformed. At the same time the motor bus had ceased to be an obvious adaptation of the horse bus and the charabanc had become obsolete with the development of the touring coach.

In this chapter we shall trace the threads that went to make up this story. It is a period that has become almost legendary in the industry, and one that is cited to illustrate both the remarkable qualities that made such expansion possible and the ill effects that are said to result from unrestrained competition. According to *Garcke's Year Book*, there were 331 operators existing in 1916 and 3,962 in 1930. Capital invested rose from 9 million to 55 million pounds in the same period.

THE AREA AGREEMENTS

The concept of an operating territory has been characteristic of the motor-bus industry from its earliest days. Some faster-growing operators tended to expand along the best traffic routes until they had established a network of services. Often this would lead to the opening of a branch in a neighbouring town; in this way Crosville, having started in Chester, began to expand by setting up first in Nantwich and then in Mold and Warrington. The aim was always to establish a territorial monopoly and the opposition came from operators who were either content with a limited horizon or seeking a quick profit by imitating the methods of the pioneers. But while territorial ambitions marked the activities of such men as E. B. Hutchinson of United, and W. P. Allen of Silver Queen, the aims of the BET directors were even wider, taking the whole of Great Britain as their potential operating area. As early as 1900 they had divided the British Isles into eleven territories, each under a district superintendent of senior status.

It was never, of course, intended that BET operating companies should compete with each other, and when in course of expansion they met the territories of other substantial operators capable of negotiating from a position of strength, competition was equally avoided. The settlement of 1913 between BET and Stanley's LER combine was the first expression of a policy which later extended throughout the BET provincial developments, in dealing with Tillings, the larger independents, and, later on, the railways. On 17 December 1913, the Provincial Omnibus Owners' Association was formed to safeguard BET and other large companies and to watch or promote legislation in their general interest. It was this organisation which provided for the definition of mutual boundaries between its member companies.

Sidney Garcke, son of the founder of BET, was to a great extent the architect of the area agreements. Born in 1885, he was at first associated with the manufacturing of buses and then became a pioneer of operation, as has already been described. He provided the counter-balance to J. F. Heaton at the time when Tillings and BET were in more or less uneasy harness together. He returned to his early interest in manufacturing in 1943, when he joined the board of Dennis Bros Ltd, of which he became chairman two years later. He died in 1948.

During the war years, BET interests in the south-east had crystallised into the Southdown, East Kent and Maidstone & District companies, with Tillings holding an interest in the first two, and it was between these three that the first area agreements were reached. Considerably more than a matter of financial arrangement between BAT and Tillings, these agreements, like others that were to follow, were negotiated individually between pairs of companies having common boundaries and took the form of contracts with the force of law. (It is conceivable that the courts might have refused to enforce them as being contracts in restraint of trade, but their value to the parties concerned was such that they have never apparently been challenged—the circumstances of one manifest breach of contract in 1950 will be described in a later chapter.)

An area agreement leaves a company that subscribes to it master in its own house, so far as competition from firms of its own standing is concerned, and leaves it free to compete with its smaller neighbours or to buy them out. It also usually provides for the division of any undertaking lying astride a boundary which may be purchased by either party to the agreement. The boundary will be defined as far as possible to run through towns where traffic can be exchanged, lengthy services being unusual at the time most of the agreements were being made. Thus the boundary between the East Kent and Maidstone companies passed through Faversham, Ashford, Rye and Hastings, and 'penetrating' operation across this line was a development of much more recent years.

The area agreement system has always been flexible, and open to newcomers; an agreement between the Trent and Barton companies was made after 1950. It has never committed any operator to financial involvement with another, and it is thus incorrect to regard it as a form of combine. It is instead rather a special form of cartel; a producers' association designed mainly to protect its members' revenue. It envisages a state of affairs where no new competition can appear and so is a first step towards further combination, provided this can be achieved. In so far as it brought an element of stability into the development of road passenger services, the system has benefited the travelling public, while its other effects will be examined in the following pages. In its early days it was necessitated by the licensing system which then existed, but its usefulness outlived this aspect of its creation.

It was largely during the 'twenties that the territorial companies defined their boundaries, first in the areas where development had been greatest before 1916 and then, as further expansion took place, in the more remote parts of the country. Only at the end of the decade was it possible to divide up the map of Great Britain, company by company, and even then the areas claimed by some were by no means reflected in their actual operations. The process began quite soon after the war had ended and was marked by a growing association between Tillings and BET.

Richard Tilling, who had inherited the family love of horses and yet had presided over the conversion of the family business to motors, had the same wide horizons as the BET directors, but decided in 1916 to work with rather than against them. In the early months of 1919, a group of businessmen at Ipswich, interested in the prospects of developing bus services, approached Tillings with a view to a joint enterprise. The Tillings sent some vehicles down and began operating in June 1919, but the Eastern Counties Road Car Company Ltd, which was formed on 30 August 1919 to take them over, was, in fact, promoted in association with BAT. During the next few years, BAT's direct operations were transferred to the management of local subsidiaries and Tillings obtained an interest in each of these; Ribble Motor Services Ltd was formed in 1919, and absorbed the BAT Preston branch the following year; the Thames Valley Traction Company Ltd was registered on 10 July 1920 to take over the Reading branch; and the North Western Road Car Company Ltd was formed on 23 April 1923 to take over the 'Peak District Committee' services at Macclesfield, Buxton and Stockport. In 1916, BET had assisted in the formation of Bournemouth & District Motor Services Ltd which began running in 1918 and when, in 1920, this company was re-named Hants & Dorset Motor Services, Tillings obtained an interest. In 1922, Tillings acquired a considerable holding in BAT and nominated two directors to its board; thereafter, a joint policy of development was followed. BAT was not, however, responsible for all BET bus operations. Various tramway companies were developing bus services during this period and these remained in the direct ownership of BET.

By 1928, BAT was interested in nineteen bus companies and was associated with Tillings in eleven of them, as well as being itself partly owned by Tillings. To simplify this rather clumsy arrangement, BAT was reconstructed in 1928 with the new title of Tilling & British Automobile Traction Ltd. Tillings exchanged its shares in the various operating companies for an increased holding in the new company, which also acquired control of a number of other BET companies, such as the Peterborough & District Traction Company Ltd and the Yorkshire Traction Company Ltd, whose bus operations had in the meantime become more important than their tramways. Sidney Garcke remained chairman of Tilling & British, but Richard Tilling, who had been the driving force in his company, died in June 1929. He had been one of Thomas Tilling's eleven children and he himself had seven, one of them achieving her own fame as Mabel Constanduros. He had remained active in the business to the end, as well as riding with the Essex Hunt at the age of seventy-five, but with the conversion to motors and the various negotiations, first with Ashfield and then with Sidney Garcke, power had increasingly passed to his nephew, Walter Wolsey Jr, and to J. F. Heaton.

Heaton was born in Yorkshire in 1880 and educated at Bradford Technical College. At twenty-three he became secretary of a colliery at Dewsbury and while in that post took eighth place in the examination list for the Society of Incorporated Accountants and Auditors. He was associated with the Harrogate Road Car Company before joining Tillings as accountant in 1915, became secretary (on a temporary basis) a year later, and was appointed a director in 1924. He worked in close association with the second generation of the Tilling family, but there was no obvious successor to Richard and the third generation was not sufficiently united (nor perhaps sufficiently ruthless) to use the power it possessed. John Tilling (Richard's grandson), in his book, *Kings of the Highway*, refers to 'a division of opinion on matters of great importance within the family, which came to a head on Richard's death', and adds : 'It is sad that within twelve months (of this event) the company should be left without one director bearing the name of Tilling'. At the monthly board meeting that fell due on the Monday after Richard's funeral, two of his three sons chose to be absent. Harry, the eldest, seems to have expected his cousin, Walter Wolsey, to be elected chairman, which he was, but to have assumed that he or his younger brother Reginald would be made vice-chairman. When this position went to J. F. Heaton, he 'seemed to feel his position acutely', and resigned from the board a few months later, to be followed within a year by his brother. Wolsey remained on the board until 1950 and repeated his success as a negotiator when the settlement between the combine and the railways was reached in 1929. He died in 1964 at the age of ninety-two.

Tilling & British did not include all the Tilling and BET bus interests. The London undertakings remained separate, as part of the LER pool, and Tillings continued to operate a few coaches for private hire work in London, including six acquired from Pickfords in 1925. Their Brighton services were also kept entirely under their own management. BET, on the other hand, retained a few companies in its direct control, either because they remained predominantly tramway concerns or, as in the case of the Potteries Electric Traction Company Ltd, because of the need for re-organisation following the severe competition which had undermined tramway finances. Northern General and Midland Red were two substantial companies retained in direct BET ownership because of their association with BET tramway interests.

Throughout the 'twenties, a number of other companies were developing to territorial status. United expanded throughout Norfolk and into Lincolnshire, as well as in County Durham, and by 1922 had opened branches in Newcastle to serve south Northumberland, and at Ripon, from which it expanded northwards in Yorkshire. A subsidiary, W. T. Underwood Ltd, was set up at Clowne, near Chesterfield, and later became the East Midland Motor Services. The National Electric Construction Company Ltd, a holding and development company similar to the BET, was responsible for establishing City of Oxford Motor Services Ltd and the Devon General Omnibus & Touring Company Ltd as bus operators and, in South Wales, was associated with the predecessor of the Western Welsh Omnibus Company Ltd.

A third important development was the provincial expansion of the National, which took place after Thomas Clarkson had severed his connection with that company in 1919. The directors decided to abandon steam buses and a new agreement was reached with the LGOC whereby operation in London was given up. National remained free to operate outside the LGOC's 'special area', but it was also agreed that it should develop the country districts in the north and east of this area on behalf of the General.

The 1919 settlement also provided for the outright transfer to the National of a depot at Bedford, which the LGOC had acquired from the New Central Omnibus Company Ltd but could not continue to use because of the 1913 settlement with BET. This, together with the group of services already working at Chelmsford, formed the basis of the National Omnibus & Transport Company Ltd, as the National Steam Car Company became on 13 February 1920. Subsequent development was rapid (though no dividend was paid for the three years prior to 1925) and the company was not content merely to develop the territory it had acquired. Many of the more promising districts had already been occupied by developing companies, but one of the largest areas where expansion was still possible was the West Country, and by 1921 NO&T had staked its claim and established itself at Yeovil, Stroud, Taunton, Bridgwater and Trowbridge.

Further west, Commander F. T. Hare, RN, had established the Devon Motor Transport and Cornwall Motor Transport companies, which had rapidly expanded in an area west of Okehampton and Totnes, subject to a boundary agreement with Devon General. By 1927, Commander Hare controlled a fleet of some 250 vehicles and had started a subsidiary company in Jersey. In that same year, he sold the two English companies to NO&T and joined their board, assuming responsibility for the company's Devon and Cornwall area. At the same time, NO&T bought up a number of other operators in Devonshire.

Thus in six years NO&T had become the territorial company of the western peninsula, where the only other substantial bus operator was the GWR. This achievement was the more remarkable in that the NO&T depots were not opened in towns close to existing areas of operation, but were established by sending one or two men and some buses into an unknown area and leaving it to them to recruit staff, hire premises, obtain the necessary licences and get started.

Another grand individualist among the pioneers of those days was W. P. Allen who, while still a young man, established bus services in various parts of England. He operated in London from 1913 to 1916 and also at Folkestone and Farningham in Kent, at Colchester and Clacton in Essex, and in Lincolnshire and

Worcestershire. By 1928 he had withdrawn from active participation in the industry, having sold his various concerns to the local territorial operator, but for many years remained a director of the Aldershot & District and East Kent companies, as well as chairman of the Lincolnshire Road Car Company Ltd which had been formed from his Silver Queen undertaking. He died in 1959.

Many companies had managed to make some progress during the war, and Midland Red was one of them. A local operator was taken over at Malvern in 1916, and at Shrewsbury in the same year a single bus was sent to take over an existing service between Shrewsbury and Bicton Heath and develop new traffic from various villages on different days of the week, thus laying the foundations of the future Shrewsbury group of services. Plans at the end of the war provided for new garages to be built at Bromsgrove, Shrewsbury, Nuneaton, Leamington, Coventry, Hereford, Stafford, Wolverhampton and Banbury, with central workshops at Edgbaston in Birmingham. These, with the operations at Worcester, indicate a clearly defined territory which remained recognisable until recent years. The only omission is Leicester, where BMMO opened its first services in 1922 and, by 1927, was finding it necessary to build a 100-bus garage. At Worcester, agreement was reached with the Corporation for BMMO buses to replace the trams in 1928, the council receiving the balance of receipts over expenditure and being responsible for any deficit. In the Black Country, the BET tramways had naturally been left alone in the early expansion of Midland Red services, but when in the middle 'twenties other operators started competitive services, BET decided to close down the tramways and BMMO buses gradually replaced them from 1926 onwards. In the following year, an agreement was reached with the Hereford Transport Company Ltd as a result of which the Midland Red services that had been developed at Abergavenny, Ross and Monmouth were exchanged for HTC routes nearer to Hereford.

Midland Red was exceptionally fortunate in its management, even in a period when exceptional men were not rare in the industry. At that time it had no general manager, traffic being in the hands of O. C. Power, and engineering in those of Wyndham Shire, each man reporting direct to the chairman, R. J. Howley. The two were not the easiest of colleagues but, between them, they gave an impetus to their company that lasted for many years. On Shire's retirement in 1940, he was succeeded by D. M. Sinclair, and when Power died in 1943 Sinclair became the company's first general manager. He had joined Midland Red from the Northern General company, where he had been assistant chief engineer since 1931.

In general, Midland Red in the 'twenties was too busily engaged in developing new routes of its own and administering new areas to find time to take over other operators' services. It would not in any case have been a wise policy since there was nothing to stop new competition appearing the day after one had been bought. The same consideration restrained most of the other territorial companies, their purchases being limited to the acquisition of larger firms, where amalgamation offered immediate and substantial economies, or where a considerable amount of new territory could be won. For most of them, however, this was a period of steady expansion and development, during which they concentrated upon establishing management and maintenance facilities capable of supporting the new services as they were opened.

The railway companies played relatively little part in the expansion of the 'twenties, except for the GWR which introduced over 100 new services between 1920 and 1928. In central and south Wales and west of Bodmin in Cornwall, the GWR was the principal operator, as it was in the Kingsbridge peninsula in Devon. Other services were scattered throughout the railway's territory, some of the heaviest being at Slough and Maidenhead, while an exceptionally long one for the period ran from Banbury via Chipping Norton, Burford and Lechlade to Swindon. Between Oxford and Cheltenham, the bus service ran in connection with trains from London and offered a more direct route than could be taken by rail. The GWR also purchased a number of small businesses, as well as inheriting services from the Cambrian Railway in consequence of the grouping. It had a mixed fleet which numbered over 300 vehicles by 1928 and included seventy Burfords, a small and now forgotten vehicle marketed by a company belonging to one of the directors of NO&T.

One or two local authorities also developed services well outside their boundaries during these years, but in the main, municipal transport departments were more cautious than the commercial undertakings. Frequently this was because of heavy capital investment in electric tramways which they were reluctant to write off, but in the absence of general powers, tramway undertakings were also faced with the expense of parliamentary procedure before they could start running motor buses. In some cases, the trolleybus was adopted as a half-way replacement for the trams, since it offered a continued load for the municipal power station; the Corporation of Ipswich, for example, retained electric traction in this way until its generating station was nationalised and only introduced motor buses when the cost of electricity for traction was sharply increased. All the same, the eighteen local authorities in Great Britain which were running motor buses in 1914 had become ninety by 1928, accounting for most of the municipal transport departments in the country. By 1930, eighteen municipal tramways had been abandoned entirely. Relatively few company trolleybus undertakings were established, but NEC's Mexborough & Swinton Traction Company started running them in 1915, and gave up its trams entirely in 1929. Others were at Llanelli and Nottingham, and larger company undertakings in Lancashire and west London were developed in the following decade.

THE RISE OF COMPETITION

The difficulties of establishing a motor-bus service before 1916 had been such that only those with considerable reserves of capital had stood any chance of success. Here and there, small carriers' businesses were mechanised with varying success and some of these continued into the post-war years. More often, these men started running motor buses after 1920 and contributed much to the development of rural bus services all over the country. Not infrequently they were assisted by the manufacturing companies, whose salesmen played a great part in the post-war expansion.

But by no means all the newcomers were established concerns seizing the opportunity to mechanise their fleets. The industry attracted a great many men who found in it a job offering greater freedom than they could expect in a factory or on a farm. Many drivers and conductors recruited by the large firms at this time chose the job because of this, and because they assumed there would be a security in it comparable with that offered by the railways. Some however wanted rather more; they wanted the independence of running their own business and the expanding bus industry seemed to offer them just this opportunity. In towns and villages all over Great Britain such men would buy a bus and set up in business—it was as easy as that. Some had the ability to make their way in the trade, others were more hopeful than able. Some found luck was on their side, others failed when they deserved better results. Sometimes a full public service would be started at once; others kept out of that sort of work and only undertook private parties. Often they met with opposition.

In some places, small operators were solely responsible for starting bus services in an area where they had taken the lead over the territorial companies; in others, there were large operators who were providing too good a service to leave any opening for new competition. Probably there are types of operation best suited to large or to small-scale business, but in a period of rapid expansion such distinctions are not always clear, and the tendency is towards experiment and adjustment. In fact, the very speed of the expansion which took place accounts for the impression of disorder afforded by most reminiscences of the 'twenties. And it was this impression which, in the eyes of the Royal Commission of 1929, justified State intervention to 'rationalise' the industry, and so led to the discriminatory clauses in the Road Traffic Act of 1930 which put an end to the days of competition.

What, in fact, did this supposed disorder amount to? W. J. Crosland-Taylor, in an admirable history of his family business,

F

Crosville Motor Services, refers to the bitter competition that raged for a time on the Ellesmere Port to Chester route between Crosville and Hudson's Bus. J. M. Hudson had been a chief engineer in the Merchant Navy, which he left in 1919 to seek a living ashore. Crosville had started running between Chester and Birkenhead via Ellesmere Port in 1911, and Hudson was presumably attracted to the industry by the success of this service. Crosland-Taylor does not tell us, but it would be likely that, by September 1919 when Hudson began to run, the Crosville buses were unable to satisfy public demand, as the company was then expanding in new directions. In any case, Hudson did quite well and started a second service shortly afterwards. The reaction of Crosville was to put a bus on the road painted in Hudson's colour, running on his timetable but just in front of him: Claude Crosland-Taylor, Crosville's managing director, was living up to the threat he had made to Hudson's face that he would 'run him off the road'. Hudson thereupon abandoned his timetable and for a while buses ran haphazard, with both sides losing revenue. Finding that Hudson was not giving up, Crosville put on a second bus, with a third on Saturdays, and followed this by running every half-hour and cutting the return fare from 1s 4d to 1s 2d. The effect was to induce more people to travel, and Hudson found to his surprise that his revenue was increasing.

But when employers become involved in close competition like this, their staff may be tempted to go further. The Crosville drivers began to try, literally, to drive Hudson's buses off the road, even when Hudson himself was driving, and the situation soon became such that the Ellesmere Port Council, which had licensed both operators, had to intervene. Taylor and Hudson were firmly told to co-operate and, in the upshot, Taylor bought Hudson out and recruited him to his own staff. The 'war' had lasted from August 1920 to January 1922, and resulted in an expansion of traffic that might otherwise have taken far longer to develop. Others followed, and in spite of or because of them, Crosville prospered and the travelling public benefited from more frequent and cheaper bus services.

Not far away in the Potteries, a different aspect of competition appeared. Here the BET tramway company, Potteries Electric Traction, with a virtual monopoly of urban passenger transport, had experimented with motor buses as early as 1900, and again between 1904 and 1906. Because of the many low railway bridges in the area, its tramcars were single-deckers, and while it had built up its traffic on low fares, it was not financially well prepared to face a period of competition. In accordance with BET policy, the company developed an omnibus branch, but its vehicles were soon outnumbered by those of its competitors and by 1925 it owned twenty-seven vehicles as compared with eighty-six in other hands. To make matters worse, the majority of the buses were operating along the Longton-Tunstall route, the 'main line' of the tramways.

No dividend had been paid on PET's ordinary shares since 1922, the people of the Five Towns clearly preferred the motor buses, yet the company was handicapped by the fact that its buses were limited to the routes it had itself developed, and these, naturally, were away from the tramlines. At the beginning of 1926 a special committee was set up by the Council of Stoke-on-Trent to negotiate with PET for the removal of the tramways, but without success. The company then applied for endorsement of its bus licences to allow the vehicles to run over any tram route, and when this was refused PET appealed to the Minister of Transport. Sir Henry Maybury, Director-General of Roads, was appointed to conduct an inquiry, as a result of which the company agreed to withdraw the tramways and was allocated licences for seventy new buses.

Conversion was carried out during the following two years, and the last tram ran on 11 July 1928. A financial reconstruction was put through on 4 January 1932 (by which time the Road Traffic Act had assured the stability of the company) and although this involved a substantial loss to shareholders, it represented the true position and payment of dividends was resumed in the following year. In May 1933 the company's name was changed to Potteries Motor Traction Ltd.

Elsewhere, private operators competed with each other with the same vigour that marked their competition with the territorial companies. On the road between Colchester and West Mersea, where the GER had for a while operated its steam buses, there were in the 'twenties four small concerns running daily services. From time to time the proprietors would see the advantages of co-operation and would agree a co-ordinated timetable, but with the next bank holiday and a rush of seaside traffic this would fall apart. For a while, all would go well but eventually one of them would run an extra journey and the route would once again become a free-for-all. Fares, too, were subject to sporadic rate wars, one of which brought the return fare down to eightpence for the sixteen miles, and dangerous practices were by no means unknown.

Clashes between the larger companies were prevented by the area agreements, while the municipal undertakings were in many cases protected by the refusal of the local authority to license buses in competition with its own services. Thus the dangers and disadvantages of competition came to be associated with the independents, who were referred to as 'pirates', 'jitneys', or in some other term that implied irresponsibility. Yet it was they as much as the territorial companies, who pioneered the industry, were responsible for much of the expansion of the 'twenties, and helped to lay the foundations of sound services which continue to the present day.

In Scotland the story was similar. The Scottish Motor Traction company had owned thirty-five vehicles in 1914, but through purchase and expansion its fleet numbered fifty by the end of the war. The 'twenties saw a great expansion of bus services north of the border, but the area agreement system was late appearing and, meanwhile, SMT established itself firmly, based upon Edinburgh. The corporation of that city, which in 1922-3 converted its cable tramways to electric traction, was strict in its licensing policy, but its relationship with SMT has been described as 'most cordial' and this no doubt contributed to the company's virtual monopoly of services into the city from the country around. By the end of 1927, SMT had established itself throughout the borders, had reached Glasgow and had an isolated enclave at Dundee.

Elsewhere, development was more sporadic, the period of greatest growth being between 1924 and 1927, when most of the companies that were later to form the Scottish combine appeared, along with a host of independents. The scale of the expansion may be illustrated by the growth of Glasgow General Omnibus & Motor Services Ltd, which started in June 1926 and was running 221 buses by the end of 1928. Many services were also developed by tramway companies, including several owned by BET. Glasgow itself had built up one of the most efficient tramway systems in the country, which the corporation had electrified between 1898 and 1902, but its reluctance to use motor buses invited pirate operation, and this was substantial when it came. Glasgow General, which had the technical support of the LGOC, was the response of local business men to this situation, and the number of buses in the city, negligible in 1923, had reached 600 by the end of 1925. Further north, Walter Alexander & Sons started running at Kilsyth in 1923 but did not emerge as a substantial operator until the end of the decade.

The development of motor-bus operation in Ireland was delayed by the political troubles of the period, and when it came it gave rise to State intervention by the governments at both Dublin and Belfast. The development here will be better understood as a consecutive story, and this will be found in Chapter 8.

THE POLITICS OF LONDON'S TRANSPORT

The development of the bus industry in London after the first world war saw a struggle between different interests that once again was to affect the subsequent history of buses throughout the United Kingdom. Lord Ashfield seems to have had at the heart of his policy the amount of capital invested in the tube railways and tramways, and to have been prepared to go to any lengths to protect it. By 1916, helped by the difficulties of pre-war and war-time operation, the LER had secured an effective monopoly in a wide area round London and had reached formal or implicit agreement with its remaining competitors, the Metropolitan and main-line railways, the LCC and other municipal tramways. In his financial management of the LER combine, Ashfield was aided by Sir Ernest Clarke, upon whom he came to lean very heavily.

For a time during the first world war, Ashfield (who had been knighted in 1914) moved in wider circles, being President of the Board of Trade from December 1916 to May 1919, where he was responsible for the introduction of war-time controls. He took his seat in the House of Commons as member for Ashton-under-Lyne. Subsequently he was associated with the objectives of Sir Eric Geddes, especially in the creation of the Institute of Transport, in connection with which Lord Hurcombe was later to refer to '. . . his vision for the future and his belief in the unity of transport . . .'. Frank Pick accompanied him to the Board of Trade and later became chairman of its Council for Art and Industry.

The LCC, from its foundation in 1889, had turned its back upon the *laissez-faire* policies of its predecessor, the Metropolitan Board of Works. Shaw Lefevre who, as a member of Gladstone's first Cabinet, had been responsible for the Tramways Act of 1870, was an early member of the Council and, whether or not through his initiative, the Progressives (the LCC's equivalent of the Liberal party in Parliament) made tramway ownership a main plank in their platform. In this they reflected advanced political opinion throughout the country, which saw in the tramway a means of social reform. By 1895 they had established favourable terms for the purchase of tramways, but when they lost their majority in the same year, a compromise was reached whereby the tramway companies leased back their lines. In 1896, an Act was passed giving operating powers to the Council, and with the return of a Progressive majority in 1898 the LCC adopted as its policy the ownership of all lines in its area, and their direct operation wherever possible. Electrification soon followed, the first LCC electric line being that between Tooting and the Westminster and Blackfriars bridges, opened in 1903.

In 1902 an attempt by the LCC to establish itself as a bus operator was fairly easily thwarted by the concerted action of other bus interests in London, as the Council had, in fact, no

powers. Its tramways, however, were treated with respect and the
LER group's motor buses never seriously challenged them. It is
not clear whether there was any formal protection agreement,
but after its early attempts the LGOC made no further move for
tramway powers. In co-operating with the associations, it opposed
the authorisation of tramways in its area, and, in accordance
with association tradition, came to terms with those that were
successful. Apart from the LCC, the municipal undertakings received little protection. Those lying to the east were slow to co-
ordinate their systems and in the early days of the motor bus
a journey to Ilford by tram involved three changes of car. The
motor bus was not slow to take advantage of this with through
services that attracted a great deal of traffic away from the
trams.

The LER group was not well prepared for the post-war boom
when it came. Many vehicles, including all the Daimlers that
had come on to the road after the LER/BET settlement of 1912,
had gone to war service and those that did return were mainly
B-types that could only be regarded as obsolete. The number of
buses in London fell from nearly 4,000 in 1914 to 1,758 in 1919.
The pressure of demand was so great that over 100 lorries were
converted for use as buses (thus making possible the withdrawal
of the National fleet) but the public could not be expected to take
kindly to transport of this kind. The LGOC was still committed to
the products of its sister company, AEC, and the 'K' and 'S' types
of 1919 and 1920 were the successors of the 'B' with increased
capacity (the 'S' had fifty-four seats compared with the thirty-
four of the 'B'). The straight-sided body of the 'K' and the
forward-control driving seat marked a break with horse-bus
tradition, but the 'K' was not an unmixed success, nor could the
AEC factory produce sufficient vehicles to meet the ever increasing demand. The size of the Tilling and BET fleets was limited
by the pooling agreement and in any case both were now turning
their attention to provincial operating. No doubt the inspection
of B.43 by King George V in February 1920 gratified the LGOC
directors, but Londoners wanted something more practical than
patriotic memories.

The LER monopoly had been established by bargaining with its larger competitors at a time when, for technical reasons, the smaller ones had been unable to survive, but in the altered circumstances of the 'twenties it was distinctly vulnerable to the new 'pirates'. It is only surprising that the post-war London independents failed to appear sooner than they did. It may be that if the LGOC had broken its agreement with AEC and bought vehicles from other manufacturers, it could have held off the new competition, for the scale of the independents' activities reflected the desire of Daimlers and others to re-enter the London market. But it was not only the long queues for buses that might turn out to be lorries when they arrived that made the General vulnerable for the first time since its earlier unpopularity had brought the Road Car company into existence. There was also a notorious gap in London's bus services, for the LGOC's policy of protection meant that where there were tramways there were very few buses, and it was this gap which the independents quickly filled.

The first of the independents was the 'Chocolate Express'. On 5 August 1922, A. G. Partridge drove his chocolate and primrose bus on Route 11 and the combine, producing the time-honoured response, put two 'Generals' on to 'nurse' the pirate. Partridge, who was operating with Leylands, was financed by the manufacturer's hire-purchase facilities, as well as by a London coach builder, Christopher Dodson. It was the morning queues on Route 19 that had first impressed him and his two partners, and his business proved one of the longest-lasting independents of any period in London's history and was not acquired by the LPTB until 10 August 1934. Like Shillibeer before him, Partridge was honoured by his imitators and became chairman of the Association of London Omnibus Proprietors, the pirates' trade organisation.

Seventeen months after Partridge's arrival on the scene there were some 500 pirate buses at work in London, and the LGOC had been driven to abandon its protection of tramways rather than see the group lose any more of its revenue to outsiders. Meanwhile, the term 'pirate' had won connotations of respect and even affection in the minds of the public. In concentrating on the protection of its capital the LER had failed to take full advantage of the development of the omnibus as a public service vehicle. The tramways in particular had been made obsolete by it, even though they had many years of mechanical life before them, and Londoners were not slow to abandon them as soon as they were offered an alternative.

Furthermore, the pirates' buses were often superior to the General's. Their Dennises and Leylands were faster, and many were operated by firms which aimed to rival the LGOC in technical improvement. Thus the introduction of covered tops, pneumatic tyres, four-wheel brakes and other advances all owed their origin to the enterprise of independents. The City Omnibus Company, in particular, was responsible for many advances and carried out mechanical work for several smaller operators, while Birch Brothers, who returned to bus operation early in 1925, built many of the bodies on other operators' vehicles, sharing this trade with Christopher Dodson. At their best, the pirates set a high standard in bus operation, and many became well known for the efficiency and courtesy of their crews. The Chocolate Express buses, for instance, were swept out after each trip and their freshly whitened tyres and step-boards were typical of Partridge's high standards of maintenance. Neither could the safety of pirate buses be criticised, for the Metropolitan police, as the licensing authority, saw that they were maintained to as strict a standard as applies to the London taxi of today. If anything, it was the police themselves who tended to restrict improvements, as in limiting the width of buses to 7 ft 5 in until 1929 (buses used on tram routes had to be within 7 ft 2 in) while the rest of the country was permitted 7 ft 6 in. This restriction was ended only when it proved almost impossible to mount pneumatic tyres on the older buses and still keep within the permissable limit.

But while many of the independents were estimable enough, giving good service and spurring the General on to better things, some were less responsible. The rough and tumble of competition had returned to London, and the drivers joined in in the business of 'racing and chasing' in the spirit of their employers. And some of the independents being virtually one-man-one-bus firms, it was not unusual for the 'gov'nor' to be at the wheel of his bus when a combine vehicle 'cut him up'. But the worst fault of some of the pirates was generally held to be their practice of operating where traffic was thickest. Some buses would carry no route number, or (like true pirates) they would have a selection of stencils available so that they could imitate the numbering systems of the larger companies. They would then switch from route to route and when passengers began to thin out, those remaining would be told that the bus was going no further. This was called 'skimming the cream of the traffic', and was considered unethical by the larger firms (and not only the LGOC) which were 'bearing the heat and burden of the day'; 'turning short' is, of course, not unheard of, even among large companies, today.

No serious rate war developed in London, although there were occasions when the independents reduced their fares. The Association of London Omnibus Proprietors acted as a co-ordinating body, and a meeting of the association in 1925 authorised a general reduction of 25 per cent of the fares charged by the LGOC. On the whole, however, the fare structure in London remained stable throughout the period of competition.

It was also charged against the pirates that their activities reduced the revenue of the 'more responsible' operators, and so made it harder for them to provide outer area and off-peak services. Modern traffic costing, however, would argue that, since the pirates carried part of the peak load without in any way reducing takings off-peak, the operator who carried on throughout the day, running to the outer terminus of every route, would require fewer vehicles and men for peak-only operation, idle the rest of the day. His total car-mileage would then no doubt be less but his net revenue would be greater because of the better use he would be making of his staff and equipment. It is of more than historical interest to question the generally accepted condemnation of the 'irresponsible' pirates, for it was used to justify subsequent legislation and is still repeated with a good deal of conviction. Dangerous the days of competition may have been, but it is doubtful whether they were as disastrous for the LGOC and the territorial companies as some of their directors were inclined to think. And if, in fact, the LER combine might have been better off in competition than it realised, there is less to be said for the developments that followed.

In fact, it was the tramways that took by far the hardest knock from the pirate buses. In less than a year they had lost so much traffic that, in June 1923, the companies announced their intention to cut the men's wages. Ernest Bevin, then general secretary of the Transport & General Workers' Union, had already succeeded in organising the bus and tram men and, in December, submitted a claim for an 8s a week increase in tramwaymen's pay. The LCC, which was by then having to subsidise its tramways from the rates, was thus brought into the dispute, and the power at County Hall was Herbert Morrison, newly elected MP for Hackney. Lord Ashfield, the third personality in the clash to come, was far from being the traditional capitalist ranged against the union leader and the socialist; Tony Corfield in the TGWU magazine described him as 'the ideal prototype of Burnham's managerial revolution; the manager who saw dividends as a drain on the industry's development funds, and who announced publicly that transport was a service and should not be exploited for financial reasons'. Events were to show that Bevin and Ashfield were pursuing complementary aims, and the settlement that followed the 1924 strike was to have wider repercussions than anyone expected at the time.

Ramsay MacDonald's first Labour government was then in office, and it was known that the Cabinet was not happy about the report of the Royal Commission on London Government of 1923, which had recommended the setting up of a single authority for passenger transport in the capital. H. A. Clegg, in his study of labour relations in London Transport, tells us that a draft Bill to set up such a body was already in existence when Bevin fired his opening shot, coupling the wage claim with a plea for 'the establishment of a single traffic authority for London under public control'. The companies' notice duly expired, yet no reduction was made. Bevin's claim still stood, and the LCC and the municipal tramway departments replied with a much lower offer, but the companies remained silent. Obviously the claim could not be resisted when tram drivers generally were earning over a pound a week less than bus drivers, but Ashfield was playing for bigger stakes than men's wages. So for that matter was Bevin and, refusing arbitration, the union called the tramwaymen out from midnight on 21 March 1924 and appealed to the bus crews to strike in sympathy. This they did, and London once again had cause to bless the independents, even though it was they who were the cause of the dispute.

Throughout this part of the episode, Bevin was under pressure from Ramsay MacDonald, who was fearful of losing the Liberal support essential for the survival of his government. Bevin was irritated by this intervention, but compromised by withholding strike notices from the railwaymen, so that the tubes and other LER lines could be kept running. Eventually he forced the government's hand by announcing on 24 March that the Underground workers would join the strike at midnight on the 28th, which so alarmed MacDonald that, invoking the Emergency Powers Act, he threatened to use troops to run services with army lorries. On 27 March he set up a court of enquiry which reported that the only basis for re-opening negotiations was 'a definite undertaking by the government to introduce and press forward legislation placing the passenger traffic of the metropolitan area under some co-ordinating control'.

This was not only what Ernest Bevin had asked for, but also what Lord Ashfield had offered. He was prepared, he said, to submit the LGOC to statutory control of fares and limitation of dividends provided an overall licensing authority were set up, and only on these terms would he consider the tramwaymen's wage claim that was the overt cause of the dispute. In fact, both men were aiming at the same target—the pirate—but neither was able to mount a direct attack on the independents, who were by no means all villains indulging in dangerous practices and paying starvation wages. Many, in fact, paid better rates than those negotiated between the union and the LGOC.

The Prime Minister had now abandoned his policy of non-intervention, and the draft Bill was brought forward with almost indecent haste, having its first reading on 25 March. If the

Liberals had caused it to be set aside before, they made no difficulties about its passage now and it became the London Traffic Act 1924 by a majority of ninety-nine. Only Herbert Morrison saw through it, attacking it in the House as a Tory Bill which Labour had previously condemned, and going into the division lobby against his own party. He accused Ashfield of exploiting the strike to secure his own ends and deplored the power of the combine to hold a threat over the House of Commons. Morrison was not, of course, opposed to the idea of monopoly, but was concerned that it should be under public control and resented the LCC's restricted representation on the Traffic Committee set up to advise the Minister of Transport in implementing the Act. But even Herbert Morrison does not seem to have remarked upon the atmosphere of intrigue which today seems to have permeated the whole episode, with the union and the combine playing smoothly into each other's hands to coerce the Labour government.

The strike ended on 28 March 1924, and if the union regarded it as a victory, Lord Ashfield certainly did not regard it as a defeat. For it lead directly to the passage of the London Traffic Act 1924, which he saw as the coping stone of his policy of monopoly for the LER group in London.

The London Traffic Bill was defended in Parliament as a measure intended to reduce congestion. It was, however, as its history shows, really a protectionist measure designed to put an end to competition in London bus operation. The machinery for this was to be found in Section 7, which gave power to the Ministry of Transport to declare any thoroughfare a 'restricted street', upon which no additional buses were to be allowed. The first Restricted Streets Order was announced on 17 February 1925, and applied mainly to the busier streets in the central area. It was to apply retrospectively from 1 January, and this was a considerable hardship for a firm like Birch Brothers, which had ordered ten Leylands in 1924, two of which had gone into service on 21 January on a new joint service between Highgate and Brockley Rise. Through the Association of London Omnibus Proprietors, the independents protested against such high-handed treatment, and after questions had been asked in the House the London Traffic Advisory Committee set up a sub-committee to consider hard cases. Early in April, Chief Constable Bassom, who was responsible for much of the administration of the Act, provided operators with a list of suggested routes through unrestricted streets, with a hint that they would be wise to get any new services they wanted going before the Minister published another Order. This may have reflected a statement made by the Minister to the House on 12 March, in which he undertook to avoid injustices in the working of the Act. On 21 May, Sir Henry Jackson defended the working of the Order by saying that, of those proprietors who had been injured by it, all had been found new routes and were satisfied. 'They are earning livelihoods on routes which, apart from stabilisation, would not have come into existance at all', he said; a remarkable statement indeed, for if these routes had been so unprofitable that no one had wanted them, they could hardly have suddenly become able to offer a livelihood.

As early as 17 April, the Minister had advised the operators of his intention to make a second Order, which would include most tramway routes. Ths came into force on 3 June, but the retrospective effect of the first Order was later amended to avoid some of the hardship originally caused (Birch Brothers, who had accepted Bassom's hint and, jointly with others, started on one of his routes, now re-instated the service which earlier they had had to withdraw). But the Minister, having placated his critics, returned to his earlier policies in the New Year and ordered operators on a number of tramway routes to cut down their services. His requirements bore particularly heavily upon the independents and there was considerable public indignation, followed by a Commons debate on 1 April 1926. On Route 17, Cornelius Beatty found that he would not be able to operate his one omnibus at all, and when he refused to comply with the Order his prosecution was dismissed with costs against the police.

At this point in time, the reputation of the pirates was entirely changed by their behaviour during the General Strike. All the LGOC buses were withdrawn for the first two days of the strike, while the members of the Association of London Omnibus Proprietors continued to run their full complement of 450 buses, a hundred of them being driven by their owners. On the third day, not surprisingly, intimidation became a problem, and the Association was therefore given the use of Regent's Park as a base, to avoid the police having to protect over ninety garages in different parts of London. A considerable organisation was set up in the park, and used also by the combine companies when they began using volunteer staff. The Metropolitan police arranged to test drivers there, and eventually 600 drivers and conductors were sleeping in the park, under canvas or in their buses. *Modern Transport* commented:

> Despite the fact that the LGOC lost no time in getting their vehicles on the streets with the aid of volunteers, and thereby performed admirable service, the 'independents' may justly claim that they stuck to their posts. In this way they won a large measure of public sympathy at a critical period in their own affairs, and it is, therefore, not surprising that the Government should have decided to allow the cases for the retention of their services on specified routes to be reconsidered by the London Traffic Committee.

In this way the administration of the Act came to be softened, and after this there was rather more give and take between the operators and the Ministry. But there can be no doubt that the London Traffic Act was in concept and execution directed at the independents, who were seen in official circles merely as nuisances (although not, it would appear, by Chief Constable Bassom).

There were other results of the London Traffic Act which were not at once apparent. Throughout its previous history, the LGOC had treated competition in the traditional manner. If a newcomer appeared, life was made difficult for him and only if he became established was the possibility of buying him out considered. It paid best to force him out of business, for a quick sale would merely encourage another to appear. But with the Act of 1924, both the LGOC and the pirates acquired statutory monopoly rights, and such rights were saleable. The LGOC soon reacted to this, taking over Cambrian, one of its larger competitors, as early as

January 1926.* In the following year it was offering £2,500 apiece for vehicles said to have been worth, on average, no more than £700; such is the value of a monopoly. The best of the purchased vehicles were repainted in General livery, but they were usually replaced with outmoded K-types in the colours of the independents for a short time, which must have given the public a poor idea of the LGOC's standards. Older and non-standard acquired vehicles were sold.

The best of the independents (and they were probably in the majority) looked upon their businesses with pride and derived satisfaction from efficient bus operation. But they were irked by the restrictions of the London Traffic Act and when A. T. Bennett, managing director of the Admiral company, offered what looked like a chance to organise on a scale that would ease their problems, many of them took him at his word and sold their vehicles and goodwill to the London Public Omnibus Company, which he formed in July 1927. The idea was that they should remain in the employment of the LPOC, which soon came to own 273 vehicles. Their disappointment must have been considerable when, within a few months, control of the LPOC passed to the LGOC (it was finally absorbed in 1930). A total of seventy-four firms had been merged to form the LPOC and in many cases independent proprietors who had been in competition with the General now found themselves working as its employees. But there remained a number of operators who preferred a continued 'livelihood' to takeover bids from the LPOC or LGOC and of these fifty-two survived until the formation of London Transport. They included Birch Brothers, with whom the LGOC reached an agreement on 31 December 1930, demonstrating once again their willingness to negotiate in the last resort.

The period of independent competition in London was one of rapid expansion and improvement. Partisan feelings ran high,

* The position of 'Cambrian' and other firms relying upon the Straker Squire chassis was weakened by the purchase of Straker Squire by Sir William Joynson-Hicks (later Lord Brentford); Home Secretary, 1924-9. Universally known as 'Jix', he was the son of Henry Hicks, who had been vice-chairman of the LGOC at the end of the nineteenth century, and had himself been the company's solicitor. He refused to permit the sale of Straker Squire spare parts to pirate operators.

and the events are still recent enough to stir men's memories. There is no doubt that anti-social practices existed, but there is no evidence that they would have continued for long if they had been met with severe repression in the courts. They reflect rather the negative side of the LER monopoly, which would no doubt have come to terms with its new competitors had not the State stepped in to protect it. For the pirates were only attracted because the LGOC and the tramways were not offering as good a standard of service as could have been provided and for which the public were prepared to pay. Under Ashfield, the LER had become inward-looking, putting an ideal of service evolved within its own walls in place of the constant adjustment to effective demand that is the best attribute of competition. Neither can the LCC escape this criticism, although the statutory bar upon its operating buses committed it to an obsolescent system of transport. The real reason why the State intervened was that the trams were becoming obsolete long before they were worn out (open-top cars of 1905 were still at work in London in the late 'thirties).

Faced with the same problem, notably in the Potteries, the BET approach was more logical, and in the long run more profitable. Cutting their losses, they abandoned tramway operation and substituted motor buses capable of competing with the independents. There comes a time in the working of any economic system when it is necessary to scrap quite new equipment (in theory, it may even be brand new), because some alternative will produce a higher net revenue. Thus while the first lesson of the 'twenties is that the LER abused its monopoly by failing to offer the public as good a standard of service as possible, given the technical resources of the time, the second is that, having in consequence attracted competition, it failed to take the next logical step and replace its trams by vehicles more acceptable to the public. Perhaps really up-to-date tramcars, running only on the most profitable routes and combined with a more rapid development of the AEC bus, might have been the answer; instead, Ashfield and Bevin forced the hand of the Labour government to intervene in a way that was neither socialist nor capitalist.

G

ROAD AND RAIL: THE COLLISION AVERTED

The pressure of the motor-bus industry upon the tramways was never likely to have affected national policy, for the tramways were in numerous hands and only in London was there a management determined to protect them at all costs. BET, the largest of the provincial tramway operators, took the view that it was wiser to cut its losses, re-invest in motor buses and avoid the sort of compromise with State control that had been part of the LER settlement under the London Traffic Act. The LCC under Morrison was still aiming for public ownership for all public passenger transport in London, while the other tramway-owning municipalities were either changing to buses or trolleybuses, or trying to manipulate the law so as to protect their own systems from competition. In so far as the pirates reduced their gross revenue, they complained through their association, but they were not organised to bring any real pressure upon the government.

The railways were a different matter. Between 1921 and 1923, before the full impact of motor bus competition could have been felt, the 'four main lines' had been created, carrying a step further the trend towards combination that is evident throughout railway history. One consequence of this was the preoccupation of railway management with the problems of re-organisation, at a time when the impact of the motor bus was at its strongest. Sir Herbert Walker, as general manager of the Southern Railway, welded the three main SR constituents into a new undertaking as successful as any, but (according to Sir John Elliot) his chief commercial manager was 'never the man for the road-rail competition that lay ahead'. The Southern, too, was fully occupied with electrification and the docks. The Great Western was the only one of the four to remain unaltered and, being uniquely involved in the industry, continued to develop its own bus services. The LNER and LMS were faced with great problems of adaptation, and even the genius of Sir Josiah Stamp was never able to overcome the mutual antipathies of Midland and North Western men, or to unite the three Scottish companies whose only point of agreement is said to have been a common hatred of Euston.

It thus seems likely that the impact of the motor bus as a competitor found the railways ill prepared. Certainly they did not respond as the GER had done when, in July 1920, it introduced the 'jazz' service on its suburban lines to meet the competition of trams and buses and the threat of a new tube. Instead of retrenching where the bus or coach had the advantage, at the same time improving the product where rail services were more likely to be profitable, the companies decided to follow Lord Ashfield's policy and that of the GWR, and aimed to take a share of the road profits to balance losses on the rail. The General Strike of 1926 demonstrated that the country was no longer entirely dependent upon railway transport—it was this that marked the end of the railway age—yet despite this warning, rail policy seems to have continued to concentrate on the all-inclusive service characteristic of that age, blithely assuming that there was room for this as well as the nation-wide networks of bus and coach services that were growing up. Events were to prove that both could not be profitable.

The railway companies, knowing that such powers as they had to run bus services were of doubtful legality, decided to clear this major issue, and in 1928 the four main lines and the Metropolitan promoted Bills to allow them to operate both goods and passenger vehicles. They met with strong opposition and a Select Committee of both Houses sat for thirty-seven days. The Metropolitan's Bill was thrown out (because of its special position in relation to the LER combine) but the Railway (Road Transport) Acts of the main-line companies became law on 3 August 1928.

At this time the railways owned only a tiny proportion of the motor buses licensed in Great Britain. The GWR owned 232 buses in 1927, when the total number must have run into five figures, and the other companies had only a handful between them. It is doubtful whether they seriously intended to operate more, for subsequent events repeated on a national scale the near-collision and settlement of 1912 between the BET and the LER. The railways' legislation did not really give them equal terms with other operators, for not only were they virtually prohibited from competing with a local authority undertaking within its own boundary, but provision of a railway bus service had to be notified to the Minister of Transport, and the service could only be withdrawn following publication of a notice of intention in the *London Gazette*, and with the consent of the Minister. Furthermore, an entry into the trade such as the railways openly threatened to make would have been still more disastrous for their train services, especially if accompanied by a major rate war.

The railways had, however, the alternative of investing in the industry as it then stood, and this the four companies decided to do. On 7 November 1928 a meeting held at 35 Parliament Street was attended by numerous representatives of the railways, and of Tilling & British Automobile Traction. It was established that the railway interest in T&BAT companies should be exactly equal to that retained by the holding company, and a negotiating committee was set up to forward the settlement and to provide the railways with financial and other information. The T&BAT representatives on this committee were Sidney Garcke and Walter Wolsey.

Little progress had been made by the committee up to the middle of 1929 and J. F. Heaton became uneasy. On 1 January the LMS and LNE railways had formed joint operating committees with Sheffield and Halifax corporations, and he suspected that the railways were trying to obtain control of the principal independent companies and to use them as a base for competitive operatings against the Tilling & British group. At that time there were several large independent concerns and it would have been perfectly possible for the railways to have done this, and so to have been able to force the combine to accept a much lower price for a settlement.

Heaton may well have had early warning of the railways' intentions. On 5 February 1929 the LMS offered the directors of the Crosville Motor Company 27s 6d per share for outright purchase and the business changed hands on 1 May. Negotiations with the National Omnibus & Transport Company Ltd must have started even sooner, for on 28 February 1929 the Eastern, Midland, Northern, Southern and Western National Omnibus Companies were registered. This was done because the NO&T was operating within the areas of each of the four main lines and it was thought desirable to simplify the railway holdings by associating one of the National companies with each of them (Northern National was registered only to protect the name). In the event, Southern and Western National were operated as one company, with headquarters at Exeter, while Midland National never functioned, since it proved impossible to separate the NO&T services in the area north of London so as to reflect the complex of LMS and LNE railways. The Bedfordshire services passed to Eastern National, with headquarters at Chelmsford, and NO&T retained direct operation of the LGOC services for which it was responsible, as well as certain routes in south-west Essex whose future ownership was in dispute. Sir John Jarvis, Bt, who had built up the NO&T in so short a time, remained its chairman and the transfer to the subsidiary companies did not actually take place until 1930.

By June 1929 Heaton had reason to suspect that a railway approach had also been made to United Automobile Services Ltd, another company whose buses operated over a wide area of the country. With NO&T and Crosville, the control of United would have given the railways a considerable advantage, so Heaton himself wrote to E. B. Hutchinson, United's chairman and managing director and a former railwayman, and invited him to call at the Tilling head office in Victoria Street for a chat. Thereafter developments were rapid, the future of the motor-bus industry turning for a few months upon the personalities of Heaton, Hutchinson and Sir Ralph Wedgwood,* general manager of the LNER. At the interview at Victoria Street on 14 June, Heaton was perfectly frank about the negotiations between Tilling & British and the railways, and asked whether any approach had been made to United. Hutchinson replied that the sale of UAS to the LNER had been agreed, even to the price, the only matter outstanding

---

* It is interesting to note that Wedgwood's railway career started in 1896 under Sir George Gibb of the NER.

being the amount of compensation he himself was to receive for loss of office.

Though pressed to reveal the price offered by the LNER, Hutchinson would give no indication and Heaton was thus faced with a delicate situation to which he reacted by offering, subject to confirmation by the Tilling board, a price of 27s 6d per share. He put this in writing on the following day, and in a second letter offered Hutchinson a substantial sum in compensation and a continuing seat on the board of United Automobile Services. Hutchinson made no secret of his embarrassment at the situation, but undertook to submit the matter to his board, which he did at a meeting held immediately afterwards at the UAS registered office in Upper Regent Street. This meeting subsequently stood adjourned until 19 June, when Heaton was invited to be present.

Meanwhile, the offer Heaton had made was referred to a special board meeting of Tilling & British. Here the BET representatives were not at first prepared to go along with Heaton, but the Tilling side affirmed their intention of proceeding alone if necessary, whereupon the BET directors agreed and further negotiations were entrusted to Heaton alone. His foresight is underlined by Hutchinson's reference, in a letter written to *Motor Transport* in 1955, to the railways' 'great anxiety to secure (his) company and use it as a base to threaten, and if necessary operate against, the other big bus groups'.

At the UAS board meeting it was finally decided to recommend the shareholders to accept the Tilling & British cash offer, rather than the more complex shares-and-cash offer made by the LNER. Two directors declined to attend, although they were present at the offices of the company during the meeting, and let it be known that they would advise the LNER to make a counter offer. In spite of this, the board sent a circular letter to shareholders on 20 June advising acceptance of Heaton's terms and enclosing forms of acceptance. With it went a letter from Hutchinson, strongly recommending acceptance and stating that Stock Exchange quotations for UAS shares had ranged between approximately 22s 6d and 24s 6d per share during the previous two months.

Heaton now made a direct approach to the LNER, calling upon

Sir Ralph Wedgwood on the morning of 21 June. He informed Sir Ralph of the situation, offered to resell 50 per cent of the UAS shares to the railway at net cost and expressed the hope that the negotiations of the previous seven months might then be brought to fruition. The LNER directors, unimpressed by this, the same day made an offer of 30s per share and on the following Sunday, 23 June, announced this in the newspapers. Their justification must be taken to be the value of UAS to the railways as a counter in their negotiations with Tilling & British, for it does not seem likely that outright competition would have been in the railway interest.

On seeing the Press announcement, Heaton issued a statement through the Press Association, in which he advised shareholders of United to await a further offer from Tilling & British. Hutchinson, on hearing of the new LNER terms, had also written to them on 21 June advising them not to accept this offer or any other, but to await a further communication from his board.

Heaton, now playing his final card, sent the following letter by hand to Sir Ralph Wedgwood on 24 June :

Dear Sir Ralph,

United Automobile Services Ltd

It was very unfortunate that we should be at cross purposes with regard to the control of the above. As I told you on Friday last, my Company would have been prepared to assign to your Company unconditionally and at net cost 50% of any shares they had acquired. I now suggest as an alternative and in order to put an end to this bidding of one against the other that your Company might agree to sell us on similar terms 50% of any shares you might obtain as a result of your latest offer.

It is only right that I should tell you, but not in any way as a threat, that a counter offer, considerably more attractive than the one you have made, is now contemplated from our side, but I felt that it would be in the best interests of both parties if we could first explore the possibilities of a settlement. As the matter is pressing I should be glad of a reply during the course of the day and if you wish it, I will come along again to see you.

Yours very truly,

(sgd.) J. F. HEATON

The effect of this letter was, as Heaton must have hoped, to re-open talks, and later on the same day he was at King's Cross station, where he saw Sir Ralph and also the LNER chairman, Mr Whitelaw. He told them that Tilling & British could not tolerate railway ownership of United and subsequent competition, and that whatever figure the LNER offered for the shares, Tilling & British would outbid it. He added that, whatever final price was reached, his offer to resell 50 per cent of the shares still stood.

Sir Ralph then countered by expressing the fear of his board that Tilling & British control of United would be used to drive up the price of the shares in other companies in the group. Heaton denied any such intention and, on being pressed, suggested as a formula the price which would be paid by a willing buyer to a willing seller, subject to the agreement of the T&BAT directors to such a basis. In the event of disagreement, the figure would be fixed by three well-known chartered accountants, Sir William Plender, Sir William Peat and Sir William McLintock.

This basis proving acceptable to both parties, it was agreed to make a joint offer of 30s per share to the UAS shareholders. The agreement was expressed in a memorandum signed on 3 July by the respective solicitors, I. Buchanan Pritchard and E. S. Herbert, which formed the basis for the general settlement reached on 30 October 1929 between the railways and Tilling & British. Hutchinson resigned from the United board on completion of the sale and took no further part in the activities of the motor-bus industry. He died in November 1967, aged 85.

During this period, the LNE and LMS railways had been negotiating with the larger bus operators in Scotland, but as this development was linked with wider changes in the organisation of the industry there, which continued into the following decade, it is described in Chapter 8. The outcome of the settlement with the railways was to give the four main lines a substantial source of revenue and some degree of protection from competition, while the English and Scottish combines enjoyed an injection of new capital, together with a higher status than that of their smaller competitors. It was very soon to be seen that this matter of status was important and to have lasting effects.

One of the incentives to a rail-road settlement was the creation of the Royal Commission on Transport of 1929, whose deliberations were to produce, with unprecedented haste, the Road Traffic Act of 1930. This Act was based upon a draft Bill which the Ministry of Transport submitted to the commission, and which had been prepared by the Departmental Committee on the Licensing and Regulations of Public Service Vehicles of 1925. All the major interests in public transport were aware of its contents, for it had been circulated by the ministry for comment. It was designed to carry out a much-needed reform of the antiquated procedure for licensing buses and coaches, which was based on the Town Police Clauses Acts 1847-89, intended to deal merely with horse-drawn vehicles. The second report of the commission appeared in October 1929 and included a strong recommendation that the draft Bill, modified in some respects, should become law.

It was thus clear that Parliament was likely to set up the 'controlled monopoly' that R. J. Howley, on behalf of the Provincial Omnibus Owners' Association, had said in evidence he would accept—the *quid pro quo* being the protection of the 'established operator' (whether large or small) from new competition. Along with the combine, the railway companies and the trade unions had endorsed the draft Bill, (the TGWU having first said it would prefer outright nationalisation), and the local authorities quarrelled merely with the loss of their licensing powers. Little foresight was needed to see that the effect of the Act would be similar to that of the London Traffic Act 1924, in giving saleable monopoly rights to all existing operators. Thus it was reasonable for the railways to invest in the industry with the prospect of more settled times to come when the full logic of combination, as envisaged for London by Sir George Gibb, would be applied to the whole of Great Britain.

Looking back, it is difficult to understand the readiness of Parliament and industry to accept the highly protectionist philosophy expressed by the Royal Commission. Its chairman, Sir Arthur Griffith-Boscawen, PC, had been a minor figure in various Conservative governments from 1895. In 1921, he had been appointed Minister of Agriculture and Fisheries but had been defeated when he stood for re-election. In the following year he was, according to Francis Williams, the only member of the Conservative group in the Coalition to share Baldwin's conviction that the Conservatives should cease to 'fight under Lloyd George's banner'. In spite of this, he was again defeated in the subsequent general election, and did not return to Parliament. As Royal Commission chairman, he was (judging from the minutes of evidence) inclined to accept uncritically the arguments of ministry witnesses and those of the railways and territorial bus companies, and to discourage any searching examination of them that his fellow commissioners tried to make. The commission certainly tidied up the draft Bill which the ministry submitted to it, and in this it was greatly assisted by the evidence of R. J. Howley. It did not, however, make any serious attempt to balance the arguments for and against the creation of a monopoly structure in road transport; indeed, it does not even seem to have conceded the existence of arguments against its own proposals.

The philosophy behind the draft Bill, which inspired much of the policy of the Ministry of Transport, derived from the convictions of Sir Eric Geddes, the founder of the ministry. Opening the debate on the second reading of the Ministry of Transport Bill in 1919, he had said that it was 'nothing short of criminal to permit a continuance of the old system of competition between light railways and roads, railways and canals'. He had stated that railways and canals which were working at a loss had to be made to pay, and he envisaged the division of the country into 'non-competitive zones'. As originally drafted, his Bill had provided for the ministry to control 'railways, light railways, tramways, canals and inland navigations, roads, bridges, vehicles and traffic and the supply of electricity'. Powers of nationalisation (by Order in Council) were included, although at the report stage the Government gave an undertaking that they would not be used. Geddes himself became the first minister (he was a close associate of Lloyd George), and in addition to the imprint of his thought that marked the ministry thereafter, it came, in the words of W. Rees Jeffreys, to be dominated in its early days by 'men of

railway experience, training and mentality'. Thus it is hardly
surprising that a policy of protection of existing investment, even
at the expense of technical progress or the choice of the consumer,
should have marked the ministry's reaction to the expansion of
the motor bus industry on so large a scale.

CHAPTER FIVE

UNDER CONTROL: THE ROAD TRAFFIC ACT, 1930

AFTER 1931, the motor-bus industry found itself in a new world. For most people, things did not seem to change; their bus still came at the same time, with the same driver and conductor, even though they were wearing unfamiliar numbered badges. For management it was different; just how different varied according to the regime they were used to, but for most the Road Traffic Act imposed a new form of control on their activities (some even called it interference). Not only did drivers and conductors have to have licences (the drivers having to pass a stiff test), but the vehicles themselves had to satisfy new regulations as to dimensions and mechanical fitness. Above all, a special sort of licence had to be obtained to authorise the provision of actual services, and when one of these was applied for, other operators could object, and so could the railways. When the licence had been granted, it was an offence to depart from the time- and fare-tables attached to it, or to run more vehicles than it allowed. Buses also had to carry time- and fare-tables for passengers to consult and tickets had to be issued—although here the non-conformists struck, so that sometimes this part of the Act was honoured more in the breach.

LICENSING BEFORE 1931

The situation prior to the Act certainly needed reform. The Town Police Clauses Acts 1847 and 1889, and the Stage Carriage Act 1832, governed the provision of public road services but made no attempt to control private hire work. They applied only to vehicles plying for hire on the streets and so omitted most express coach operation, which used private land for terminal purposes. In addition, the Town Police Clauses Acts were permissive and by no means all the local authorities which were supposed to administer them had adopted the powers they gave. Others interpreted them in a number of different ways. Finally, since they were intended for the licensing of horse-drawn vehicles, they applied only within local authority boundaries, so that a service running through industrial Lancashire required buses licensed by each authority through whose area they passed. In most country districts there was no licensing at all (no counties possessed powers, and only 65 out of 644 rural districts).

At one extreme, there were authorities which stretched the Town Police Clauses to justify a system of licensing not unlike that which the Road Traffic Act itself introduced. On Tees-side, a number of councils formed a joint committee to regulate traffic, but in other parts of the country there was little co-operation and it was not unknown for a council to license a service leaving its area on one road, while its neighbour defined its route from the boundary along another. (It was the difficulty of providing co-ordination among so many authorities that lead the Royal Commission to recommend the creation of *ad hoc* licensing authorities covering wide areas). In practice, only a minority stretched the system so far and most remained content to license vehicles to ply for hire in their own areas, with more or less adequate control over construction and maintenance. Others simply licensed all comers, using the system as a source of revenue.

But there were other aspects of the Town Police Clauses as a system of control. Minor corruption was not unknown, nor should it be wondered at when councillors could always claim that their limitation of the number of licences was intended to prevent congestion. As soon as a limit is placed upon a franchise of this kind, the individual licence acquires a cash value as a result of the monopoly that has been created. In other cases, councils decided as a matter of policy to license a particular operator's vehicles rather than to provide a municipal transport system. But the most frequent use of licensing powers was to protect the trams or buses of the licensing authority itself against competition from local operators or services coming into the town from outside. Norman H. Dean, in his history of the origins of Hebble Motor Services, describes how, at its start in 1924, Halifax Corporation refused to license the company's buses. Licences were obtained from the surrounding authorities and the first services carried passengers within the borough by various devices, such as accepting only those who already held return tickets. The route to Huddersfield was licensed only by the intermediate authority of Elland, but once a Halifax passenger had travelled by tram to the boundary, he could take a return into Huddersfield. Coming home, he took another return from Elland to Halifax, after which he could travel regularly between the two terminals.

In spite of such devices, some of the Hebble services were the subject of police prosecution. Fines were imposed, whereupon the publicity attracted new traffic to the buses. Halifax Corporation was a substantial tramcar operator, and the eventual compromise whereby the tramway routes were protected by the bus company charging higher fares benefited both sides, for the buses were then able to concentrate on the longer distance traffic. But the story illustrates the main weakness of the system, the lack of adequate powers of enforcement. For many operators in the 'twenties it was reasonable commercial policy to run an unlicensed service, treating the occasional fine as part of its overhead costs. No real attempt was ever made to defend the Town Police Clauses Acts; they were intended to deal with the hackney as a taxi rather than as an omnibus, in which sense they are the basis of most taxi licensing today.

All the same, the state of affairs prior to 1931 had its advantages, the greatest being the freedom given to operators to back their own judgement and provide services wherever they saw a prospect of reward. This enabled the industry to grow to maturity quickly and to develop a comprehensive pattern of services in a very short time. The express coach industry grew up without effective licensing. The same freedom favoured the territorial companies equally with the independents, both large and small, and the Town Police Clauses had the advantage of leaving large areas uncontrolled outside the towns, just where flexibility was most needed.

THE ROAD TRAFFIC ACT

The Road Traffic Act contained a great deal that is still part of our motor legislation. Compulsory third-party insurance was introduced and the obsolete speed limits were revised. There was little controversy during the passage of the Bill through Parliament and few people showed any awareness of the enormous significance of one small group of clauses. Only Sir Arnold Plant, writing in the *Journal of the Institute of Transport*, remarked that they would lead to the impoverishment of the consumer. Some have argued since that they have undermined the prosperity of the industry as well.

The industry at the time, through its spokesmen, generally welcomed the Act. The local authorities, once reconciled to the loss of their licensing powers, realised that their transport undertakings would be protected by the system; the territorial companies made common cause with the railways. The independent operators were never consulted, nor were the interests of consumers ever given direct attention either by the Royal Commission or by Parliament. It was argued that what was good for the industry was good for its passengers, and what the public transport industry (with the possible exception of the independent busmen) wanted was monopoly. Thirty years before, or thirty years later, Parliament might not have been so ready to grant it, but in an age of protection no political party seriously questioned the principle. There was the precedent of the London Traffic Act of 1924 and the assumption that the railways (and with them their newly associated bus companies) represented a capital investment with a special claim to be shielded from the competition of 'pirates' and 'jitneys'. Above all, there was urgent need for reform.

The Road Traffic Act 1930 introduced a structure of licensing that survived with little change into the 1980s. It created its own climate of thought and, for some, it became almost a heresy to criticise it. It greatly improved the standards of safety throughout the industry, but of the five types of licence it introduced one had especially wide effects. This was the *road service licence*, without which it was illegal to run a regular bus service or to advertise an excursion of any kind or a tour. It did not apply to private hire, although the definition of this type of work proved extremely difficult. It set out the route to be followed, the time- and fare-tables and, for most express services and excursions, the number of vehicles that might be run at any one time or on any one day. It distinguished between 'stage carriages' and 'express carriages' by restricting the latter to services with a minimum fare of one shilling single (this gave rise to anomalies). It was a licence that conferred upon its holder the privileges and the responsibilities of a State-controlled monopoly.

The other types of licence introduced by the Act brought a much-needed reform of the law regarding the construction and use of public-service vehicles. They required drivers and conductors to hold licences and to wear numbered badges; medical and character certificates were needed to obtain these licences and drivers had to pass a stiff test, as well as to hold a normal driving licence. The vehicle required a certificate of fitness, which was renewed for shorter and shorter periods as it grew older; it was examined annually, with additional rigour when the certificate was due for renewal, and was subject to spot checks at any time. To obtain a certificate, it had to comply with regulations which however restrictionist in comparison with Continental or United States practice, resulted in greatly improved standards of safety.

The certificate of fitness related to the vehicle and passed with it to a new owner, but another licence, the public service vehicle, was necessary before it could be used for hire or reward. This was issued to the vehicle's owner and could be suspended or revoked if the holder was not considered to be a 'fit and proper person' to operate buses. It was only valid if a certificate of fitness was also in force for the vehicle and its main purpose was to exert some control over the operator's general standards. It was also the connecting link between the minister's representative, the certifying officer, who was responsible for the issue of the c.o.f., and the traffic commissioners, who were responsible for all other types of licence. The commissioners presided over what are known as 'traffic areas'—there were ten in England and Wales and one for Scotland—and although appointed by the minister, they were largely autonomous. In most areas they consisted of a full-time paid chairman with a panel of representatives of local authorities (counties and county boroughs), whose chief function was to provide one or two of their members to sit with the chairman at the public enquiries known as 'traffic courts'. In the Metropolitan traffic area, the police had a special function, and since there were no 'panel' commissioners, the licensing authority was known as the traffic commissioner, in the singular. The Metropolitan area also differed from the rest in that the Commissioner of Police for the Metropolis was responsible for licensing drivers and conductors.

Because of the nature of the road service licensing system, the duties of the commissioners extended from the purely administrative world into the judicial. When considering applications of individuals or of companies for public service vehicles licences, or deciding on an appeal against the refusal of a driver's or conductor's licence, the only question they had to ask was whether or not the applicant could satisfy certain objective standards. Similarly, the operator whose vehicle conformed to the regulations regarding construction, equipment and maintenance had to be granted a certificate of fitness by the certifying officer. If it was refused, any appeal to the minister would turn upon matters of fact. In the early days of licensing there were a few hard cases, but soon the standard vehicle, providing it was properly maintained, came to be automatically certified and licensed. The power of the commissioners to refuse a public service licence on the general ground that the applicant was not a 'fit and proper person' was rarely used, although it did provide a strong sanction in reserve to deal with any serious malpractice.

The grant, refusal or variation of a road service licence depend upon no such objective criteria. The Act required the commissioners to look to certain general objectives in reaching a decision, but none of these was measurable and each must, in the last resort, be a matter of opinion. They had to have regard to the suitability of the route and the extent to which it was already 'adequately served', and to such generalities as 'the extent to which the proposed service was necessary or desirable in the public interest' and 'the needs of the area as a whole, including the provision of adequate, suitable and efficient services, the elimination of unnecessary services and the provision of unremunerative services'. (It will be noted that the final pair would seem incompatible.)

Applications for road service licences were published in a periodical called *Notices & Proceedings,* which was issued fortnightly in most traffic areas but weekly in the busier ones. Any operator 'along or near the line of route', and any appropriate local authority, might object and in the absence of any definition of a valid objection the usual form was to complain that the proposal 'would abstract traffic from services of the objector'. Thus while the commissioners had the arduous duty of satisfying a set of abstract principles, the arguments laid before them by applicant and objector, however much they might pay lip service to the Road Traffic Act, really turned upon who was to obtain or protect a profitable monopoly. The commissioners were further hampered by the fact that the railways had a right of objection but did not come under the jurisdiction of the Act.

The success of the Road Traffic Act (in the sense that it worked smoothly and was reasonably equitable) was due to the co-operation of the industry and the personal qualities of the men chosen to act as chairmen of the traffic commissioners. The first appointments covered a wide range of professional backgrounds and no attempt was made to introduce a strictly legalistic interpretation of the Act. Decisions were made upon the facts of each application (in so far as this was possible), and since appeal decisions had no binding force beyond the case at issue, precedent had very little importance. From an early date it was established that the commissioners need not be limited by the evidence produced before them, but might use any additional knowledge they or their departments might have. Crosland-Taylor recalls A. T. James, the first chairman of the South Wales Commissioners, who was immensely knowledgeable but very deaf, and who, though probably hearing little of the cases argued in his court, clearly commanded the respect of those who appeared before him. Because of the capabilities of the men who held the posts, the area traffic commissioners came to exercise considerable control over the industry and, in general, tried to let justice be seen to be done. It was not entirely their fault that the average small operator always shunned traffic court procedure, feeling with some justification that the dice were loaded against him.

The traffic courts themselves (officially known as public sittings) involved quasi-judicial procedure, although the normal rules of court did not apply. Evidence was called from the applicant and objecting operators, and the applicant was usually expected to provide support from the public, calling as witnesses private individuals or representatives of public bodies. Cross-examination and re-examination permitted, but since the witnesses were not under oath and no operator would want to intimidate or annoy a member of the public, the atmosphere was fairly informal. Anyone could appear as an advocate and while barristers and solicitors did practise in the traffic courts, lay consultants worked alongside them. But the operator who conducted his own case was not at a disadvantage if he had sufficient confidence to make up for his lack of forensic skill. (Michael Robbins has pointed out that the same was true of parliamentary proceedings in the early days of railways.) The effective constraints upon the freedom of the industry were, in practice, two-fold: the cost of traffic court procedure and the principles that the commissioners found enshrined in the Road Traffic Act and applied in reaching their decisions.

The cost involved in the traffic court appearances was always regarded by the territorial companies as part of the price for the monopoly the Act gave them. In the early days, contested cases took up the full attention of traffic staff, with sittings continuing late into each evening and resuming next day. The railway companies made full use of their powers of objection, opposing every application that remotely affected them, even though the applicant might be a company which they partly owned. As time went on, the pressure dropped (there were about half as many sittings in 1938 as there had been in 1932), but the cost factor became more important, for while it was worth spending heavily to obtain one's licence in the first place, it later became a matter for calculation whether or not an application for an entirely new licence was worth the cost, always supposing one was successful. The traffic staff of the territorial companies quickly became familiar with court procedure, which meant that the smaller cases were less expensive for the bigger firms, whereas many small operators found they needed a professional advocate for their rare appearances and were thus at a disadvantage.

The cost and complexity of traffic court procedure undeniably discouraged change and development in the industry, but so also did the pattern of decisions. D. N. Chester, writing in 1935, deduced from them the principles of priority, protection and public need as guiding the minister and the commissioners in their interpretation of the Road Traffic Act. The first of these, priority, had particular importance in the early days of the system. When the licensing of goods vehicles was introduced under the Road and Rail Traffic Act of 1933, 'grandfather rights' were given to existing hauliers, who automatically received a licence authorising them to run vehicles up to the same aggregate tonnage as they had had in 1932. The Road Traffic Act, on the other hand, made no such provision, and although an operator who applied for a road service licence by 31 March 1931, was permitted to continue any service operated at 9 February 1931, pending a decision, the mere fact of operation on a given date provided no certainty of success. Services started on or after 9 February, however, had to be withdrawn on 31 March, so the earlier date put an end to most of the jockeying for position that began as the implications of licensing became clear to the industry.

Road service licensing was introduced when the depression was reducing demand, particularly over the longer distances, and the commissioners found themselves faced with a general over-provision of services. To reduce this, they asked which operator had been operating on any route longest; which had been licensed to do so, where licensing had previously existed; and how satisfactory the operators' record had been as to maintenance and regularity of operation. In the area of Tilbury, Grays and Purfleet, where twenty-seven small operators had shared the local services (in addition to the National and several others who ran into the area from elsewhere), no less than nineteen were either refused licences or withdrew their applications. Here the criterion seems to have been the condition of the applicants' buses, some of which were dangerous, but where a decision could not be made on this basis it depended upon which could be said to be the 'established operator'. In this way, the 'claim jumping' services originating just prior to the Act were distinguished from those with a longer history, or those that were genuine new development. Where there remained little to choose between the claims of several operators, the commissioners would generally encourage them to agree on a co-ordinated service. If this involved a territorial company and a number of independents, the former would probably take the initiative, but often the attempt would fail because of the suspicion (and sometimes the stubbornness) of one or more of the smaller proprietors. The commissioners would then be driven to a 'Judgement of Solomon', which usually resulted in a division on the basis of each operator's traffic figures for 1930.

The principle of priority was a fair one, and generally acceptable to the industry, which was probably spared the worst consequence of the recession as a result of the Road Traffic Act. The principle of protection applied more broadly and has had a longer life, for arguments about priority became less important when the initial shareout of licences had been completed. Protection, on the other hand, can be said to be the basis of road service licensing, which was intended to constrain competitive forces in the industry. Local services were generally protected from longer distance ones, and regular from irregular or seasonal ones, and various methods were devised to achieve these ends. In some cases the carriage of passengers on a certain section of route, or between certain points, or on certain journeys was entirely prohibited; in others, a minimum fare was laid down to discourage short-distance riders; finally, a compromise might be reached.

But priority and protection together had a more serious consequence, for between them they made it almost impossible for a new operator to start a service. However much the industry had tried throughout its history to limit the effect of competition by agreement, there had always been the potential 'pirate' to act as a stimulant and to prevent the mutual protection associations from lapsing into inertia. Road service licensing set a ring-fence round the trade, and although its administration was generally just and far-sighted, the effects of such interference, good and evil, were evident. Behind such lofty phrases as 'bringing order out of chaos', 'responsible operation' and 'limited competition' lies the absolute effect of the Road Traffic Act in creating a monopoly, and the fact this was equitably shared amongst those in the trade in 1930 does not really alter the position. Also it must be recognised that the monopoly was directed to protecting the capital of the railways who were in a privileged position, just as the London monopoly of 1924 had been directed to protect the capital of the Underground group.

The monopoly was limited to regular service operation, leaving charter work unrestricted. Here again, the Act leant towards the larger operators and the railways, for the smaller, specialist firm is generally more successful in the private hire trade, while few of the territorial companies obtained more than a fraction of their revenue from it. But the boundary line between genuine charter work and regular bus or coach operation has always been hard to define. Originally, public-service vehicles were classified as 'stage carriages', 'express carriages' or 'contract carriages', but even before the first licences were issued it was found necessary to make provision for 'excursions and tours' (which might be either stage or express) and for these to include extended tours of more than one day. Private hire ('contract carriage') operation was defined as the hiring of a vehicle as a whole, but because the hirer usually re-imburses himself from the passengers, this definition had to be extended. The Act stated that separate fares could be charged when a vehicle was used 'on a special occasion', without it ceasing to be a contract carriage, but it is not easy to define a special occasion. Hore-Belisha's Road Traffic Act of 1937, which also introduced pedestrian crossings and driving tests for motorists, tried to improve this definition, although with limited success.

Problems of definition bedevilled the enforcement of road service licensing, for the law set out to make specific distinctions where common practice makes none. We are all used to generalisations such as bus services or coach services, but because of the flexibility of the vehicles in everyday use it may not be easy to classify a particular operation exactly. The attempt to make physical distinctions between different types of vehicle along these lines was never more than half-hearted, for the Act permitted certain types to be used in the function of others, and most vehicles were licensed on the most generous definition, so that their use was not unduly restricted. The hard cases arose when a private-hire operator strayed over the border into the forbidden world of service operation, as he was tempted to do by the very fact that it was a jealously guarded monopoly (he would also be attracted by the steady, if unspectacular, revenue of most service operations). The enforcement of this part of the Act led to many prosecutions, none of them easy to explain to the public, and many arising from the activities of the minister's traffic examiners, since evidence was not always easy to come by. Understandably, prosecutions of this nature, which were most common during the decade after 1945, were unpopular with the public and served to give the Road Traffic Act a bad name.

Chester has relatively little to say about his third principle, that of public need. In practice, the first two have had far more significance, for together they sum up the whole spirit of the Road Traffic Act. Public need, which might be expected to play the lead, is in fact very difficult to define and usually more a matter of opinion than fact, which accounts for its limited value as a criterion. Operators of public transport are all too familiar with petitions for new services accompanied by long lists of signatures: only too often the service, when it is put on, fails to attract more than a handful of passengers. Inevitably in traffic court procedure, public need tended to be a matter of various witnesses' ideas of what might happen if a service were to be provided, which in turn would depend upon how well the applicant had prepared his case and upon the objectors' ability to destroy it. It is not surprising that the commissioners would frequently refer to their own knowledge of the situation rather than to the evidence before them. And this became more common the longer the system continued in being, for a strong-minded chairman, with the accumulated knowledge of his officials to draw upon, would tend to use the power of his office to influence the provision of services in his area. Thus the authoritarian provisions of the Act made a mockery of any concept of public needs being expressed by the effective demand of the consumer, or being met by matching different types of production to different forms of demand.

By the Road Traffic Act of 1934 the traffic areas were adjusted in the south of England. The Metropolitan area was enlarged to include the whole of the territory of the new London Passenger Transport Board, and the Southern Traffic area, over which Sir Rowland Harker had presided, was abolished.

The Road Traffic Act may also be seen as a step towards the 'professionalisation' of the motor-bus industry, in the sense that operators were able to escape from the hurly-burly of a competitive market into the formalities of the traffic court. D. S. Lees, in his monograph, *Economic Consequences of the Professions*, observes:

> . . . restrictions on competition make life more comfortable for producers. That is one of their main purposes and, as a community, it is an option open to us. A competitive economy is not

a comfortable place : efficient, vigorous, tolerant of diversity and idiosyncracy—but not comfortable. Competition can never be eliminated but there is nothing written in the stars that says it must be priority number one.

He points out that touting is regarded as beneath the dignity of the professional (and quotes the legal and medical professions as examples), and yet without it 'a powerful facet of the drive of enterprise would go'. Touting was always one of the activities held against the pirates by the establishment, until it was ended (apart from some continuance in the day excursion trade) by the road service licence. It is not too much to compare the effect of the Act in making the industry 'respectable' with the consequence of registration, the status achieved by solicitors in 1729, by doctors in 1858, by nurses in 1919, and by hairdressers in 1964.

On the other hand, the Road Traffic Act was a workable and acceptable alternative to nationalisation, or to the outright ownership of the industry by the railways. Management remained in the hands of 'first generation' busmen, not a few of whom could well remember what it was like to be out working on the road. In Northern Ireland, where the management was handed to a board without transport experience, and in Eire, where the two railways ran the buses themselves, progress by the end of the decade was far less by comparison with the developments which had taken place in Great Britain. Crosland-Taylor has described the difficulties of working under railway management :

> We were a new toy and lots of railway officials came round to look at this queer thing—a motor-bus business. . . . The road engineer came to see if he could do our vehicle maintenance. Traffic staff came to see what the inspectors did and whether it would be a good thing to copy railway methods. Individual railway officers were very acceptable, but they had been brought up on tradition, whereas we had been brought up on expediency.

The Tilling & British settlement, combined with the Road Traffic Act, had the great virtue of leaving the young industry to manage itself with the minimum of constraint compatible with their protectionist philosophy.

THE INDUSTRY UNDER THE ROAD TRAFFIC ACT

The work involved in setting up the licensing system was substantial. Many of the territorial companies loaned staff to the traffic commissioners to help trace the multitude of small businesses, many of which figured in no public records. The commissioners for the Northern Scottish area had to make personal visits to some of the Hebridean islands to persuade the local operators to apply for licences at all, and not a few small proprietors throughout the country gave up their services in 1931 and subsequent years, because of the formalities the Act imposed upon them. In 1953 the author sent a letter to 218 operators who had left the industry in East Anglia alone, asking what were their reasons for retirement; out of twenty-one who replied, eleven said they had been discouraged by the 'red tape' element of the Act. In this connection, Crosland-Taylor recalls that for three weeks he and his staff worked until 8 or 9 pm every night, preparing applications for the Crosville licences, and that a lorry was needed to take the forms to Manchester.

In many ways the Road Traffic Act of 1930 was a major reform in a field where it was urgently needed. It proved to be an effective means of controlling the less scrupulous or the careless operator, and of preventing the public from being exploited or put in actual danger. Both large and small firms, and even municipal transport departments, have been subjected to the ultimate sanction of having their vehicle licences revoked or suspended. The system is a tribute to those who designed it and it has been copied in many other countries.* It is therefore the more necessary to underline the distinction between the enforcement of adequate standards and the control of actual operation, for it is the latter which has had the greatest impact upon the development and organisation of the industry.

The system of controlled monopoly enshrined in the road service licence extended to the whole of Great Britain the

---

* E. K. Hawkins, in *Roads and Road Transport in an Undeveloped Country* (HMSO 1962), argues forcefully that restrictive licensing on the model of the road service licence is harmful in a developing economy.

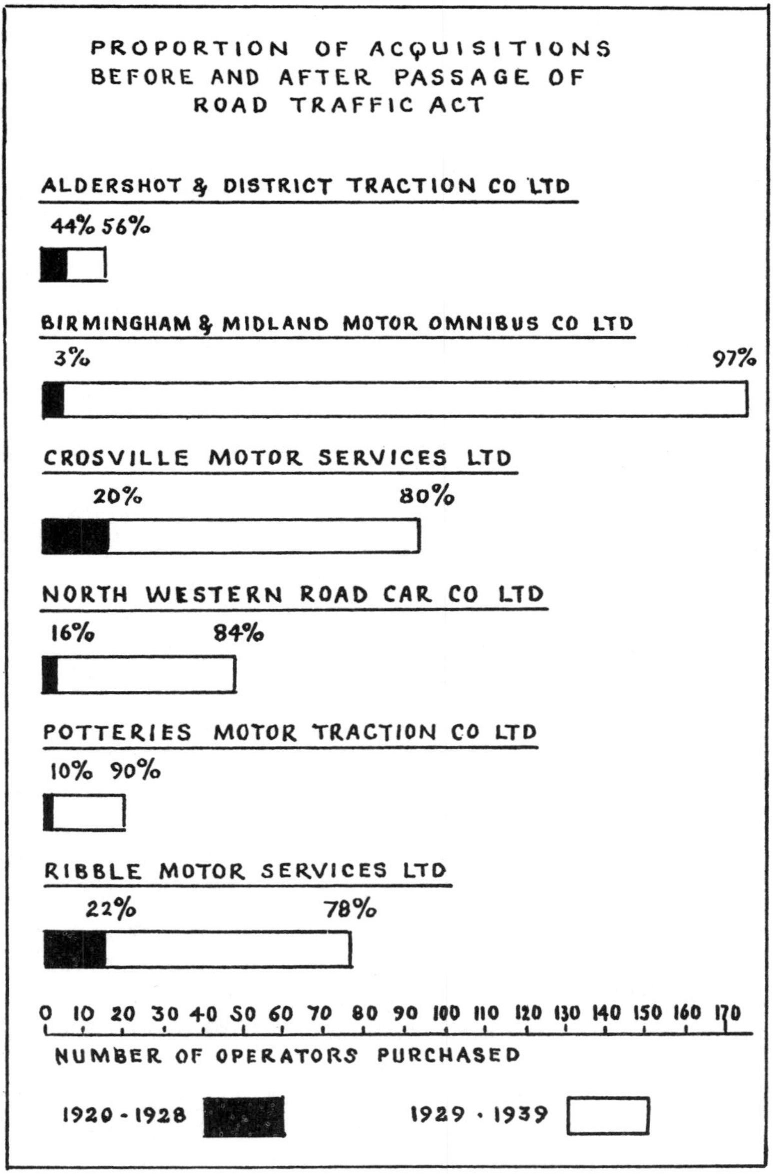

PROPORTION OF ACQUISITIONS
BEFORE AND AFTER PASSAGE OF
ROAD TRAFFIC ACT

ALDERSHOT & DISTRICT TRACTION CO LTD
44% 56%

BIRMINGHAM & MIDLAND MOTOR OMNIBUS CO LTD
3%   97%

CROSVILLE MOTOR SERVICES LTD
20%   80%

NORTH WESTERN ROAD CAR CO LTD
16%   84%

POTTERIES MOTOR TRACTION CO LTD
10% 90%

RIBBLE MOTOR SERVICES LTD
22%   78%

0 10 20 30 40 50 60 70 80 90 100 110 120 130 140 150 160 170
NUMBER OF OPERATORS PURCHASED

1920 - 1928   1929 · 1939

FIG. 3. *Proportion of acquisitions before and after Road Traffic Act*

principles of the London Traffic Act of 1924. By putting the railways in a privileged position, the legislators made it plain that they were to be protected from the competition of the motor bus, just as the tubes and tramways of London had been protected from the pirates. And the effect of the two Acts upon the industry was exactly the same, for within a short time the territorial companies began to buy up their competitors, just as the General had done in London. It was always maintained that the road service licence was not a saleable asset and there were cases where the transfer of a licence to the purchaser of a business was refused, but, in practice, it was always safe to assume that an application for transfer would not attract any objection, since it would be against the interest of operators themselves to interfere, provided no modification was proposed at the same time.

The Road Traffic Act thus had the effect of giving statutory backing to the system of area agreements devised originally by Sidney Garcke, and further strengthened by the settlement between the combines and the railways. One of its immediate effects was to enable the territorial companies to buy the majority of the express-coach services that had been started by independent operators, as described in Chapter 7. Another was the opportunity which now arose of consolidating the territories assigned under the area agreements, and the scale of this may be judged from the fact that the 367 independents originally licensed in the Eastern Traffic Area in 1931 had been reduced to 192 by 1939. Figure 3 illustrates the extent to which certain companies increased the rate at which they bought other businesses; so long as there was the possibility of new competition arising, there had to be powerful reasons for spending money on purchase. Before 1930 a business had to be big enough to have a virtual area of its own, or to have sufficient nuisance value, before it could find a buyer in this way, and if it were in difficulty, it would pay its neighbours to let it fail rather than to buy it up. The Road Traffic Act therefore gave hundreds of small proprietors a security and an assured value that they had never had; in short, protection.

In suitable cases, considerable economies could be made from a merger, and this encouraged the territorial companies in their policy of purchase. They were also under some pressure from the railways to reduce the number of independents, the LMS and to some extent the LNE being chiefly committed to this policy. Carried to its extreme, as in the cases of Crosville and Eastern

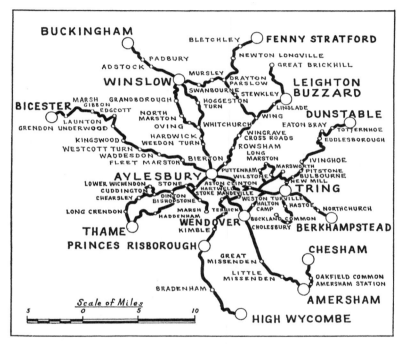

MAP 2. *Bus services of the Aylesbury Motor Omnibus Company Ltd in 1929, prior to their subsequent partition between the area agreement companies*

Counties, it meant that numbers of small businesses were acquired in rural areas which would probably have been better left alone, for services from country districts are more economically provided by operators based in the villages they serve than by large, town-based companies. A side effect of the system was the tendency to leave operators on the area agreement boundaries alone, so that even now the independents are often to be found in greater number in such places than elsewhere. Map 2 illustrates the complications that followed when the Aylesbury Omnibus Company Ltd was bought by Eastern National in 1933; because Aylesbury lay at the meeting point of five companies, its routes had to be distributed between them.

CHAPTER SIX

MEN AND MACHINES

THE story of how the motor-bus industry began, and how it established itself as an independent part of the whole business of transport, is a story of individual effort both on the part of those who perfected the vehicles and those who sought out their most effective use. As time went on, various subsidiary activities grew up: ticket issue and accounting grew more sophisticated; vehicles grew more specialised; bus and coach stations were built; and publicity became ever more important. In addition, the industry had to adapt itself to changing circumstances imposed from without; physically, by the condition of the roads and later by growing congestion, and legally, by the regulations for the time being in force. Finally, the human side of the story is all-important, not only in respect of the lives of the pioneer busmen, but also of the multitude of men and women who work the buses, and the trade unions within which they have been organised.

PIONEER VEHICLES AND THEIR PROBLEMS

The 'emancipation' of 1896 was brought about by the pressure of those (including some of the highest in the land) who wanted to drive their motor cars without risk of prosecution. It was by no means a charter for the development of the commercial motor vehicle, which was still subject to many restrictions, and the motor was still regarded as a pleasure vehicle for young people with money. Pioneers such as Walter Flexman French, who were convinced of the commercial possibilities of motor transport, turned at first to very small vehicles, which were either horse buses with a motor or motor cars with wagonette bodies, and which seldom seated more than ten passengers. The main exceptions were the steam buses of the period, but as C. E. Lee has pointed out, the buses placed in service before 1904 were 'individual, and largely experimental, vehicles', or one-off jobs.

The wagonettes lingered on in provincial towns, but from 1904 the heavier buses began to establish themselves by virtue of their greater seating capacity. For a year or two the single-decker ruled supreme, but before long the age of the double-decker had begun. This was made possible by the Heavy Motor Car Order of 1904 which, in its way, marked the emancipation of the commercial motor vehicle. Numerous makers of both petrol and steam buses now entered the field, but the first standard vehicle to achieve lasting success was the Milnes-Daimler which had reached this stage of development by 1905. The de Dion and Straker-Squire were its most important contemporaries.

After 1905, the motor bus took on a distinctive appearance which was to last until the 'twenties. It was square as to bodywork, with a pronounced 'snout' housing the engine, and although it owed a good deal to its horse-drawn predecessor, it had clearly established a new tradition of design. Among eccentric variations were buses at Liverpool which were built to look like electric trams, while the first buses to run in Northern Ireland were built in the Derby works of the Midland Railway (for the Northern Counties Committee), and had standard railway carriage ventilators on the roofs.

In spite of the Locomotives on Highways Act of 1896, a man still had to walk with a red flag in front of vehicles of three tons and over until the level was raised to five tons in 1904. This was an embarrassment to early operators, the Milnes-Daimler, for example, weighing $3\frac{1}{2}$ tons. The GWR dealt with the problem by removing sufficient equipment for their buses to show 2 tons 19 cwt on a weighbridge, whereupon this weight was solemnly painted on the side and the missing equipment replaced. Since this procedure appears to have been perfectly legitimate, it was no doubt common practice, but much of the success of early bus operation depended upon the zeal with which the law was enforced. Many of the railway companies, as we have seen, had no parliamentary powers to run motor buses—even the GWR was without powers of its own until 1928—but the obvious value of their services was such that no one challenged their legal standing.

The Birmingham police were at first ill-disposed towards the BMMO buses, which made the difficulties of maintenance even worse. During August, September and October 1905, forty-five BMMO buses were ordered off the road under local byelaws, forty-two for excessive noise, two for dropping oil on the roadway, and one for running without a front tyre. The company was not allowed to repair a breakdown on the spot but had to tow the vehicle to the depot in Ladywood Road; perhaps it is not surprising that their motor buses were withdrawn in 1907. Everywhere the low speed limit was a hindrance, varying in degree with the attitude of police and magistrates, and it was not unknown for an operator to suffer the indignity of hearing that the evidence against him had been obtained by a constable on a bicycle. In towns where municipal services alone were running, there was, understandably, less trouble of this kind.

It is not easy today to picture the mechanical problems of early operation. An engineer had to be his own mechanic, and a driver had to be something of an engineer. Lubrication was a matter for skilled judgement—or instinct—the driver of a Milnes-Daimler having to pump oil to the engine sump from a glass bottle on the dashboard as required. The internal-combustion engine was a much more delicate mechanism than the steam engine and would not tolerate the same rough treatment. The breakthrough in developing a satisfactory petrol bus was achieved by a handful of men; Searle with the X- and B-types for the LGOC, and again through his association with the Daimler 'Silent Knight'; Frost-Smith, Stevens and Brown with the Tilling-Stevens; Thomson with the 'Lothian'; and, to a greater or less extent, the designers of the Leylands and other makes that were to become important later on. These men achieved what many thought impossible, among them A. L. C. Fell, chief officer of the LCC tramways, who said in 1909 that 'twenty years hence motor buses will be exhibited as curios in museums'.

The importance of tyres cannot be over-estimated. Early vehicles were invariably steel-shod owing to the high cost of solid rubber—in 1902 a set of solid tyres for a one-ton vehicle imposed a running cost of about tenpence a mile. This high cost almost caused the GWR to abandon its early buses, but the foresight of the company's road motor engineer, F. C. A. Coventry, and the conclusion in 1904 of a mileage contract (at 3·0576 pence per mile) combined to prevent this. When tyres came off, as they did from time to time, one result was to alter the class of the vehicle and bring it within a speed limit of four miles an hour. Wheels were usually made of wood, and Alfred Baynton recalls that these 'shrunk during the hot weather and were therefore taken off nightly and soaked in pits filled with water to prevent them falling to pieces'. Cast steel wheels became standard in London after 1910, but Baynton's reminiscence relates to the East Kent company during the first world war.

Searle's buses, designed for the LGOC and for Daimlers, established the petrol engine over the steamer and, apart from Clarkson's buses, the number of steamers declined after 1909 until the last of all ceased to run in the Isle of Wight in 1923. More successful was the petrol-electric which shared with the steam engine the advantage of being very much easier to drive than the orthodox vehicle. Dispensing with any gear-changing device, it avoided the need for one of the fundamental skills of motoring. Thomas Tilling was associated with the development of the petrol-electric bus from 1907 and standardised it from 1911, although Tilling-Stevens Motors later became a separate concern. The use of the same model by Midland Red from 1912 has already been mentioned; a driver who joined the company when petrol buses were being introduced after 1921 recalled how superior he felt to the 'tramwaymen', as he called the Tilling-Stevens drivers, because of his ability to drive a real motor bus.

The chief faults of the petrol-electric lay in its performance on hills; going up, the motor ran too slowly to deliver enough power to the electrical equipment, and (more seriously) in coming down the engine could not be used as a brake. All the same,

Tilling-Stevens vehicles introduced in Douglas in 1928 ran on very hilly routes until 1949 and the foundations of two of the most important companies in Great Britain were laid with these machines.

Buses before the first world war offered limited comfort to their passengers, and this was not only due to their inherent limitations. It is true that the early pneumatic tyre was incapable of carrying a vehicle heavy enough to convey an economic load, and the first double-decker to use pneumatic tyres ran in Wolverhampton for the corporation of that town in 1927. The design of buses in the early days was heavily influenced by the London market, which all manufacturers desired to enter, and here the inflexible attitude of the Metropolitan police delayed progress. Apart from two very early examples, no buses were allowed to ply for hire in London with a covering over the top deck and this condition was re-inforced by police regulation in 1909, some months after the first double-deckers with completely enclosed top decks had been put in service by Widnes Corporation. It was not until October 1925 that the restriction was withdrawn in London and the first to appear in the provinces, apart from Widnes, was a vehicle owned by Liverpool Corporation which entered service in January 1920.

Another regulation of the Metropolitan police forbade enclosed cabs or even windscreens, so that the driver remained exposed and uncomfortable until the 'thirties. On the other hand, because of the skill required, the early drivers enjoyed a considerable prestige, and some kind of uniform was usually provided by the larger firms. Working conditions were improved over the worst of the horse-bus era, although there was still no legal limit to the hours a man could be expected to work and standards varied widely. The London & Provincial Licensed Bus Workers Union was formed in 1913 and had some success in the capital, where it negotiated its first agreement with the LGOC, the 'Busmen's Charter', in the following year. There was a short-lived strike in London in 1917, but the scattered development of the industry and the nature of the job outside the larger towns did not make the organisation of labour easy. Apart from the Londoners, only the 'railway busmen' achieved formal agreements, being provided for within the National Union of Railwaymen by a settlement with the GWR in 1916.

SOME EARLY BUSMEN

Amongst the pioneers, a few names stand out because of their contribution to the wider story, and their careers have been described elsewhere in the text. But many of the early busmen, who can never be thought of as 'lesser men', made their mark in narrower paths, while some made contributions that were less spectacular but still of lasting importance. Among the latter were A. D. Mackenzie and A. E. Cannon, who left their mark not only upon Southdown Motor Services Ltd, which they served for a grand total of eighty-one years, but upon the Hants & Dorset and Wilts & Dorset companies as well. Mackenzie, a consulting engineer, became general manager of the Sussex Motor Road Car Company, a predecessor of Southdown, in 1907, and appointed Cannon, who had had experience of bus operation in London, as his engineer. The two men formed a partnership as fruitful as that between Power and Shire of Midland Red, but without the antipathy that lay between the Birmingham pair. Mackenzie was the traffic genius and his maxims have passed into the language of the industry. A. F. R. Carling, who joined his staff in 1931 and succeeded Cannon as general manager of Southdown in 1947, describes how the company's network was built up on the basis of buses running every hour on almost every main road (and many others) in its territory. Mackenzie appreciated that an hourly headway would be easy for everyone to understand and he firmly believed that 'facilities create traffic'. In those days of expanding demand, he realised that frequency mattered, and if a service were unsuccessful running every hour, he might well improve it by running every ten minutes. He is also credited with the maxim : 'If there is anyone walking along one of my routes, there is something wrong with the service', and he believed in 'anchoring' routes at each end, either in a town or at an exchange point with another service, so as to avoid 'thin ends'. On such a combination of flair and commercial ability he established Southdown, and with it all he remained, in Mr Carling's words, 'surely one of the kindest pioneers who ever lived'.

Mackenzie's first area manager at Brighton was Major H. E. Hickmott, who had been introduced to the company by W. F. French. After the first world war, Major Hickmott was chosen by BAT to establish Ribble Motor Services, of which he became managing director at the age of thirty-seven. He retained the post until his retirement in 1944 and W. J. Crosland-Taylor has described him as a one-man-band; certainly his achievement in building up one of the largest of the territorial companies indicates a man of exceptional energy and foresight. Hickmott's genius lay in the field of co-ordination, and to this day there are small firms working in close and successful partnership with Ribble; so much so that on the route worked jointly with Pennine Motor Services, Pennine conductors even pay in at Ribble offices. He was responsible for a tripartite agreement between Liverpool Corporation, Crosville, and Ribble which is a model of its kind, and when the traffic commissioners for the North Western area were reviewing Lancashire bus operation in 1931, Hickmott declared that Ribble was a party to no less than eighty-six schemes of co-ordination.

The north-west of England saw the careers of other busmen of Hickmott's stature. 'Ned' Edwardes became resident engineer of South Lancashire Tramways in 1901 at the age of twenty-six, and general manager nine years later. He saw the company pass through the stage of running trolleybuses to become, as Lancashire United, one of the independent territorial firms and remained in charge of it until he retired in 1955. After the death of Sir Arthur Stanley in 1945 he became chairman as well, an office Stanley had held for forty-five years. A retiring man with a gruff exterior, he was well liked and respected, and Crosland-Taylor speaks of his love of people, 'even officials of the Transport and General Workers Union, who are so much more human than they were thirty years ago'. Many busmen have been exclusively dedicated to the industry they served, but Edwardes was a man of many interests, including golf, shooting, fishing, music and the arts.

The foundations of Crosville were largely laid by Claude Crosland-Taylor, who must surely have reached the heights of the management profession had he not died at the early age of forty-five. Here was another man with wide interests who became the youngest mayor the city of Chester had known for 700 years. His neighbour at North Western was George Cardwell, whose later career is described in Chapter 9, but whose early years were marked by sound foundations he laid for that company. Cardwell was responsible for the special relationships that North Western came to have with the local authorities in its area, whereby he avoided fruitless competition and succeeded in getting his buses into the centre of towns and cities at a time when municipal policy was often directed to keeping company vehicles out.

A pioneer whose reputation was made with one company was J. Coventon Moth, who remained a director of Trent Motor Traction until his death in 1963 at the age of seventy-five. In 1909, Commercial Cars Ltd of Luton found itself with a number of unsold vehicles on hand and so formed a company called Commercial Car Hirers Ltd to operate them, with Moth as secretary and general manager. A fourteen-seater was leased to a Scottish landowner, and one of his guests, who came from Derbyshire, hired another to connect his home with Ashbourne and Derby. What might have remained a private affair was developed by Moth into a public service between the two towns, to which were added services from Derby to Alfreton and between Alfreton and Chesterfield. Moth also ran his company's Commer buses in various other parts of the country, but these services were sold to other interests for development. The Derbyshire services, however, attracted the attention of BET, with the result that Trent Motor Traction was formed in 1913, joinly by BAT and Commercial Car Hirers, with Coventon Moth as its first secretary. He became a director in 1915 and was also on the board of the CCH freight haulage company. After 1920 he became associated with certain laundry businesses and, in 1934, assisted in the formation of Advance Laundries Ltd, which came into BET ownership in 1955. He remained on its board until his death.

Next door neighbour to Trent is Barton Transport Ltd, one of the largest independent family businesses to have survived. What is more, there have been few family businesses that have contributed so much to the history of the industry. One of its later directors was involved in it at the age of eleven, when he was making regular journeys to Derby on behalf of his father, and on one such occasion returned with a pony and trap to Mablethorpe, where the family then lived. His father, T. H. Barton, had left the firm of Hornsby & Sons to manage the family's quarry but retained his interest in automobile engineering; as early as 1894 he had been working on the development of an oil engine. He used the pony and trap to ply for hire in Mablethorpe, replacing it in 1900 with a 9-hp Benz wagonette.

This was sold shortly afterwards when, for health reasons, the Bartons moved to Weston-super-Mare and bought a 6-hp Daimler twelve-seater which was used on local services and for tours as far afield as Glastonbury and the Cheddar Gorge. The business thus established was sold in 1903, and the family returned to Derbyshire where, among other trading activities, they ran a Durham-Churchill char-a-banc on excursions. They replaced this with a more powerful model of the same make in 1908, and the father and son decided to use it on a regular service between Long Eaton, Beeston and Nottingham during the Goose Fair. In spite of railway competition, the service was so successful that they went on with it, earning £475 profit in the first three months and adding a second vehicle in the following year. Other routes were opened, but they were not the first claim on the firm's resources and when twenty Gloucester vehicles in new condition were acquired as the result of a bankruptcy, they were resold at a profit and not used for purposes of expansion. On the other hand, the family took a great interest in bus operation, all four of T. H. Barton's daughters working at one time or another 'on the back'; almost certainly the first conductresses the industry had known.

When war broke out, the services were all withdrawn and the buses transferred to carrying workers to the Chilwell Shell Filling Factory. Pioneer work was done in converting them to run on coal gas, carried in a bag on the roof, and for a time the firm was making 100 such bags a week for sale to other operators. When peace returned, the bus services were re-opened, although as late as 1924 gas was still being used as a fuel to some extent, because of the high price of petrol. Still pre-occupied with technical experiments, including a 'road train' which was a failure because it was too heavy, Bartons turned again to the idea of heavy oil and in 1928 they ran one of the first diesel-engined buses in Great Britain. A rebuilt Lancia with a Black-stone engine carried the title 'Barton British Fuel Oil Bus' with the slogan 'No Petrol—No Danger'. During the second world war, coal gas was once more used as a fuel instead of the more general producer gas, with its clumsy coke-burning trailers.

A pioneer who left his mark on the London area and survived a remarkable series of changes of employment while retaining essentially the same responsibilites, was A. H. Hawkins, founder of the East Surrey Traction Company Ltd. Having left school in 1894 at the age of thirteen, he saw the possibility of a bus service between Reigate and Redhill, where he lived; a route which was then being worked by horse buses on a fifteen-minute headway. In 1910 he wrote to a trade journal for advice on starting a motor bus service, asking 'whether any of the bus makers supply buses on the deferred payment system, as my capital is limited'. His company was formed the following year and by 1913 had developed sufficiently to meet the southward expansion of the London General Omnibus Company in the neighbourhood of Merstham. An area agreement between the two was signed in 1914, and after the war they began to work closely together, since the General had decided to farm out its country operations to other operators as agents (the National and Thames Valley companies were similarly chosen for this purpose).

In 1929, East Surrey became a subsidiary of LGOC, and in 1932 it was renamed London General Country Services Ltd and took over the other agency routes. Hawkins remained in charge and in 1930 became the first and only managing director of Green Line Coaches Ltd. With the formation of London Transport he was made general manager, country buses and coaches, and held this post until he retired in 1946, still with his headquarters at Reigate. He died in 1963 and in his obituary J. B. Burnell doubted whether his years with the General and the LPTB were the happiest period of his life, recalling how depressed Hawkins had been one day in the early 'thirties when one of his drivers who for over twenty years had greeted him with 'Good morning, Arthur' addressed him for the first time as 'Mr Hawkins'.

One of the most remarkable characters in the industry during the 'thirties was Edward Hillman, who is reported to have been hardly able to read or write and to have been attracted to the coach trade by the success of operators for whom he acted as booking agent at his shop in Stratford. He bought his first coach early in 1928, and on 7 December of that year he started a service between Stratford and Brentwood which, by the end of 1929, had been extended through Chelmsford to Colchester. In the spring of 1930 it was pushed on to Clacton, and by this time there were fifty-four departures a day from Stratford. Hillman's concern to develop traffic meant that local fares were available all down the road, and although special coaches ran for long-distance passengers when trade was brisk, at other times everyone used the same coach. Not all journeys covered the whole route, the timetable thinning at Brentwood, Chelmsford and Colchester.

Hillman's fleet consisted entirely of Gilfords, the standard vehicle for many independents, and during 1930 the business became closely linked with the Gilford Motor Company Ltd. New vehicles were rapidly acquired, so that the fleet grew from eighteen in March to fifty-seven in December 1930. During that summer the service was again extended, with six journeys a day to Ipswich, and two each going on to Yarmouth and to Norwich. The single fare to Ipswich was fixed at 5s (the same as Clacton), with Yarmouth at 6s and Norwich at 7s 6d.

In the same year the London terminal was moved to a new coach station near Tomlins Grove, in Bow. After some financial infighting, Hillman also acquired a service between Aldgate and Upminster, which he began to work early in 1931.

At the beginning of 1932, Hillman's original service provided seventy departures a day from Bow, with a fifteen-minute headway as far as Brentwood from 6.15 am to 11.30 pm. At Brook Street Hill, it was said that there was never a Hillman coach out of sight. In August, Hillman parted company with Gilfords and formed a limited company with an authorised capital of £50,000 and a registered office at Romford. By the end of 1931

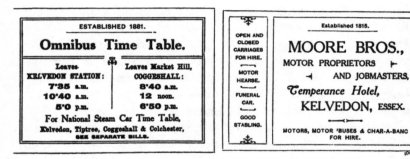

FIG. 4. *Omnibus connections with the railway in the early years of this century*

he had taken a lease of Maylands Aerodrome, between Romford and Brentwood, and in the summer season of 1932 he started an air service to Clacton which was operated on similar lines to his coaches. In 1933 he added air services to Paris and to Margate, and R. D. S. Higham has commented that he 'carried the war against the railways into the third dimension', adding that he 'became unpopular with Imperial Airways (and) Railway Air Services, because of his ability to fly faster and cheaper on the cross-Channel routes than the monopoly'. The remark applies with equal force to his coaching activities.

In January 1934 the newly formed London Passenger Transport Board took possession under its Act of Hillman's Upminster business and of more than half his activities on the Colchester route. By then, he was running 113 coaches, a remarkable expansion from nothing over six years. The LPTB acquired the Romford garage but not the Bow coach station, and Hillman proceeded to sell the remainder of the business, with twenty-eight vehicles, to Eastern National. Under the area agreement, the section to Ipswich and beyond should then have passed to Eastern Counties in some form, but that company was retrenching in the express coach field and the licences for Bow-Ipswich, Bow-Yarmouth and Bow-Norwich were surrendered. George Ewer & Company objected to the transfer of the Colchester and Clacton licences, and succeeded on the ground that this would have given Eastern National an unfair advantage, so that by August 1934 Hillman's former business had been reduced to a Bow-Chelmsford route, with no local fares between Bow and Brentwood. Later in that year the airway company 'went public', but Hillman died a few days afterwards; he had been backed by the London banking house of d'Erlangers, who continued to develop the business until in November 1935 it became part of the newly-constituted British Airways Ltd. Another bus operator who turned to the air was Fred Wright, of Louth, who for a few years in the 'thirties flew a biplane from an airfield near the town, and also owned a 'Flying Flea' (which apparently never took to the air).

Hillman's policy of carrying short-stage traffic on his coaches brought him into conflict with local bus operators, and not least with the firm of Moore Brothers of Kelvedon, who were one of the oldest established businesses in the whole of the industry. Their original business had been set up on 20 February 1815, with a 'fleet' of three donkeys and a cart. A horse bus was introduced between Coggeshall and Kelvedon station in 1881, and a similar vehicle later ran between Braintree and Colchester, while a carrier's cart served the main road between Colchester and Chelmsford. In 1912 a Daimler shooting-brake was bought, but mechanisation really began in 1914 with the purchase of a Clarkson steamer which carried the title 'National' as a fleet name. With this the first of the firm's motor services was started, but at about the same time two Coggeshall carriers bought motor buses and began to run between Braintree and Colchester. Moores followed suit, and after the war the fleet was built up until, by 1963, they owned forty buses, including twenty-five double-deckers. In that year the business was sold to Eastern National, since (according to a member of the fifth generation of the family) they had 'run out of Moores'.

Mention has already been made of Commander F. T. Hare, RN, who began his transport career by setting up a haulage business at Okehampton in January 1920, employing ex-service men and running four Maudslay lorries. The venture proved less profitable than had been expected, but the possibilities of bus operation looked better and two AEC twenty-seaters were bought and used for services to Launceston, Tavistock and Hatherleigh markets, also running to Exeter two or three times a week. From this grew Devon Motor Transport, a business which was developed with a strong individual bias. Every effort was made to secure what the Navy would call a 'happy ship', and a form of profit sharing was introduced in 1925 after the staff had accepted a temporary cut in pay to meet financial difficulties arising from severe competition. Ingenious methods of attracting traffic included a poster showing 'Felix the Cat' boarding a green bus, with the caption 'He has stopped walking—and now rides by DMT'.

In 1923, Commander Hare bought a business further west and formed Cornwall Motor Transport, a certain amount of co-ordination following between the two companies and the GWR and Devon General. Thus the westward expansion of the National Omnibus & Transport Company was checked by the existence of substantial operators in the western peninsula, until, in 1927, DMT and CMT passed to National ownership, Commander Hare joining the NO&T board and remaining in charge. In the meantime, he had been operating a steamship service to the Channel Islands and in 1923 had formed the Jersey Motor Transport Company Ltd. Faced with unrestrained competition, he sold this in 1928 to the island's principal railway company and took a holiday in Kenya.

This led indirectly to the establishment of bus services first in Malta, which were withdrawn when General Motors unleashed a flood of cheap vehicles, and then in Cairo, where the Egyptian

General Omnibus Company SA was started on 1 January 1931. In this case, the British government gave financial support to Thorneycrofts for the construction of the buses, the working capital being provided by Commander Hare and his Egyptian associate, who was legally required to own 51 per cent of the shares. Although an immediate success in terms of traffic, local difficulties lead to the sale of EGOC to the Belgian interests responsible for the Cairo tramways, and Commander Hare turned to what was then known as British East Africa. He had obtained an exclusive agency for the sale of Morris cars in Kenya and, in conjunction with Major K. A. Brown, acquired a garage business in Nairobi.

In his African ventures, Commander Hare insisted upon an exclusive franchise and this he obtained in 1934 for the operations of Kenya Bus Services Ltd in Nairobi. Albion buses with Gardner diesel engines were imported, fitted with high-pressure pistons on account of the altitude, and were probably the first diesel buses to be used in Africa. Services in Mombasa followed and on 1 January 1939 the Uganda Transport Company Ltd was launched, a condition of its franchise being that all its initial services should commence on the same day.

Commander Hare returned to the Navy during the second world war, leaving his partner (by then known as 'Bus Brown' in East Africa) to supervise the various operations of Overseas Motor Transport. After a while, the native staff in Uganda approached the management with the request that twenty cents a month should be deducted from their pay and sent to the boss, who they had heard was hungry. From this gesture arose the idea of sending help to Britain, and with a subscription raised from all the OMT staff, a mobile canteen was bought for the Tavistock Women's Voluntary Service, which was used during the air raids on Plymouth and Exeter, and later for the 'meals on wheels' service. Christened a 'chula wagon', it was handed over in the presence of the driver and conductor of the first DMT bus to run between Tavistock and Plymouth, symbolic of the link maintained between Commander Hare's far flung operations.

THE PROGRESS OF THE VEHICLE

By the end of the 'twenties, the motor bus had become an established form of transport; the railway age was ended. But the vehicles themselves had changed and the technical advances of the decade were as remarkable as the commercial ones. The word 'char-a-banc' has by now almost passed out of the language, and few people today will be able to recall one; by 1929 the char-a-banc was already obsolete. Its replacement was the 'all-weather saloon' or the 'sun-saloon' (which had a sliding roof)—the type of half-cab coach already obsolete. Pneumatic tyres were first fitted in 1923 and the improvement was recognised in 1928 when the maximum speed for buses was raised from 12 to 20 mph provided pneumatic tyres were fitted. Covered tops for double-deckers became general by the end of the decade (some die-hards complained at this). Roads were also improving, and in the absence of serious congestion motor buses and coaches could operate under ideal conditions. Petrol was the universal fuel.

The manufacturers who contributed to this rapid development were not always the pioneers of the pre-war years. Buses were imported from France, Italy and the United States, but the main British suppliers were far more numerous than they are today. Leyland, Albion, Daimler (by then a British company), Dennis and Guy were familiar; aec had ceased to be part of the ler group, and after a brief link with Daimler (as Associated Daimler) had come to stand on its own. Thornycrofts had formed their own operating company, Venture Ltd of Basingstoke, to gain direct experience, and Gilford was a name closely associated with the independents, many of whom it had financed. Reo, Lancia and Chevrolet were familiar foreigners. Tilling-Stevens ceased to belong to Tillings and turned from building petrol-electrics to more orthodox construction. To a great extent the rapid expansion of the industry was made possible by the continuous development of the public-service vehicle and the pirates were frequently successful because of the light, fast buses the industry produced for them. Hubert Allen, chairman of Yelloways Motor Services Ltd, has also pointed out that the establishment of express coach services would not have been possible without the 'lighter low-loading chassis—in particular, the Reo, Lancia and Leyland "Lioness".'

Compared with the present day, when there are virtually no more than three major manufacturers, the number of firms in the market before the war seems extraordinarily large. Figure 5 gives some idea of the range available to operators at different periods of the history of the industry. But the settlement of 1931 was accompanied by a big step forward on the technical side of bus operation, for operators were at last able to choose vehicles that were really reliable and economic. The period of experiment was at last coming to an end.

A. F. R. Carling has suggested that the 'paragon of vehicle virtues' at this time was the Leyland 'Titan' T.D.1, 'a well-sprung, low-loading double-decker, with a six-cylinder engine, designed from the first for pneumatic tyres, which offered, if not quite the capacity and durability of the tramcar, certainly something much nearer them than anything available before, and it combined these advantages with the greater comfort and far greater mobility of the bus'. It was upon this vehicle, and similar developments by the other principal makers, that the territorial companies standardised for the most part, in so far as they were able. Their problem was complicated by the choice of vehicle that had been available to the smaller firms whose businesses were bought after the Road Traffic Act came into force, so introducing non-standard elements that were frequently in too good a state to be written off quickly. Thus when the Eastern National company bought the bus undertaking of A. W. Berry & Sons Ltd of Colchester in 1937, at a time when ENOC was starting to standardise on the Bristol chassis, it acquired three Dennis, one AEC, two Bedford, two TSM, one Commer, two Gilfords and a Morris. Five of these were disposed of in a year or two, but one of the TSM's ran until 1945, and one of the Dennis's (new to Berry in 1934) remained in service until 1952.

But despite the choice available, several operators had been unable to satisfy themselves and decided to build their own ve-

FIG. 5.

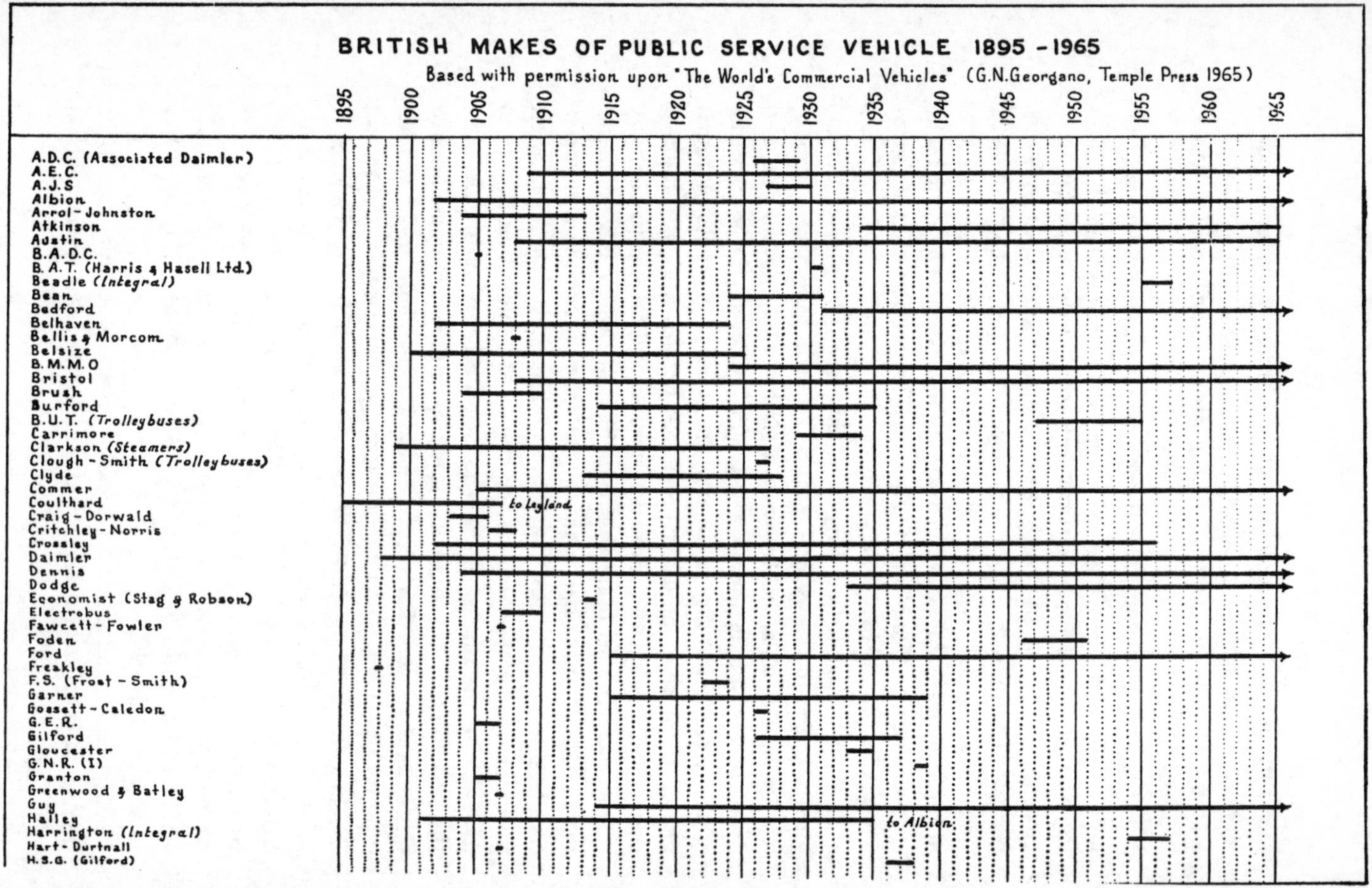
BRITISH MAKES OF PUBLIC SERVICE VEHICLE 1895 - 1965
Based with permission upon "The World's Commercial Vehicles" (G.N.Georgano, Temple Press 1965)
1895
1900
1905
1910
1915
1920
1925
1930
1935
1940
1945
1950
1955
1960
1965
A.D.C. (Associated Daimler)
A.E.C.
A.J.S
Albion
Arrol-Johnston
Atkinson
Austin
B.A.D.C.
B.A.T. (Harris & Hasell Ltd.)
Beadle (Integral)
Bean
Bedford
Belhaven
Bellis & Morcom
Belsize
B.M.M.O
Bristol
Brush
Burford
B.U.T. (Trolleybuses)
Carrimore
Clarkson (Steamers)
Clough - Smith (Trolleybuses)
Clyde
Commer
Coulthard
to Leyland
Craig - Dorwald
Critchley - Norris
Crossley
Daimler
Dennis
Dodge
Economist (Stag & Robson)
Electrobus
Fawcett - Fowler
Foden
Ford
Freakley
F.S. (Frost - Smith)
Garner
Gossett - Caledon
G.E.R.
Gilford
Gloucester
G.N.R. (I)
Granton
Greenwood & Batley
Guy
Halley
to Albion
Harrington (Integral)
Hart - Durtnall
H.S.G. (Gilford)

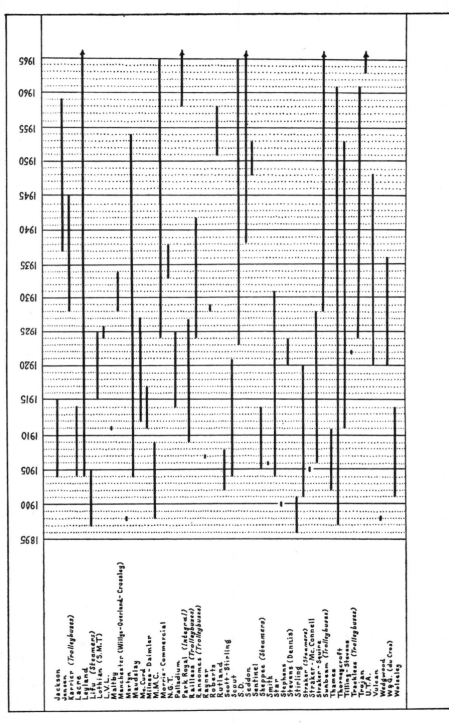

K

hicles to their own specification. The Bristol Tramways & Carriage Company produced a bus in its own shops in 1908, and thereafter almost all its vehicles were home-made; by 1932 over 1,000 had been built, many of which were sold to other operators. When the company passed into the Tilling group, the 'Bristol' became the standard chassis for many associated companies and the factory became complementary to the coach works at Lowestoft which had been established by the United Automobile Company and hived off under Tilling management as Eastern Coachworks.

At Birmingham, the exceptionally brilliant chief engineer of Midland Red, L. G. Wyndham Shire, had designed his own bodywork as early as 1914. After the war he sought for his ideal chassis, which had to be both light and simple, qualities rare in the products of the period. At first he thought he had found what he wanted in a Tilling-Stevens light goods chassis with normal transmission—he had by then abandoned his early enthusiasm for the petrol-electric vehicle—but the manufacturer was not prepared to accept his alterations to the standard production model. Arthur Twidle has remarked that in this case the chief engineers of both manufacturer and potential customer were obstinate men.

Shire's obstinacy, however, brought him his greatest success, for he was able to obtain permission from his board to design and build his own bus, altogether contrary to BET policy in matters of vehicle equipment. The 'SOS' was one of the most successful designs of its time; it had an engine of advanced design (Shire sought Ricardo's advice over this), and was not only capable of competing with the small, fast buses of the pirates but was more efficient and economical than anything else available. It also gave passengers a very smooth ride and Shire's triumph was complete when, after 1924, Midland Red supplied numerous 'SOS' buses to other companies in the BET group.

Some have said that the letters 'SOS' stand for 'Shire's Own Specification', but Twidle records that Shire originally wanted to call his design 'EOE', standing for 'Experience Over Experiment'. The company's chief accountant, having pointed out that it was more commonly associated with 'Errors and Omissions Excepted', Shire adapted the phrase to ' 'Sperience over 'Speriment', and the 'SOS' was born. He remained with Midland Red until his retirement in 1940 and died in 1963, having trained many of the engineers responsible for the motor-bus industry today.

One of Shire's brightest young men was John Petrie, who in 1926 became assistant general manager of the Northern General Transport Company. He had in the interim been in charge of the Sociedad General de Autobuses in Madrid, and of the China General Omnibus Company. Northern General was another company that had taken to building its own vehicles, starting after the first world war, and although he bought large numbers of 'SOS' vehicles, Petrie used NGT's Bensham works to produce a highly specialised machine to work the many routes in County Durham where low bridges prevented the use of double-deckers. This was the 'SE 6', a forty-four-seater saloon, which first appeared in 1933, almost twenty years ahead of its time. It had three axles, since regulations restricted the length permitted with two, but the main departure from traditional practice was the side mounting of the engine, which allowed the full extent of the floor space to be used for seats, as in the underfloor mounting of many present-day engines. An example of the fleet of 'SE 6' buses and coaches operated by NGT is to be seen in the Transport Museum in London. Petrie was a notable traffic man as well as engineer, and although he remained with the company barely ten years, he left his mark upon Northern General. When he retired, he returned to Spain to live but came back to England during the war years and worked with Devon General. He died in France in 1949.

A similar vehicle to the 'SE 6' was the AEC 'Q', which first appeared in London in 1932. Whereas Petrie's design placed the engine somewhat out of the vertical line, the 'Q' had an upright engine placed outside the chassis frame, and the consequent lateral seat on the offside became familiar to many Londoners. Five double-deckers were built, one of which never entered service, but the saloon model was ordered for quantity production by London Transport and used on both central and country services. Although the experimental vehicles had petrol engines, all the production batches were given oil engines from the start, for by this time the automotive diesel had proved its advantages in heavy traffic.

The adaptation of the heavy oil engine for commercial road transport was the biggest technical advance of the 'thirties, and development was remarkably rapid. The first diesel bus in Great Britain entered service with Sheffield Corporation on 9 March 1930; Barton Transport's followed in the same month. Not only did the compression-ignition engine burn fuel more economically than the petrol engine but, partly because of a tax difference, diesel oil was cheaper than petrol. Moreover, the reliability of the diesel engine makes it particularly attractive to the operator of high annual mileage, although its greater initial cost means that this mileage must be high enough for it to earn its keep. For some time the diesel coach was regarded by many operators as too noisy to satisfy passengers on luxury services, but Midland Bus Services put a fleet to work on the Glasgow–London express night service as early as 1932. In Neville Chamberlain's budget of 1935, the principle was established of equal taxation of fuel oil and motor spirit, and this long remained unchanged. The diesel engine was so well established that, in the year ending September 1935, nearly one-third of the new registrations of public-service vehicles were so equipped. The advantage had been proved in a number of conversions, such as that made at Sheffield where, when a Karrier bus was fitted with a Benz diesel engine, fuel consumption improved from 3·9 mpg to 10·9 mpg, and lubricating oil consumption from 73 mpg to 326 mpg.

UNIONS AND MANAGEMENT

Outside London, trade union organisation came late to the motor-bus industry. The railway busmen were members of the National Union of Railwaymen, as indeed some of the territorial companies' staff still are. In consequence, the impact of the General Strike of 1926 was limited outside the capital, and it was in London that most of the incidents of the strike took place. Buses there went on runnng with boarded windows and police protection, and damage was serious in some cases, as when a Tilling double-decker was set on fire near the Elephant & Castle. In spite of the bitterness that marked the strike, and the violence that included fighting between strikers and volunteers, H. Webb records that, at Tillings, there was no legacy of antagonism between those who came out and those who went on working. The impact of the General Strike in the provinces is not well documented, although Leyland Motors seem to have used numerous vehicles from their works to provide transport for their employees.

One of the effects of the Road Traffic Act was to stimulate the growth of trades union membership amongst busmen throughout the country. This co-incided with the spread of the combines for, in the words of H. A. Clegg, 'Many of the companies which were taken over were paternalistic, easy-going little companies, and the new owners introduced methods of rationalisation which were opposed by the men who turned, in many cases for the first time, to union organisation for protection'. The municipal side of the industry was easiest to organise, since there already existed the National Joint Industrial Council for the Tramways which, in May 1937, was re-named the NJIC for the Road Passenger Transport Industry. The Transport and General Workers Union on its formation in 1921 had absorbed what had originally been the London & Provincial Licensed Vehicle Worker's Union (the 'red button' union), but for some time its strength had lain largely amongst the London bus and tram crews. When the provincial men began to seek union support, the TGWU naturally welcomed them, but since Ernest Bevin's policy was built firmly round the policy of a national agreement with standard terms and conditions, the union was not always sympathetic towards local disputes. By 1936, this had caused some disillusionment, and a number of unofficial strikes. At Northampton, where United Counties busmen struck, it was specifically the union's agreement with the firm that was at issue, and Clegg quotes a striker as saying : 'When the union officials assured us that this was all the company could afford to pay and all we had a right to expect, we began to wonder whose side they were on . . . it was decided to disown the damn thing altogether and get in a spot of direct action .. .'.

In London, it became very clear that Bevin's policy of encouraging the growth of a large organisation with which he could bargain was not approved by all the men. There is a strong leaning towards syndicalism in many busmen, perhaps because the nature of the trade attracts the individualist who is not happy in a monolithic union. The *Busman's Punch*, the organ of the Rank & File Movement, saw the LPTB as State capitalism. The Movement was accused by Bevin of being under Communist domination, although Clegg doubts this, but it was never wholeheartedly syndicalist. It organised a series of small strikes that were directed as much against the TGWU as against the new board, and Bevin was inclined to take any opposition to himself as evidence of Communist activity. The Movement's strength lay in the extent to which it reflected the busmen's suspicion of the union as something remote, and sympathetic towards the bosses.

By 1936, though, the TGWU had adopted the Movement's aim of a seven-hour day for the busman as its own, and was pressing for it in negotiations with the board. By March 1937, this had been modified to seven and a half hours, but the board was not prepared to discuss any reduction. The union gave one month's notice of strike action on 31 March, and the Movement at last found itself able to act with Bevin's apparent approval. Contact had been maintained with the provincial busmen, where unrest was still common, and even before the official strike began in London, the dispute had broken out in other parts of the country. Maidstone & District and Eastern National men struck on 14 and 20 April respectively; Eastern Counties men at Cambridge and Norwich joined them, and some City of Oxford, United Counties and East Yorkshire men as well. These strikes were ostensibly against the conditions which the TGWU had negotiated with the companies concerned, and Bevin firmly refused to recognise any of them as official, although a delegate meeting held at Chelmsford on 28 April petitioned the union's executive.

In many places, emergency services were provided by independents and one small firm actually issued a printed timetable for its 'strike service' between Cambridge and Bedford which carried the imprint: 'Approved by the Traffic Commissioners and the Strike Committee'.

Bevin refused to recognise the provincial strike, and when the delegation asked to meet union representatives, he arranged for it to end in such a way as to further his aim of a national agreement with the territorial companies. In London, meetings were held between the union and the LPTB, but on 23 April the board refused to discuss the subject of shorter hours and asked for the dispute to be suspended until after the Coronation. A delegate conference the following day refused to suspend the strike notices and, in spite of the intervention of the Minister of Labour, these expired at midnight on 30 April. Next morning and for four successive weeks no buses ran in London Transport's central area. The Minister of Labour immediately appointed a court of enquiry, whose hearings commenced on 2 May. During the first two days, Bevin argued that the reduction in the hours of driving buses in London was justified on grounds of health, and that, whether or not the board could afford it, it was demanded by common humanity. On the following two days, Frank Pick argued that the cost would be beyond the board's resources, at the same time casting doubts upon the injury to health argument. Both of them called witnesses, but in an interim report on the fourth day of the hearing the court gave neither side a clear victory. It said that the medical evidence had been inconclusive, and called for an independent enquiry; if this found the busmen's health at risk, then steps should be taken to meet the situation. If these steps implied the reduction of hours, the court felt that the LPTB 'would be assured of the goodwill of the public when budgeting for any extra cost involved'. The board accepted this report and offered to negotiate 'easements', provided the issue of reduced hours was dropped until after the medical enquiry.

In a ballot at branch level, the busmen refused this offer. The executive of the union advised them to reconsider their decision, but this advice was rejected at a delegate conference by a majority of forty-six votes to four. The strike continued but, although there was some evidence of support from the tramwaymen, the leaders of the Movement seem to have been unable to raise the support they had expected there. The trams and trolleybuses continued to run, as did the Underground (which was, of course, the province of a different union), and London managed without buses just as it had done in 1917 and 1924, even though this time there were no pirates to help out. It was even said that the buses were better out of the way during Coronation week; a strange contrast to the London of the Great Exhibition. By the end of the month, however, Bevin seems to have decided that the strike had lasted long enough—over £100,000 had already been spent in strike pay—and the end came quickly. The conduct of the strike had been entrusted to the Central Bus Committee which was dominated by the leaders of the Movement, and on 26 April the executive of the union revoked the powers it had granted to the committee, met the board's representatives at the Ministry of Labour, and arranged for a return to work, which took place on the 28th.

If Bevin was not exactly leading the busmen during the Coronation strike, neither was he being lead by them; rather was it a case of the two following parallel courses for a while, which enabled Bevin to achieve his own ends. In 1924, these had been the security of the union and the establishment of a single transport authority with which it could negotiate. In both these aims he had succeeded, but it quickly became clear that the busmen were uneasy about the union's paternalist attitude to their problems. Papworth, Snelling and the other leaders of the Rank & File Movement were less syndicalist than communist in their outlook (whatever their actual affiliation), but the spirit of the men they represented was (as Clegg remarks) much nearer to 'The Miners' Next Step'; the first issue of the *Busman's Punch* carried an article entitled 'Against Permanent Officials'. The spirit behind the strike was certainly stronger than its ostensible cause could account for, especially as the medical report, when it appeared in 1939, found little evidence of any special risk to busmen's health. But the executive acted to put an end to the Rank &

File Movement, or anything like it and, high-handed though
it may have been, it was successful in establishing its supremacy
for the future. The dispute must be regarded as part of the long
struggle between Bevin and those who disputed his leadership,
but it is doubtful whether either the busmen or their passengers
secured any immediate benefit.

Outside London, the earliest attempt to establish joint negotiating machinery between employers and unions was the formation
in 1919 of the National Joint Industrial Council for the Tramways Industry, which included company as well as local authority
representatives. Although its constitution allowed it to cover trolleybus as well as tramway operation, motor-bus employees were
excluded from its scope. This may seem surprising in view of the
extensive development of the industry even at this date, but probably reflects the continued importance of the big independents
and the fact that the GWR men were covered by an agreement
with the railwaymen's union. In 1934 the TGWU approached the
larger company undertakings with a view to obtaining a national
agreement, and two years later the companies seceded from the
NJIC for the tramways, while the council took a broader title and
continued to exist to provide for industrial relations in the
municipal sector.

Discussions between the TGWU and the territorial companies
continued, assisted after 1939 by the Ministry of Labour, and in
1940 the National Council for the Omnibus Industry was set up.
This included the TGWU and certain other unions representing
maintenance and other staff, while the employers represen-
tatives were nominated by the Conference of Omnibus
Companies, which included BET, the Transport Holding
Company and certain independents. A third negotiating body, the
National Joint Council for Craftsmen in Municipal Passenger
Transport Undertakings, was set up in 1950, while London
Transport Board continued to negotiate its own terms with the
unions with which it was concerned.

The national agreements which regulate wages and conditions
of service amongst the undertakings belonging to one or other
of these councils (and for the LTB) were complex documents, and

there is an important distinction to be made between firms that were parties to them and those that were not. The TGWU tried to negotiate separate agreements with the outsiders, and these would generally reflect the more flexible nature of the small firm's operations. Some degree of control was also exercised by the 'not less favourable' clauses of local authority contracts (usually for the carriage of schoolchildren) and of government departments and, since contract work of this kind is very important to most of the smaller firms, there exists a general minimum standard throughout the industry. This is re-inforced by the fact that both small and large firms are competing in the same labour market, and the general absence of disputes among firms outside the national agreements indicates that their wages and conditions were broadly acceptable. They were invariably much simpler than the agreements themselves which, in practice, means that there was less scope for argument on points of interpretation.

The employers have quite separate organisations to deal with their commercial interests and negotiate with government departments on matters other than industrial relations. These bodies also include most manufacturers of vehicles and equipment, and suppliers of tyres, fuel and lubricants to the industry. The oldest and largest was the Public Transport Association, which took its title on the merger, in 1943, of the Omnibus Owners Association with the Public Service Transport Association, each of which had been formed in the last decade of the nineteenth century. The PTA covered England and Wales, including the territorial companies, a number of municipal transport undertakings, and twenty-three independents, some of them quite small. In addition, local authority undertakings in England and Wales had their own body, the Municipal Passenger Transport Association, which originated in 1902 as an association of municipal transport managers. The Scottish Road Passenger Transport Association emerged in 1921, largely at the instigation of R. Stuart Pilcher; it included the four municipal transport departments north of the Border, the Scottish Bus Group companies and a number of individual members. Finally, there was the Passenger Vehicle Operators Association, consisting of many of the independents and the descendent of a number of loose groupings which had existed since the re-appearance of competition in the 'twenties.

The years of the second world war saw buses and coaches running long after they would normally have been withdrawn, and the first new vehicles to appear with the return to peace were little changed from the best 1939 practice. By the end of the 'forties however, competition demanded a better standard, and to meet this demand came a major development, the appearance in 1950 of a satisfactory horizontal oil engine. The 'Q' had not been an unmixed success but now, at last, coaches could be designed around an engine placed on its side in a flexible mounting beneath the floor of the vehicle. Here was a revolution comparable with the appearance of the all-weather saloon which had displaced the char-a-banc, and the typical coach of the 'thirties, with its cut-away half-cab for the driver and its maximum thirty-seven seats (thirty-three or thirty-five were more usual) became obsolete overnight. The new underfloor-engined coaches seated forty-one, or if designed as buses, forty-five, and were able to take advantage of the increase in permitted width from 7 ft 6 in to 8 ft, and in length from 27 ft 6 in to 30 ft. They also presented design problems, for the single-decker no longer had an inescapable engine cowling up front, from which all design had sprung, but was simply a box on wheels.

The 'thirties had also seen the appearance of a second standard form of single-deck coach, with a bonneted engine protruding in front of the windscreen and a 'normal control' driving position in place of the 'forward control' of the half-cab type. This was a smaller vehicle, usually seating about twenty-six, and had evolved from the fast, light buses so popular with the pirates of the previous decade. After the war it was developed, especially by Duple Motor Bodies who gave it the name 'Vista' and produced large numbers of twenty-nine seaters on a standard Bedford chassis in collaboration with Vauxhall Motors. The 'Vista' soon became the standby of almost every independent operator and not a few were owned by the territorial companies; it was a maid of all work, and most traffic commissioners were prepared to allow its use on bus services without a conductor. The last Bedford/Duple 'Vista' was produced in March 1951, and as no similar vehicle has since been designed at so attractive a price, second-hand machines long kept their value in spite of all changes in the market.

Post-war years have seen the spread of oil-engined buses and coaches to all types of work, for even after the tax on petrol and diesel oil was equallised, the slightly lower price combined with better consumption continued to make the diesel more attractive as other operating costs rose. The petrol-engined double-decker is now extinct, and there are few operators who find that the quieter running of a petrol engine is sufficiently attractive to passengers to outweigh its higher running cost. The petrol engine remains on the market mainly because of its lower initial cost, and because it is easier to maintain and repair; only an operator of high annual mileage can justify the first cost of diesel vehicles, and a skilled diesel fitter can command good wages anywhere. For the smaller operator, therefore, especially in the country, the petrol engine retains its attraction and Vauxhall Motors, the American-owned producer of the Bedford chassis, concentrated on petrol engines for some years after the war, although now offering a diesel alternative. Commer, the Rootes subsidiary, produced what may yet be the engine of the future, a vertically-opposed design which was notably economical and particularly easy of access.

The past 35 years have also seen the concentration of British bus manufacturers, followed by the return of European producers to the British market. While smaller firms have come and gone, the larger and better known bus builders have almost all come into the Leyland stable, starting with the Scottish firm of Albion Motors, acquired in 1951. Guy Motors, one of the few companies allowed to produce buses during the second world war, became a subsidiary of Jaguar Cars in 1961, and some six years later Jaguar became part of the British Motor Corporation, and so in due course passed to British Leyland, as BMC was to become. Then, in 1962 AEC and Leyland were merged, and although the AEC badge remained on certain types of vehicle for a while, that name too disappeared. In 1969, after the formation of the state-owned National Bus Company, Leyland and Bristol designers combined to produce the Leyland National, a fully integrated single-decker, using a new purpose-built plant at Workington; after early problems, it became a popular model.

Among coach operators, the market has been dominated by Bedford for so long that the name is almost synonymous with a class of vehicle. It therefore felt like the end of an era when Bedford Commercial Vehicles announced that no more PSV chassis would be produced after the end of 1986, despite the growing popularity of the 12 metre *Venturer,* and the long-standing loyalty of coach operators to the OB, SB, VAM, VAL and YRT. The return of Fords to coach production in the 1960s did not lead to a lasting contribution to the lightweight coach market, where the independent operators predominate. Yet the 1980s have seen the growing importance of DAF, Scania and Volvo in the coach market, with Volvo offering a well-liked double-decker as well. Body-builders, of whom there were once so many, have been greatly reduced in number, with Duple holding its own despite problems, but here the European firms, including some in Holland and West Germany, and even in Portugal, have contributed to the development of a new generation of super-luxury coaches that offer a standard quite as high as first-class travel by rail.

The new coaches are not only extremely expensive, but they have produced the same shock wave through the industry as it experienced when the first under-floor engined coaches appeared around 1950, and made the half-cab saloons out of date in a year or two. The difference is that they are not so easy to use for less-than-luxury traffic, and so are already proving an embarrassment to some of those who have bought them. The other principal design change came after 1968, when the government began to offer a 'new bus grant' to assist stage carriage operators, and tied it to the acquisition of approved types of vehicle. This was in turn used to expedite the introduction of rear-engined double-deckers, suitable for one-person operation (a policy that will be examined further in Chapter 10).

The general tendency in bus and coach design has, since about 1960, tended towards greater sophistication, accompanied inevitably by greater first cost and more expensive maintenance. But the most recent development has been the return of the small bus, for urban operation, where, as we shall see, the value to the consumer of high frequency has been recognised. Many such services have been provided by vehicles based on the Ford Transit, or have used Mercedes minibuses. The days of the British double-decker are said by some to be numbered, but it would take courage to foresee the future now.

CHAPTER SEVEN

THROUGH THE GREEN FIELDS: EXPRESS COACH SERVICES AND EXTENDED TOURS

WHILE the motor bus is still largely regarded as a plebian vehicle, the 'luxury coach' has become an accepted means of travel for all classes, throughout the world. It is an integral part of air travel at all but a minority of terminals and it is not unusual for fleets of coaches to carry distinguished personages from place to place when bridges are opened or other civic and military ceremonies performed. Compared with the bus, the coach has moved far from its early associations with the 'beanfeast' and 'wayzgoose'; yet the vehicle that carries dignitaries is in no way different from the one that takes the darts team on its summer outing.

With the building of motorways, coaches have begun to rival the railways in speed, and since the 1980 Transport Act there has been a great increase in coach travel. This has gone along with the introduction of the new type of super-luxury vehicles mentioned in Chapter 6. Since the late 'twenties, coaches have left London daily (and sometimes nightly) for all parts of the country. Others have linked provincial towns and cities, connecting with each other in places such as Cheltenham to cover practically every main road in a pattern of routes more intricate than ever the railways achieved at their height. More than anything else, it was the appearance of the long-distance coach that hurt the railways' finances, taking away profitable traffic they could ill afford to lose, even though it reduced the burden of their holiday peaks. There can be little doubt that had the Road Traffic Act been passed five years earlier, very many coach services would never have been started, and it is a tribute to the energy and foresight of the pioneers that the network that existed in 1939 had been created almost entirely between 1925 and 1930.

EARLY ATTEMPTS AND SETBACKS

Because of the long tradition of the stage coaches (which had been kept alive by a 'revival' in the 'seventies) the idea of using the motor bus over longer distances was in the minds of the earliest pioneers. Clarence Freeland, who had operated buses in Hastings before inspiring the Vanguard company in London, encouraged G. S. Dicks to establish a service between London and Brighton (always one of the busiest coaching roads), and this was started on 30 August 1905. It was operated with open-top double-deckers such as were in use in London, and was a notable success. Perhaps surprisingly, there was sufficient traffic to justify carrying on through the winter and, in November, the service began to be run with a single-decker which left Northumberland Avenue at 9 am and returned from the Old Ship at Brighton at 4 pm. To this day, the provision of a winter service is taken as the criterion of a coach service that provides for something more than marginal demand.

The success of the Vanguard service was such that the London & South Coast Motor Services Ltd was formed in November 1905 to run between London and Folkestone, using a special coach with large rear wheels, designed by the managing director, W. J. Cann. This confidence in the future of long-distance services must be seen against the very poor roads of the time, before Rees Jeffreys and Lloyd George had found a solution to the dust problem. Had it not been for the Handcross disaster, the history of the public transport industry in this country would no doubt have been very different.

There are few stories of disaster in the motor bus story to compare with those to be found in the history of the railways. This is no doubt partly due to the smaller scale of the early operations, but may also reflect a greater mechanical sophistication. The word 'accident' comes to mind more easily than 'disaster', and indeed the accident on Handcross Hill, although it resulted in ten deaths, would not be remembered were it not for its effect on the development of the industry. It was on 12 July 1906 that a 'Vanguard' Milnes-Daimler, similar to the buses used on the Brighton service, was on its way there with a private party from Foots Cray and Orpington. About 200 yards down the hill, the cardan shaft broke away from the casing of the gearbox, thus breaking the transmission between the engine and the wheels and preventing the driver from using the compression of the engine to assist normal braking. To stop the vehicle running away he tried to steer into the bank, choosing the off side of the road. But the heavy camber gave the bus a severe tilt and the upper-deck passengers were swept into the road by the branches of a tree, ten of them being killed. The bus itself was so stable that it came to rest still upright some thirty yards further on, at right angles to the road.

Public confidence in the idea of long-distance bus service was shaken by the disaster, although country services that ran just the same risk were not affected. Dicks at once withdrew the Brighton service, Cann dropped his plan for one to Folkestone, and an accident at Medomsley in County Durham in 1911, in which ten people were killed under similar circumstances, no doubt strengthened general prejudice against the idea. The combined effect was to delay the appearance of the express coach service for some twenty years, and correspondingly to postpone the most startling impact of the new industry upon the railways. The London & South Coast company, which ran local services at Folkestone, was bought in 1915 by W. P. Allen and subsequently absorbed by East Kent, whose board Allen joined.

In 1917, Chapman & Sons of Eastbourne, which had had a long history of omnibus operation and had started running motor buses in 1909, began to run to and from London, using vehicles driven by coal gas carried in a sort of balloon on top. This was a success, and continued to run (though later with more normal vehicles) every summer until the company sold its coach activities to Southdown Motor Services in 1932. During the nine-day railway strike of 1919, an Essex bus operator, the Mersea,

Colchester & District Transport & Bus Company, ran between Mersea Island and London for a short time, while in 1921 George Ewer & Company Ltd began to run what would now be called excursions and tours from East London, at first using converted lorries. In the previous year, Midland Red had started seasonal services from Birmingham to Weston-super-Mare and to Llandudno, and in 1921 Blackpool and Aberystwyth were added, but these services carried passengers only from terminal to terminal. Like many others, they were intended to cater for passengers who preferred both a lower fare and a less crowded journey than the railways could offer when they went on holiday and were prepared to accept a longer journey time. The post-war years saw long queues for tickets and crowded holiday trains, and when Turnham & Company began to run from London to Brighton at Easter 1919, passengers were sometimes obtained by touting outside Victoria station. This was the year when, at the August bank holiday, 300,000 people went to Blackpool alone.

Turnham's daily service to Brighton was the start of the London seasonal trade, and when Shirley James of Pickfords organised the London & Coastal Motor Services pool (London Coastal Coaches) in 1920, the original partners were Pickfords, Tillings, East Kent, Southdown, Edward Paul Ltd, the Lion Cartage Company, West London Coaches, Turnham & Company and Motor Coaches Ltd. For some years the services run by these and other operators were designed to cater for London 'trippers', and on some of them no period return bookings were accepted. A full load of day-return passengers was clearly more profitable than the chances of half loads and empty mileage involved in running a full public service, and so the express coach industry started life with a certain stigma which, though never logically justified, proved difficult to lose. To the extent that the railways lost peak traffic that required rolling stock which could have no other use, they must have stood to benefit from the competition, while the coach firms themselves, needing a broader base for their operations, soon began to accept the cost of providing an inclusive service.

PLATE 1

King of the Road. The horse bus driver retained the traditional status of the stage-coach men. To sit by him and appreciate his obiter dicta *was a privilege* © TfL (source: London's Transport Museum)

PLATE 2

George Shillibeer, the original pioneer of the London omnibus © TfL (source: London's Transport Museum)

PLATE 3

Above: *The 'Knifeboard' bus with passengers back-to-back on the top deck. The photograph was taken in 1891.*
Below: *A 'Garden Seat' bus which replaced the 'Knifeboard', standing outside the Raynes Park Hotel. 'The man on the Clapham Omnibus' has a place in history – here he is!* Both pictures © TfL (source: London's Transport Museum)

PLATE 4

PLATE 5

Great Western (Above) and North Eastern Railway buses. Each company started in 1903, the GWR at Helston and the NER at Beverley (British Railways Board)

PLATE 6

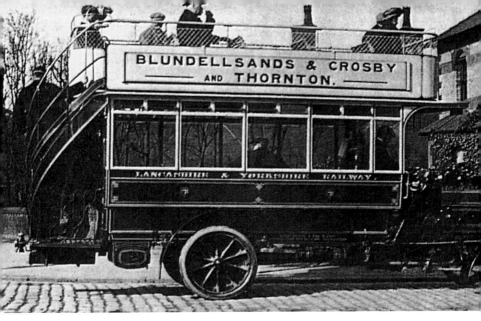

PLATE 7

Above: *One of the Milnes-Daimlers which the Lancashire & Yorkshire Railway ran for a few months at Crosby in 1907. They were later moved to Chorley, but the service did not survive long* (British Railways Board)
Below: *An historic moment in the history of long-distance services. With Milnes-Daimlers like this, Vanguard ran daily between London and Brighton from 30 August 1905 until the Handcross disaster of 12 July 1906 put an end to a promising development* © TfL (source: London's Transport Museum)

PLATE 8

PLATE 9

The Great Western Railway takes to the road. Buses at Slough station in 1905 (British Railways Board)

PLATE 10

Clarkson's steam buses taking part in the Territorial Manœuvres in 1909 (Eastern National Omnibus Company)

PLATE 11

Richard Howley, a quiet but forceful man, at the helm in British Electric Traction in the years of consolidation (British Electric Traction)

PLATE 12

H C 'Harley' Drayton, busman and financier (British Electric Traction)

PLATE 13
A 'General' bus starting its journey. The date is 1911, but the job remains the same today. © TfL (source:
London's Transport Museum)

PLATE 14

Top: *Early days of British Electric Traction buses. This service became part of the East Kent Company* (Omnibus Society Collection)

Centre: *The new bus— and its proud owner. This one replaced a horse bus in Essex before the first world war* (Author)

Bottom: *The railway bus* (Omnibus Society Collection)

PLATE 15

PLATE 16

PLATE 17

PLATE 18

PLATE 19

PLATE 20

MEN OF THE INDUSTRY

Top left: *E. B. Hutchinson, founder of the United Automobile Services Ltd*
Top right: *Sir William J. Thomson, Scottish master busman*
Bottom left: *Sidney Garcke, pioneer of British Electric Traction buses*
Bottom right: *Sir J. Frederick Heaton, creator of the Tilling combine*
(All pictures supplied by *Motor Transport*)

PLATE 21

PLATE 22

PLATE 23   PLATE 24

Top left: *Lord Ashfield, architect of London Transport* (British Transport Museum)

Top right: *R. Stuart Pilcher, who left his mark on municipal transport at Aberdeen, Edinburgh and Manchester before becoming a well-known chairman of traffic commissioners in the West Midland area (Motor Transport)*

Bottom left: *Frank Pick, who helped build up the London combine, rose to board membership, and left a lasting impression of industrial design* (London Transport Museum)

Bottom right: *John H. Watts of Red & White, a leading independent busman (Motor Transport)*

PLATE 25

Above: *Railway motor. A GER petrol-engined bus on an Edwardian summer day at St Osyth in Essex.* Below: *Company steamers. These two National steam buses were in entirely different ownership in spite of the common fleet name; one belonged to the manufacturer, and the other to one of the oldest private firms in the business* (Both pictures supplied by the Eastern National Omnibus Company)

PLATE 26

PLATE 27

Above: *The long arm of the law. In spite of their different ownership, these London buses of the 'twenties were not competing with each other.* Below: *The Roaring Twenties. Trafalgar Square in the evening rush hour* Both pictures © TfL (source: London's Transport Museum)

PLATE 28

PLATE 29

PLATE 30

Top: *An outing by chara'. Drivers of these vehicles faced penalties for speeding if they did more t twelve miles an hour.* Centre: *The 'Model T' Ford, foundation of many small businesses. This belonged to an operator serving a handful of remote Essex villages.* Bottom: *The Gilford was workhorse of the independents between the wars. This 30-seater belonged to a Cambridges operator and is standing at the bus station at Cambridge, with Eastern Counties buses behind* (All pictures supplied by the author)

PLATE 31

PLATE 32

PLATE 33

THE PROGRESS OF DESIGN

Top: *Advanced for their period, coaches like this covered 160 miles a day between London and Suffolk. The curtains are typical of the 'thirties.* Centre: *The standard post-war coach, before the underfloor engine changed everything.* Bottom: *With the engine removed under the floor, all you have is a box. But it can still be a well-designed box* (All pictures supplied by the author)

PLATE 34

PLATE 35

Fighting nationalisation – a typical double-decker of the 1950s (British Electric Traction)

PLATE 36

The bus of the eighties – Strathclyde PTE in George Square, Glasgow (Author)

PLATE 37

Minibuses proliferate – Midland Red North vehicles at Shrewsbury in 1986 (Author)

THROUGH THE GREEN FIELDS

The distinction between the 'regular express service' and the rather less 'respectable' seaside holiday services still has a certain amount of validity. C. H. Preece has defined the 'true express service' in terms of regular operation to a published timetable, stage to stage fares, and individual bookings both single and return, subject of course to the criterion of distance. Add to this the rather obvious point of all-year operation and it is possible to select the first service to satisfy these conditions. It began on 11 February 1925, being run by Greyhound Motors Ltd between London and Bristol, and has continued (except for a wartime break) ever since. By a nice coincidence, it served the same route as the first mail coach, 141 years before.

Just as the success of Partridge's 'Chocolate Express' attracted a host of imitators on the streets of London, so the appearance of the Greyhound service was the signal for a general development of the express network. The territorial bus companies were far from unanimous in their reaction to the new type of service; while those along the south coast took their share of the traffic between London and the seaside resorts, many others were content to leave express operation to independents. In general, it was the smaller operators that played the greater part in the rapid expansion of these services and there is an air of adventure about the whole affair. It took courage for the partners in a firm like Cliff's Express Services, of south-east London, to open a daily service to Llanelli with only a hired garage as a base for the coach that started out each morning on the up journey to London. Many services ran from Charing Cross embankment and the new branch of the industry was remarkable for the small organisation with which it could flourish. On the busier routes competition was strong, and by 1930, there were 128 operators in England and Wales running regular services as defined by C. H. Preece, with many more engaged in the seasonal holiday traffic. Table 1 shows the number on each of the main routes out of London.

TABLE 1. DAILY EXPRESS COACH SERVICES FROM LONDON
IN THE SUMMER OF 1930

Destination	*Number of Operators*
Thanet (Herne Bay, Margate, Ramsgate &c)	20
Portsmouth and Southsea	18
Southampton and Bournemouth	17
Oxford	16
Birmingham	15
Lowestoft and Yarmouth	15
Devon and Cornwall	14
Clacton and Walton	13
Brighton	12
Hastings	11
Worthing	11
Eastbourne	9
Newcastle and the North East	9
North Essex and Suffolk	9
Leicester	8
Littlehampton and Bognor Regis	8
Folkestone	7
Liverpool	7
Manchester	7
South Wales	7
Edinburgh	6
Gloucester	6
Yorkshire (West Riding)	6
Bedford	5
Blackpool	5
Glasgow	5
Norwich	5
Preston	5
Chelmsford	4
Dover	4
North Wales	4
Weymouth	4
Yorkshire (East Riding and York)	4
Bristol and Weston-super-Mare	3
Lincolnshire	3
Medway Towns and Sheerness	3
Nottingham	3
Southend	3
Aberystwyth	2
Aldershot and Farnham	2
Cambridge	2
Felixstowe	2
Tenterden	2
Winchester	2
Worcester	2
Burnham-on-Crouch	1
Cromer and Sheringham	1
Crowborough	1
Gosport	1
Harwich and Dovercourt	1
Hunstanton	1
Maidstone	1
Rye	1
Seaford	1

Fare-cutting was not infrequent, and the return from London to Plymouth fell at one time to 12s 6d. Between London and Cambridge there was sharp competition between Varsity Express Motors and Westminster Coaching Services, and here the return fare fell to as little as two shillings. Varsity had services from London to Oxford and to Bournemouth, and Westminster served Cambridge on routes to Bury St Edmunds, Ely, Wisbech, Yarmouth and Norwich, and so each could afford a rate war over the one fare, especially as it encouraged new traffic. Services ran roughly every hour and, though taking over an hour longer than the trains, greater frequency as well as cheaper fares made them attractive, added to which they ran from the centre of Cambridge right into the West End of London. Neither were the vehicles at all primitive, for both companies had a name for being progressive. Both were sold to Eastern Counties in 1933 and some of the Varsity vehicles remained in service until 1951, having been given double-deck bodies and oil engines in the meantime. The last Westminster vehicles were sold by ECOC in 1945, having been re-bodied in 1934, and two of these were loaned to London Transport in the winter of 1940-1 : a nice irony, since Westminster had been an offshoot of one of the London pirates of the 'twenties.

Among the experiments of the early days of express coaches was the sleeper coach, which was not successful, although overnight services using ordinary vehicles quickly became established on the longer routes. Cross-country services also appeared very early and here the coach could often compete with the train in timing because it ran direct and avoided changes. In East Anglia, a number of small operators took advantage of the absence of direct railways to London in the sector between Ipswich and Cambridge to open medium-distance services. Most of these were worked from headquarters in Essex or Suffolk towns or villages, but an exception was the Brixton-based 'Limited Stop Pullman', which ran twice daily between London and King's Lynn via Sudbury, Bury St Edmunds and either Brendon or Thetford. Most of these coaches acted as local buses at the country end of the route.

EXPRESS SERVICES AND THE ROAD TRAFFIC ACT

Although the road service licensing system was administered with little of the harshness which had caused parliamentary questions about the London Traffic Act, 1924, express coach services, which were of course in the same relationship to the railways as the buses had been to the London tramways, were something of an exception. The M.T. Company, which had pioneered the route between London and Thanet as early as 1920, was given a heavily restricted licence. The intermediate stages, which were allowed to the East Kent Road Car Company, had not in fact been served by that company, which had started running some time later than M.T. The principle of priority had not been applied here, because it was argued by East Kent and accepted by the commissioners that the territorial company needed the profitable express service in order to subsidise its rural buses. On appeal, the Minister of Transport upheld the traffic commissioners view, and the M.T. directors, F. A. Flynn and F. A. Collett, published a broadsheet called . . . *and the Last shall be First*. They later sold the service to East Kent and turned to other forms of operation.

In general, however, the Act was applied for the protection of the railways rather than the territorial bus companies, the argument being that the railways needed protection in order to practise cross-subsidisation. Until as late as 1951, little attention was paid to fares on bus services, which became stabilised at 1930 levels, but the railways tried very hard to get coach fares raised when licences were first being granted. Having failed, they introduced the monthly return, which was a reduction of $33\frac{1}{3}$ per cent, first for summer traffic only but afterwards as a permanent rate. The effect was to make fare levels of great importance on express services and early in 1932 a system of regional committees was set up, representing operators of express services radiating from London. These committees, now defunct, recommended agreed fares for various destinations in the first place to the Metropolitan traffic commissioner. When an increase was proposed, the commissioners arranged for a public hearing at which two or three representative firms would make a case, after which other applications would be granted 'on the nod'. Other area commissioners followed these decisions, which to some extent affected fares on provincial services that did not touch London, so that a rough and ready national machine existed for the purpose of regulating the charge to the public.

In various appeal decisions during the early 'thirties, the Minister made it clear that the railways could expect protection from serious road competition so far as their 'backbone' services were concerned. The general policy was that express coach services on such routes should not be permitted to run merely in the summer months, carrying full loads at lower fares, and they were therefore restricted in capacity to a level related to the winter load. The restriction was first applied in September 1933 when, in connection with an appeal decision, the Minister made Order No 54 affecting services between London and Liverpool, Glasgow and Edinburgh. It laid down that the number of vehicle journeys to be licensed on any one day on each service was at no time to exceed three times the basic number that the operator was prepared to provide daily throughout the year. Perhaps because it was so clear a declaration of policy, Order No 54 came to have the force of precedent, amended by Order No 32 of 1934, which allowed the restriction to be modified where traffic was heavier in one direction than the other, provided the overall limit still applied.

What was significant about this policy was its clear distinction between 'backbone' services and the rest, which left unaffected a great number of services that ran on a limited number of days during the summer, carrying holiday-makers direct from the city to the seaside and often starting from the suburban areas, well away from main railway stations. Most of these were given some limit of duplication but, since it was related to evidence of their current carryings when they were first licensed, there was probably little restriction on the level of trade. The attitude of the Minister was virtually that taken by the railways in recent years: the coaches were welcome to their share of the peak holiday load which the railways could only carry at the cost of much idle capacity for the rest of the year. In the case of the 'backbone' services, on the other hand, the principle of cross-subsidisation was applied. The railways were expected to provide a nation-wide system, much of which lay in areas of thin traffic potential and so had to be subsidised out of the profits of their long-distance express trains. This practice had been threatened both by the rural bus, which had reduced railway traffic still more in the 'thin' areas, and then by the express coach, which had threatened the profitability of the main lines. On the other hand, the road services had become so popular that it was impossible for them to be abolished and so the compromise was imposed. It had little relevance to the level of demand, which was itself affected by the high rail fares necessary on the main lines because of cross-subsidisation itself.

The territorial companies began almost at once to buy out the independents from the 'backbone' sector. In 1930, there had been twenty-five such services provided by territorial companies and 103 by independents: in 1938 these figures were thirty-two and twenty-seven. The overall reduction in services represents the disappearance of competition from most routes, so that by 1938 the territorial companies had almost complete control of the all-year-round services between London and the nearer coastal resorts. The few independents still serving London were those running to the North West and North East, to East Anglia, a single operator to Oxford and Worcester, and one serving Crowborough in Sussex. In the provinces, the territorial companies obtained similar control over the main cross-country routes, with exceptions such as the Newcastle-upon-Tyne-Coventry and Nottingham-Manchester-Blackpool services which remained in independent hands. The process was encouraged by the traffic commissioners, who frequently deleted intermediate stages from licences granted to seasonal operators (as in the case of the M.T. Company), in order to protect the territorial companies and enable them to practise cross-subsidisation like the railways.

The Road Traffic Act gave the independents a saleable monopoly, similar to that given by the London Traffic Act to the London pirates in 1924. The territorial companies also had

new capital recently obtained from the railways and clearly it
was in line with railway policy for them to obtain control of this
field of operation : if express coach operation could not be stopped, the railways preferred it to be in the hands of their 'sister
companies'. But many operators gave up regular express services
in the early 'thirties and it is probable that economic conditions
of the time had some influence on this trend.

Not all the territorial companies kept express operation entirely
in their own hands. It soon became clear that it would be neither
easy nor desirable to apply a rigid area agreement system to
these services and various compromise arrangements were reached.
In the South East, a clear boundary was agreed between East
Kent and Maidstone & District, so that East Kent coaches from
London would not set down passengers in the M&D area; this
agreement dated from the 'twenties. Services between London
and the North divided themselves fairly easily between the
operators concerned, for the really long-distance operator does
not want too many intermediate stops and the Great North Road
does not pass through many large towns or thickly populated
areas. Services between London and the Midlands could thus
be distinguished, and although there was some overlapping,
ownership tended to remain with the company in whose territory
the outer terminal lay.

In the West of England, the situation was different. Not only
had the first true express-coach service been developed here, but
there had also been a general growth of services, both to London
and laterally, centred on the crossing of the Severn and the city
of Bristol. Greyhound Motors Ltd, the original pioneers, had
developed services from Liverpool and the Midlands to the South
West, and from Bristol to Weymouth and Bournemouth, as well
as from London to Cheltenham and Gloucester. Between Birmingham and Plymouth they worked jointly with Midland Red, which
also had services to Weston-super-Mare, while Red & White
were running from South Wales via Gloucester to Birmingham, London, Bournemouth and Plymouth. In 1926,
George Readings founded Black & White Motorways Ltd at
Cheltenham, running two services a day to London. In the follow-

ing year, H. R. Lapper became director and general manager and expanded the business rapidly, starting new services in all directions and giving passengers the opportunity for a wide range of connections at Cheltenham. In the meantime, Elliott Brothers Ltd of Bournemouth had established themselves as the principal operator between London and the South West peninsula, with the fleet name of 'Royal Blue', and they also ran between London, Bristol and Weston, from Portsmouth and Bournemouth to Bristol, and from the Midlands to Bournemouth and Plymouth. A number of smaller operators covered the same routes, including Allchin & Sons of Northampton and various operators between London and South Wales. There was thus heavy duplication over most services, and although the Road Traffic Act led to a reduction in the number of operators, there still remained a number of financial interests involved.

On 30 April 1930, control of Black & White passed to Midland Red, and the Bristol Tramways and City of Oxford companies were almost at once brought into partnership, the latter having no express service of its own. The first chairman was R. H. Nicholls, the GWR superintendent of the line, the other directors being O. C. Power (BMMO), R. G. Pittard (BT&C) and R. F. Dixon (City of Oxford). On R. H. Nicholls' retirement, O. C. Power became chairman in his place. George Readings operated coaches in London for a short time but soon returned to Cheltenham where he acquired a motor agent's and garage business; H. R. Lapper remained in charge of Black & White as general manager.

In 1933, United Counties acquired Allchins, and during the first few years of the decade Red & White bought most of the South Wales express operators, as well as MacShanes of Liverpool. Red & White made a point of developing connections with other operators' services and this was carried a stage further in March 1934 when agreements were reached with Black & White and Midland Red to pool their operations between South Wales and London and Birmingham. Almost at once this 'minor pool' was merged into a wider one for on 1 July 1934 Associated Motorways was formed by Black & White, Red & White, Midland

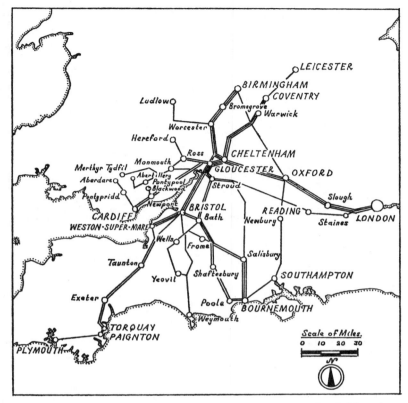

MAP 3. *Express coach services later included in the Associated Motorways system as they were running in 1929*

Red, Greyhound, Royal Blue and United Counties. Its formation was largely the result of Lapper's initiative and he became the first chairman of its management committee, a position to which he was re-elected annually until his retirement in 1953. The extent to which services were duplicating each other in 1929 is illustrated in Map 3, while Map 4 shows the network established by the new pool.

Associated Motorways grew after 1934, and came to include a number of other members. Bristol Tramways & Carriage replaced Greyhound Motors when they bought that operator, while the Western and Southern National companies replaced Elliott

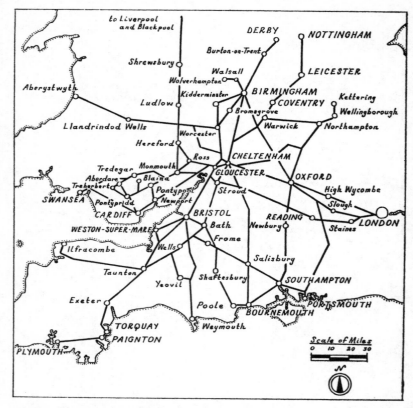

MAP 4.   *The Associated Motorways system of express coach services at its formation in 1934*

Brothers when they took over the Royal Blue business. The member companies formed a partnership of which the legal expression was the operating agreement, whereby each member had contributed certain specified services to the pool and had agreed that they should be operated together as part of a single organisation. The members then provided their own vehicles for the actual operations (Associated Motorways owned no vehicles itself) and the net revenue of the pool was divided between them on the basis of the number of car miles each had run during the year. The success of the system followed from the economies that could be made; services were concentrated on the Black & White coach station at Cheltenham opened in 1932 and this became the hub of a wheel whose spokes extended in every direction. Journeys were timed to co-incide there, so that inter-connections became possible between a great number of places; other routes tangential to the wheel were timed to connect at intersections. The result was a comprehensive network which became a household word throughout the south-western quarter of England.

In the North of England, pooled operations of this kind have an even longer history, although they are nowhere comparable with Associated Motorways in geographical or operating complexity. The Northern General service between Newcastle and the West coast was extended in 1929 to become a two-hourly, limited-stop service between Newcastle and Liverpool, worked jointly with North Western, Yorkshire (Woollen District) and West Yorkshire; East Yorkshire and Lancashire United joined the pool subsequently. Yorkshire Services was a pool formed in July 1930 to run from the West Riding and Hull to London and Birmingham. The only other example of this type of operation until more recent years was the Coastal Express (later South Coast Express), which East Kent, Maidstone & District, Southdown and Hants & Dorset established in May 1929 to run between Margate and Bournemouth, in competition with a similar service started by Royal Blue earlier that year. After 9 May 1932, it was curtailed at Portsmouth, by decision of the traffic commissioners, who also refused permission for the Royal Blue service to run east of that town.

LONDON'S COACHES

Towards the end of the 'twenties, the independents had a final fling by developing yet another special traffic—the limited-stop network round London known today as Green Line. This move followed from the restrictions applied under the London Traffic Act and the subsequent sale of many businesses to the LGOC, as well as from the improved standards of comfort and reliability that had made the long-distance services feasible. At first, when Glenton Tours started to run six journeys a day between Victoria and Sevenoaks, it was not apparent that this was anything but another express coach service, for pre-booking was required (thus taking the service out of the control of the Minister under the Restricted Streets Orders). Glenton began to run in August 1927, followed by Redcar Services of Tunbridge Wells, who ran from there to London from 16 September but withdrew on 1 January 1928. A. W. Priest started a service between London and Luton in November 1927 but the first sign that something different was emerging was the appearance on 3 March 1928 of Gray's service between London and Oxford. For the first time, tickets could be issued on the coach and pre-booking was not required. The regulations were avoided by a minimum fare of threepence and when no prosecutions followed, there was a rapid growth of similar services. Redcar re-opened the Tunbridge Wells route and, by the end of 1928, there were services to Aylesbury, Redhill, Biggleswade, Bishop's Stortford, Welwyn Garden City, Brentwood and Guildford, all operated by independent companies. Birch Brothers went further afield with a service to Bedford which, in the absence of pre-booking, could still be said not to be an express operation in the usual sense.

Between 1927 and 1931 there were seventy independent operators running services of this kind, in addition to the General, National and East Surrey companies. A few appeared only briefly or sold the goodwill of their services to others, but most were operating at the same time, their activities being comparable with those of the earlier pirates in central London—which many of them had been. The LGOC was slow in reacting to the new development, for although an express department was formed in 1928, its first service did not appear until 2 October 1929. This ran every fifteen minutes between Watford and Golders Green, connecting with the tube on to which through bookings could be made. Its success seems doubtful, for it was withdrawn on 12 November, to be re-opened on 18 December on a thirty-minute headway, while on the same day the first LGOC through service appeared, running every forty minutes between Watford and Charing Cross. At this time the LER combine was extended by the purchase of East Surrey which, from 1928, had controlled

Autocar Services Ltd of Tunbridge Wells, and during 1930 each of these operators developed limited-stop services. In July 1930, the LGOC registered its subsidiary, Green Line Coaches Ltd, to operate on this basis, at the same time taking the precaution of registering Red Line, Yellow Line and Blue Line to protect itself from competition. (Some years before, action had had to be taken against the proprietors of the London Genial Omnibus Company, whose return tickets kept turning up on LGOC buses). This did not prevent a Cream Line service being started in September 1930, which ran during peak hours only between Brookman's Park and Charing Cross.

Green Line started operating on 17 July 1930 with a Guildford-Charing Cross service of its own creation and the two LGOC services from Watford. Subsequent developments are confused, since both National and East Surrey operated with the Green Line fleet name and the LGOC started further services in its own name to take advantage of existing licensing rights, subsequently transferring them to Green Line as going concerns. A Green Line coach station was opened in Poland Street, W1 on Christmas Day 1930, partly because of the traffic congestion in central London which was being blamed on the new coach services. The Skylark company had already managed to avoid this by linking its services to run from Hertford to Guildford and from High Wycombe to Dorking. Green Line followed suit, for the Poland Street station was badly sited in narrow streets and caused as much congestion as it saved. The success of all these services was based upon frequent operation with no pre-booking, thus combining the advantages of the stage carriage with the comfort of the express coach. They demonstrated once more the flexibility of the motor vehicles and were yet another variation on the twin themes of plying for hire and regular operation.

Nowhere in the provinces did a comparable network of limited-stop services grow up. Midland Red introduced its 'X' services quite early, and these were similar in that pre-booking was never required and a minimum fare was usually applied to discourage short-stage traffic. They were, however, a different sort of compromise, running over routes such as Shrewsbury-Hereford, Northampton-Birmingham-Shrewsbury, and Birmingham-Nottingham, with headways rarely as close even as every sixty minutes. The Cardiff-Swansea service of Neath & Cardiff Luxury Coaches, and various services between Lancashire and its coastal resorts, were other examples of the limited-stop service as a compromise between stage and express operation, each adjusting itself to local demand. The type of vehicle used also varied, although the tendency was towards the more comfortable express coach of the period rather than the somewhat austere buses associated with the Green Line service of later years.

EXTENDED TOURS AND COACH CRUISES

The boundary between the express coach service and the extended tour is not always easy to define. On the one side there were two-, three- and four-day services between London and Edinburgh which were really tours and hardly competed with the regular day and night services. On the other, there are many 'period excursions' which are, in fact, seasonal coach services with no single or day-return fares and which definitely do compete with the regular services. But there is still a clear and distinct section of the industry which provides for extended tours, both at home and abroad, and it has a long and fascinating history.

Chapman's of Eastbourne seem to have been the first operator to advertise a tour, which ran in 1910 to North Wales, the coach being a twenty-two seater Dennis. It was evidently a success, as it was followed by an extensive programme during the next few years, including a twenty-one-day tour to John o' Groats. In 1919 the first Standerwick tour, from Lancashire to London and the South Coast, was driven by E. V. Standerwick himself. In the following year, Cannon and Mackenzie, pioneers of Southdown and other companies, ran a number of tours based on Worthing, including one to the Lake District and another of the south-west that took in both Porlock and Countisbury hills. In their 1914 brochure the hope was expressed 'that the ladies will wear hats or caps as small as possible. It is very unfair to other passengers if their view is obstructed by the hats or feathers of ladies in front of them'. A lesson no doubt learned by experience.

The first world war put a stop to the business, but by 1920 Chapmans were back in the market and operating six-day tours of the battlefields; without doubt, the earliest Continental coach tours. The following year they added tours to the French Riviera, and in 1923 to Holland, Germany, Italy and Spain. W. P. Allen's London & South Coast Motor Services Ltd also ran tours of the battlefields from various towns in Kent. Another firm operating tours at this time was Westcliff-on-Sea Motor Services Ltd of Southend.

It is noticeable that the pioneers were almost invariably based on seaside towns, where demand presumably arose from those who had gone to live there upon retirement. A remarkable pioneer was the London firm of Motorways Ltd, run by Graham Lyon and H. J. Spencer, which, in 1920, acquired a White and a Chevrolet truck from the US Army in France. These were fitted with coach bodies built in France, had twelve or fourteen swivelling armchair seats, a buffet-kitchen and a toilet compartment and were employed on a regular service between Calais and the Mediterranean. Other vehicles were added later and tours reached North Africa in 1924. An attempt to reach Istanbul was frustrated by bad roads and Belgrade remained the eastern limit (although in 1935 Motorways ran a coach tour to Leningrad and Moscow).

E. L. Taylor has recalled the great improvements made in the motor coach between 1919 and 1939 and reckons that the riding qualities of the best vehicles of the time compared very well with those of the private car of the same period. Coaches for long-distance touring were custom built, their timber bodies showing a high degree of craftsmanship, and if they had a short life the trade was sufficient to attract many companies to it. Some of the larger firms were sceptical, tending to take the view that coach operation was ethically inferior to the provision of bus services, but this merely left openings that others were not slow to fill. Neither was touring at home neglected and the trend away from 'static' holidaymaking encouraged operators to establish themselves in various parts of the country. Although no statistics are available, the volume of business was certainly far less than it is today and the majority of the population had no easy access to the originating point of a tour. All the same, the idea had taken root and awaited only the more favourable climate of the post-war years to develop into an industry of its own.

M

CHAPTER EIGHT

A CHANGED WORLD: 1931-1948

THE industry at the beginning of the 'thirties faced a period of adjustment quite apart from the consequences of the national crisis. Between 1928 and 1931 the threatened collision between road and rail interests had been averted and the territorial companies (with certain exceptions) were henceforth to be known as 'sister companies' of the railways. It was clear that the new dispensation would take time to settle down; it was to do so in the changed circumstances of the Road Traffic Act, which had subjected the motor-bus industry to a greater degree of State control than had ever been applied to the railways themselves.

ROAD AND RAIL : AN UNEASY PARTNERSHIP

The Road Traffic Act was given no 'teeth', in the sense that the traffic commissioners had no power to compel any operator to apply for a licence. In practice, this does not seem to have been a serious constraint upon the ability of the commissioners to influence the industry and they at no time made any wide use of their power to initiate the variation of an existing licence. Instead, they worked very closely with the management of the industry, whose general philosophy they seem largely to have shared while remaining sufficiently detached to establish the dignity of their office. In this, the quasi-judicial atmosphere of the traffic courts certainly played its part, but the commissioners also gained respect from certain clear lines of policy that may now be observed.

The first of these was their firm refusal to allow the doctrine of precedent to rule their decisions. This is not to deny the importance of various appeals in guiding their interpretation of the Road Traffic Act, but as early as October 1931 the Minister laid down that 'It is clearly a matter for the traffic commissioners in the first place to consider each case on its merits and to arrive at the decision which appears to them proper in the particular circumstances'. While this principle may at first sight appear to give them arbitrary power, in practice it gave the road service licensing system a degree of flexibility without which it would have been difficult for the industry to function satisfactorily. The second principle, which arose from the first, concerns the place of the small operator, and here the commissioners saw to it that he did not suffer more than could be helped from the working of the system; a guiding principle which certainly gained them respect throughout the industry. Finally, and perhaps this is their most remarkable achievement, the commissioners held the balance between the bus operators and the railways to the general benefit of the industry and in spite of the special position given to the railways by the Act.

The railway companies and the combine made no serious attempt to integrate their trading activities. Railway directors were nominated to the boards of those territorial companies in which there was a rail holding, but they were instructed by their own boards that, as representatives of railway management, they were to forward the commercial success of the bus company within its own sphere and not to seek to influence policy in favour of its railway associate. Thus at board level there was a link between the two industries, though it did not lead to co-operative action. Standing joint committees at a lower level were set up to co-ordinate commercial activities, but relatively little was done.

The British Railways Press Bureau issued a broadsheet in 1930, which was called *Co-ordinating Rail and Road Travel: How the Public will Benefit.* It listed a number of *Benefits to the Public,* and these are worth reproducing in full :

> By the agreements come to and the policy pursued the railway companies are already in a position to offer better services to the public, and by their investments in road traction they have renewed the interests of their stockholders in traffic which had been

regarded as 'lost' by the railways to the roads. The co-ordination policy being actively pursued between the railways and associated 'bus undertakings is taking a number of definite forms, including :
Interavailability of return tickets by 'bus or rail.
Service arrangements to facilitate exchange of passengers between railway and road services.
Combination of railway and omnibus timetable matter, and adjustment of services where possible to improve connections.
Employment of omnibus transport as extension of railway journeys for pleasure and other purposes.
Amplification of travel facilities by use of both arms of transport in combined tours.

In practice, all this did not amount to very much. Interavailability was attended by procedural complications and was never widely advertised where it did exist, while 'exchange of passengers' meant little more than the use of station yards as terminals, without any attempt at co-ordinating times of arrival and departure. Combination of timetable matter meant that a number of associated bus companies included lists of train departures from stations in their area as an appendix to their timetables, while the railways, with very few exceptions, continued to exclude all mention of road services from theirs. Improved connections simply failed to materialise on any scale sufficient to absolve 'both arms of transport' from criticism; this was perhaps inevitable in view of the dilemma of a bus company faced with the conflicting demands of local and rail connecting traffic, as described by David St John Thomas in *The Rural Transport Problem*. Instead, both rail and road managements accused each other of making constant minor adjustments to their timetables so that detailed co-ordination was impossible to maintain and therefore not worth attempting.

An impartial observer, familiar with both industries, would no doubt have laid the blame equally upon the management and staff of each. Such observers were rare, however, and precisely because of the state of affairs they would have condemned : a continuing state of mutual intolerance amounting at times to antipathy. To this day, it is possible to find evidence of such an attitude of mind, not least in certain trade union circles, although the activities of the Institute of Transport and similar professional bodies have done much to mitigate it on both sides. In the 'thirties the criticism was more easily justified, for the Road Traffic Act and the financial settlement had imposed an uneasy truce on a short-lived but bitter period of open warfare, and men who have seen their livelihoods threatened are not disposed to change their attitudes in a hurry.

In any case, the interest of the railway stockholders mentioned in the quotation given must be seen in all fairness as having taken precedence over the needs of the travelling public. Nowhere was this clearer than in the early days of the road service licensing system, when the railway companies objected to applications from their sister companies just as readily as they did to those of independents. In a way this was inevitable, since the traffic commissioners would probably have taken them severely to task if they had been discriminatory in their policy, but it may be doubted whether the bitter and lengthy proceedings which resulted did anything to improve the relationship between road and rail, while the managements of both industries were certainly diverted from more productive work.

The main burden of the railways' objections in the traffic courts was directed at the long-distance services, and A. F. R. Carling quotes one of their counsel as telling the Scottish traffic commissioners that 'they thought they were justified in asking for the complete prohibition of long-distance bus services. The public would not suffer', he added, 'except for the higher fares they would have to pay'. The compromise the commissioners and the minister finally reached was described in Chapter 7, but if the railways had hoped to suppress what Carling calls 'a new and dangerously effective form of transport', they notably failed. The commissioners took the view that, with the exception of a small number of express coach services, the road and rail companies appeared before them on equal terms, so far as the system permitted. They also assumed that the railways were not justified in expecting protection from the local bus services and concentrated upon the adjustment of the two systems over longer distances.

CHANGES OF OWNERSHIP AND CONTROL

The Road Traffic Act did, however, advance the railways' policy in a more general way, for it permitted the consolidation of the territorial companies as has already been described, and thereby enabled the railway companies to take a widening share in the ownership of the industry as absorption of the independents proceeded. It also lead to the gradual transfer of the railways' own bus services to their associates and to certain subsequent changes in the structure of the combine itself. The last buses in Great Britain to run in outright railway management were those on the joint GWR/SR service at Weymouth, which was transferred to the Southern National Omnibus Company on 1 January 1934. In Yorkshire, however, a number of buses remained in the ownership of the LNER and LMSR, although managed by the municipal partner in various joint committees; an arrangement which survived until the 1960s.

The companies the railways had bought outright were also transferred to the new pattern of joint ownership and placed under Tilling & British management. A period of adjustment followed, by the end of which the territorial boundaries had settled down into a form that was not to be disturbed until after the war and whose aim was to produce a series of viable concerns within the framework of the area agreements. In South Wales, the Western Welsh company appeared as a result of the merger of the NEC's South Wales Commercial Motors with the GWR services and those of Lewis & James Ltd and a number of other sizeable independents. Its territory was difficult to define, involving a great deal of interworking and route sharing with Red & White and the Glamorgan municipalities, while to the West it reached a peculiar agreement with Crosville, whereby services were divided according to the direction in which they ran. The Wrexham & District company became Western Transport in 1930, absorbing more GWR routes, including those acquired when the Corris Railway was bought by the GWR along with Bristol Tramways. But Western Transport was to have a short life, being merged into Crosville in 1933 as the Llandudno

Coaching and Carriage Company, another T&BAT subsidiary, had been two years earlier.

In East Anglia, a new company called Eastern Counties Omnibus Co Ltd was set up in 1931 to absorb the Norfolk area services of United, the Ortona Company of Cambridge, the Eastern Counties Road Car Company of Ipswich and the Peterborough Electric Traction Company. The new company had its headquarters in Norwich and also acquired the body-building works founded by United at Lowestoft.

But no sooner had the T&B/railway combine been set up than its proprietors began to develop separate groups that remained outside it. In the previous chapter it was seen that Tillings had kept some direct operation in their own hands and that BET had not parted with subsidiaries which were predominantly tramway companies or were undergoing financial reconstruction. Now Thomas Tilling Ltd, which was not bound by the agreement between T&BAT and the railways, proceeded to make some new purchases, starting in 1931 with the interest of Sir John Jarvis and his associates in the National Omnibus & Transport Company, which thus became a Tilling and not a T&BAT subsidiary. Bristol Tramways & Carriage, which the GWR had bought, became a subsidiary of Western National at this time. In the same year, Tillings purchased United Counties of Northampton, but here they did not introduce any railway interest. In 1932 they bought H. M. S. Catherwood Ltd, the Irish international operator, and in 1935 they added Westcliff-on-Sea Motor Services to their empire, allocating a part share to Eastern National, which gave the railways an indirect interest. Meanwhile, in January 1931, J. S. Austen's National Electric Construction Company had become part of the BET group and while some of its subsidiaries, such as Devon General and City of Oxford, had railway shareholdings, none of them became part of the Tilling & British combine.

In South Wales, the multitude of local authorities, each with licensing powers and many with operating ambitions of their own, had made it difficult during the 'twenties for a territorial operator to appear. The emergence of Western Welsh as the 'chosen instrument' of the railways and the combine has already been mentioned, but over a wide area of Monmouth and Glamorgan, John Watts and his associates had been developing a series of small and medium-size businesses with a careful eye to the local political situation. A Cardiff-Gloucester service had been established by 1928, and in the following year a Cardiff-London express service was bought from another operator. Although late in the field, Watts had territorial ambitions and early in 1930 established himself at Plymouth, where he formed the Southern General Omnibus Company Ltd, in connection with the local body-building firm of Mumfords. In the same year, the bulk of his Welsh interests were merged to form Red & White Services Ltd, with headquarters at Chepstow.

Before the end of 1931 an agreement was reached between Watts and the GWR under which Southern General and its subsidiary, Cornish Buses Ltd, were sold to the Western National Omnibus Company. Although Red & White did not become a rail-associated company, it achieved a certain recognition at this time, which did not however inhibit its further expansion. The purchase of Red Bus Services of Stroud took place in 1933 and in 1938 a group of eleven small businesses around Swansea which had passed into the company's control was merged to form United Welsh Services Ltd. From this basis a 'third force' in the industry was later to appear.

EVENTS IN SCOTLAND AND IRELAND

The effect of the Road Traffic Act upon the ownership pattern of the industry was nowhere more marked than in Scotland, where it resulted in a complete change in the balance of power. The Scottish combine, in the words of C. E. Lee, 'crystallised' between 1929 and 1932, but the process was complex and involved. It represented the amalgamation of the bus interests of Baillie Thomson's Scottish Motor Traction Company with those of the Alexander family, J. C. Sword and R. B. Dick, along with others in the control of the LNE and LMS, who in due course became part-owners of the new group. Numerous operators (including a confusingly large number with the word 'General' in their titles) were acquired at this time, and these included former tramway undertakings of the BET and Balfour Beattie groups. The holding company for the combine became SMT itself, which remained an operating unit as well, covering most of Eastern Scotland south of the Forth; its subsidiaries were the Central SMT Company Ltd in the Clyde valley, the Western SMT Company Ltd based on Kilmarnock, and W. Alexander & Sons Ltd occupying eastern Scotland from the Forth to Inverness. Thomson remained at the head of the group, with the Alexander, Sword and Dick families also represented. With Scottish tenacity, the three latter still had members on the board of the nationalised holding company that succeeded SMT.

The new group's territory did not, in practice, cover the whole of Scotland. Tilling & British retained a foothold in the southwest in the shape of the Caledonian Omnibus Company Ltd and the early 'thirties were marked by extensive licensing disputes between Caledonian and SMT. In the extreme north, Inverness & District Motor Services Ltd had been formed in 1925, and in 1930 its owners joined with the LMS to form the Highland Transport Company Ltd, which opened a branch in Caithness and bought out an operator on Skye. The last gap in the chain of bus services on the British mainland was filled on 1 April 1933 when Highland started running between Brora and Helmsdale, but the Skye business was not a success and was resold in 1935. Substantial independents remained in north-east Aberdeenshire and on the west coast there appeared a number of co-operatives. The Highlands and Islands remained the preserve of small independent operators, usually combining passenger operation with the carriage of Post Office mails under contract.

The remaining operator of substance outside the SMT group was the firm of David MacBrayne Ltd, best known for its shipping interests which date back to 1851. The need for subsidies to maintain essential links in the area was first recognised in 1891, when £10,200 was paid, but the appearance of the motor bus threatened the steamer trade in the coastal waters. MacBraynes put their first bus into service in 1906, running between Fort

Rothesay Tramways Co. Ltd.

Ettrick Bay

RIGHT ACROSS THE ISLAND . .

THE SAFEST, SMOOTHEST MOST INTERESTING AND COMFORTABLE METHOD

is by ELECTRIC RAILWAY from ROTHESAY, through private ground. Scenery Magnificent. **NO BUMPY ROADS OR DISAGREEABLE ROAD DUST** to contend with.

WATERS PURE AND LIMPID, direct from the Atlantic.

Or, if preferred, by the Tramway Company's Luxurious Charabancs fitted with GIANT PNEUMATIC TYRES—Smooth and Comfortable as a Rolls-Royce.

Map on other side shows the Places of Interest.

DESCRIPTIVE NOTICE BOARDS ON ROUTE.

Ettrick Bay is the starting-off place for some of the finest walks and drives on the West Coast by mountain, moor and shore.

Putting, Midget Golf, and other amusements during the season available for Tramcar Passengers.

NEW CONCERT TEA ROOMS

Now Open. Viands of Finest Quality at City Prices.

For Particulars and Bookings of **Bus Tours to All Parts of England and Scotland** (including local tours and Oban and Trossachs), enquire Bus Information Bureau, 24 East Princes Street, Rothesay, —Phone 19 ; or Tramways Office, Pointhouse,—Phone 76.

FIG. 6. *Period flavour in a Scottish operator's publicity*

William and North Ballachulish, and its driver remained on this route for forty years until he retired. As early as 1912 they were running services as long as those from Ardrishaig to Inverary and Oban, and from Fort William to Inverness. The narrow roads meant that for many years only fourteen-seaters could be used.

Great concern was felt in 1928 when MacBraynes refused to tender for the renewal of their mail contracts and no other firm could be found to do so. Subject to continuance of subsidy payments at a higher level, Burns, Laird and Company and the LMS then formed David MacBrayne (1928) Ltd to acquire the old company's assets, the Burns, Laird interest subsequently being transferred to Coast Lines Ltd. Road services were then developed more quickly, MacBrayne's buses reached Glasgow in 1929 and the company became established in what would otherwise have been Alexander's territory.

In Northern Ireland, the nine railway companies of the Province emerged from the first world war with their finances in disarray, and before the newly independent government could take action they were further shaken by the appearance of road competition on a growing scale, commencing in 1923. Bus operators were numerous and small, running light and fast vehicles, frequently imported from the United States, and they quickly covered the six counties with a network of services. Only the city of Belfast adopted the Town Police Clauses, and these it used to protect its own tramways by refusing to license any operator to carry passengers wholly within the city limits.

Competition was keen and frequently destructive, but in 1926 the government introduced a general system of licensing in the interests of fitness and safety. This enabled larger firms to appear, but it also put an end to the monopoly of the Belfast tramways and pirate buses appeared on the city streets in great numbers beginning in June of that year. In 1927, the railways were given road powers and in the following year an inquiry was held into the situation in Belfast, from which came the recommendation of a system of road service licensing which was set up in 1929. The combination of this with the railways' powers brought about a situation similar to that on the mainland, except that the railways bought their way in as bus operators themselves, along-side H. M. S. Catherwood Ltd, a firm in which Thomas Tilling Ltd obtained an interest in 1932. In this way the number of operators in the Province was reduced from 180 in 1928 to 52 in 1934.

But the railways continued to lose traffic to the roads and in 1932 they approached the government with a request for a complete monopoly. Sir Felix Pole was invited to advise and reported in favour of a State board; he would have liked it to include all inland transport but the international status of the Great Northern Railway as both rail and road operator made this impracticable. He therefore recommended a road transport board in which the railways were to invest and insisted that it should incorporate the Belfast municipal undertaking. Catherwoods and the Belfast Omnibus Company Ltd supported his concept. The Northern Ireland Road Transport Board came into existence in 1935 and on 1 October took over the bus operations of Catherwoods and the BOC, the Northern Counties Committee and the Belfast & County Down Railway, and of the GNR so far as they lay in the Province. The Belfast undertaking was not included, but instead was given substantial protection from the NIRTB. All but three of the remaining independents were acquired before the end of the year, giving the board a fleet of 692 vehicles of twenty-seven different makes, many of them so badly in need of replacement that 122 new buses had to be bought during its first year of existence.

The NIRTB was not an immediate and unqualified success, although it met its chief difficulties in absorbing the hauliers during 1936. A quarter of its fleet had come from small family businesses and a half of the remainder from the railway companies, of which the largest, the GNR, was still a bus operator on a large scale in the Free State and had not been anxious to part with experienced staff. Thus the board was short of technical and administrative staff, as well as being over-capitalised. Inquiries held in 1937 found that the intended partnership between the board and the railways had been a failure from the first, due to 'a fundamental divergence of views'. There had also been 'public antagonism and adverse propaganda by vested interests' arising from 'the general feeling of resentment at the enforced transfer of so many small existing local businesses to what was looked upon as a monopolistic authority'. The board, unlike any comparable authority proposed on the mainland, had acquired the private-hire sector of the trade along with the bus services and it was alleged that charges in this sector had been so far increased that the class of passenger used to hiring buses for sea-side outings could no longer afford to do so.

The main inquiry had been conducted by a committee chaired by Sir William McLintock and its criticisms touched also upon the failure of the government to appoint anyone with transport experience to the board; upon the 'grossly excessive' payments for goodwill; upon the omission of the Belfast undertaking; and upon the rate at which acquisitions had proceeded. The Stormont parliament referred the report to a joint select committee, which did little but prevent any action before war broke out in 1939. During the war, even the freight activities of the board were profitable, but by 1946 they were once more in deficit and in 1948 the board was wound up and its undertaking transferred to the Ulster Transport Authority, which also acquired the railways other than those crossing the border. Belfast Corporation was allowed to retain its own transport service.

The Dublin government, faced with problems similar to those in the north of Ireland, followed a firmer course. The railways, apart from those crossing the border, were merged to form the GSR in 1924, in order to achieve economies and reduce their capital burden. Bus competition appeared rather later than it did in the six counties, and it was some time before any major undertaking appeared, doubtless because of the reluctance of investors to risk their capital during the troubles. In 1926 however F. T. Woods of Altrincham bought a small business on the outskirts of Dublin and renamed it the Irish Omnibus Company. The Free State railways obtained general road powers the following year and at once an agreement was reached under which the IOC became the bus operating arm of the Great Southern Railways. This settlement arose from the onerous restrictions that the Railways (Road Motor Services) Act applied to direct operation on the part of railway companies.

In 1929, the IOC became financially linked with the GSR, and in the same year the GNR and the Londonderry & Lough Swilly Railway began to run buses in the Free State. Railway finances continued to worsen and in 1932 a restrictive system of licensing was introduced, which hastened the process of acquisition of the independents. In the same year, area agreements were signed between the IOC and the GNR, and between the IOC and the Dublin United Tramways, which had started running buses in 1925 to meet independent competition. In 1933, it became necessary to write off a half the GSR capital and the Road Transport Act of the same year gave powers of compulsory purchase to the railway companies and DUT. The latter company made a clean sweep of the Dublin 'pirates', acquiring twenty-four businesses in two years. The GNR continued to purchase operators in its territory and on 1 January 1934 the Irish Omnibus Company services were transferred to the GSR and the bus company wound up.

By 1938, the railway finances warranted a new tribunal of inquiry but the war, with its severe restriction of private motoring, gave a respite. The government realised that this would not continue and that the railways would need to be re-equipped, so in 1944 a new statutory company, Coras Iompair Eireann, or Ireland's Transport Company, came into existence. This was a merger of the GSR and Dublin United Tramways and was a compromise between State and private ownership. Still the decline in railway revenue continued and in 1948 the government appointed Sir James Milne to report on the future of transport in the state. The Milne Report, an extensive and detailed document, was distinguished by a general philosophy which bears the mark of A. W. Tait, one of the expert advisers and later a founder of the traffic costing service of the British Transport Commission. Upon its recommendations was based the Transport Act of 1950, which merged the CIE with the Grand Canal Company to form a public authority, with a board appointed by the government.

THE FIRST CONURBATION AUTHORITY

The largest merger of all was the one which, with the passage of the London Transport Act of 1933, set the seal of government approval on the policies of Lord Ashfield. The formation of the London Passenger Transport Board was not nationalisation as we have since come to know it; the models for the new board were the Port of London Authority and the BBC. But the creation of a public authority to run public passenger transport in London had been called for by Bevin and welcomed by Ashfield in 1924, while the Bill itself was inspired by Herbert Morrison. Far from being a revolutionary step, it was the logical conclusion of the policy initiated by Sir George Gibb when he succeeded Yerkes in the management of the tubes. Ashfield became the first chairman of the LPTB and held the post for two successive seven-year periods, after which he became a member of the British Transport Commission. He was also a director of ICI and of the Midland Bank. When he died in 1948, *The Times* carried an obituary notice by the Lord Chancellor which said he was 'more interested in other peoples' problems and difficulties than he was in his own'. *Modern Transport* spoke of a 'lovable and remarkable personality', and concluded its notice by saying : 'Certainly, few have contributed more in their generation to the happiness and welfare of their fellows'.

Ashfield's concern was not primarily for his shareholders whose interests he regarded as a barrier to his main policy, the integration of public transport so as to make the 'best' use of the physical resources available. But while the interest he served was not the limited one of a body of investors, neither was it the interest of the consumer, who was to be given little opportunity of influencing the provision of transport and no true freedom of choice in its use. Ashfield was a type of the benevolent despot, not avid for power, but welcoming it as a means towards his ends. If he had opposed the formation of the LPTB, it may be doubted whether Morrison's Bill could have been carried through Parliament at a time when a Conservative government (under a pseudonym) was in power. But this man, who had been general manager of the London Electric Railway Company since 1907, was, rightly or wrongly, the most public-spirited individual British transport has yet produced, and at the age of sixty-one he had achieved as eminent a position as any man in the industry.

C. E. Lee described Ashfield to the author as 'a real professional', and said that transport '*meant* something to him'. It was this emotional involvement that distinguished him from the more orthodox financiers of the industry. In general, his preference was for 'private enterprise' and, according to Lee, he would have preferred a pooling agreement with the LCC tramways to the formation of the LPTB but was converted to Morrison's idea. In his private life he suffered from constant ill health and was a man of such narrow moral outlook that he even called for the resignation of one of his officers who had obtained a divorce.

The first measure to reach Parliament providing for the further unification of London's transport undertakings was a proposal in 1928 for a common management of the LER group and the LCC tramways, with pooled receipts. This clearly reflected Ashfield's leaning, but on the arrival of a Labour government the following year Herbert Morrison persuaded him to accept a wider objective. The London Passenger Transport Bill was tabled in December 1930 and so non-partisan was it that the change of government in the following autumn did no more than delay its progress. The Conservative administration made certain changes which Morrison could not accept and he eventually voted against the Bill, but it became law on 13 April 1933 and the LPTB came into existence on 1 July.

The London Passenger Transport Board consisted of members elected by a body called the 'Appointing Trustees'. The first appointments included Lord Ashfield's closest associate, Frank Pick, who became vice-chairman and chief executive officer and made a lasting impression upon the organisation in the latter capacity. Pick had come to London from the North Eastern Railway with Sir George Gibb in 1906 at the age of twenty-eight. He became commercial manager of the LGOC in 1912 and was responsible for the development of new bus routes and for the advertising department. In 1921 he became assistant general manager of the LER group and was made managing director in 1928. He deserves special mention for his lasting concern for the principles of good design in industry and for the high standards that became associated with the name of London Transport. He served one seven-year term on the board, during which he was responsible for the evacuation scheme for London children in 1939, and he died in 1941. A solitary man, his recreation consisted in shutting himself away from the world to listen to gramophone records of classical music.

The third principal figure of the LPTB was Alderman John Cliff, a trade unionist who came to the T&GWU on its foundation in 1922 from one of its constituents, the Amalgamated Association of Tramway & Vehicle Workers. He had joined Leeds Corporation Tramways at the beginning of the century and had always been associated with wages negotiations, becoming a joint secretary of the National Joint Industrial Council for the Tramways Industry upon its formation in 1919. Assistant general secretary of the T&GWU from 1924, he resigned this office on appointment to the LPTB, first as a part-time and later as a full-time member, with special responsibilities for staff matters. He became deputy chairman in 1947,* and resigned in 1955.

The board was given a special area, within which no other person or undertaking might provide a public road service local to that area (other than taxis), without the board's written consent. Within this area, the board was freed from the necessity of holding road service licences, though it required them for any services operated in the fringes around the 'special area' in which it did not have the same monopoly rights. The whole territory was very much that of the LGOC and LGCS, with various provisions for penetrating routes, both outward by the board and inward by other operators. Apart from the Underground (LER) Group, the Act provided for the transfer to the LPTB of the Metropolitan Railway Company, the various local authority tramways, the Tilling and T&BAT undertakings, and fifty-nine independent bus firms. A standing joint committee was set up with the main-line railway companies which, in accordance with the Act, arranged

---

* By this time the LPTB had become the London Transport Executive.

N

for the pooling of all the board's passenger receipts with those of the main-line railways arising from journeys within the board's area. Settlement with the independents was not always easy and in a number of cases, including the allocation of 'C' Stock to Tilling and to T&BAT, reference had to be made to the London Passenger Transport Arbitration Tribunal.

Apart from the undertakings which were specifically transferred by the Act, some seventy small operators in the country area, including a number that had been operating Green Line type services, were refused 'consent' by the board, which was therefore obliged to acquire them. Some services of surrounding territorial companies were also acquired. A number of special services for football matches, race meetings and similar events were left to independent operators to provide under the consent clause. The board also gave consent to a number of small rural operators in the country area, with some of whom it ran jointly. Since the London Transport Act did not apply to services that had one terminal outside the board's special area (except so far as local journeys were concerned), the great bulk of express services and excursions from London remained unaffected. Private hire operation remained almost entirely in the hands of the independents, for the board was given power to run contract carriages only within its own area and a narrow fringe outside.

It is not easy to judge the success of the London Passenger Transport Board. Certainly it did nothing to relieve congestion, for the number of buses increased, as Charles F. Klapper had foreseen when he told the Omnibus Society in 1932 : 'If the proposed board is to remain solvent the number of public service vehicles in the London area will not be reduced by a single unit'. The LPTB was given a complex capital structure, with various classes of stock reflecting the various assets transferred to it. After the LER and Metropolitan Railway companies had been wound up and their holdings distributed, the largest block of 'C' stock was the £1,544,759 in the hands of Thomas Tilling Ltd. This stock carried priority in the allocation of interest, the standard rate being 5 per cent for the first two financial years and $5\frac{1}{2}$ per cent thereafter, with a maximum of 6 per cent, after which any surplus revenue was to be transferred to reserve. The board, in fact, failed to achieve the standard rate in any year up to 1939, and while this was permitted for five consecutive years, it seems likely that its solvency would have been in question had it not been for the intervention of the war.

DEVELOPMENTS IN MUNICIPAL TRANSPORT

The 'twenties had seen the growth of municipal bus operation. J. Sleeman has calculated that the eighteen local authorities running buses in 1914 had grown to ninety by 1928, and Kilmarnock Corporation in 1924 was the first to substitute buses for trams (Keighley went over to trolleybuses two days earlier). Although 1926 saw a straight change from horse trams to motor buses at Morecambe and Heysham, there was no general change to buses until the last years of the decade, and many municipal undertakings were still committed to the tram at the start of the 'thirties.

In certain parts of the country, where suitable parliamentary powers had been obtained, municipal transport departments had developed services well beyond their civic boundaries. Recognising this, the railways approached a number of them and joint operation was established at Sheffield, Halifax, Huddersfield and Todmorden. This usually took the form of a joint committee under whose direction the municipal management was responsible for operation, the railway retaining direct ownership of part of the fleet and receiving an agreed proportion of the net revenue. At Sheffield, the joint committee became a territorial operator in its own right, but no railway interest was obtained in the case of Walsall and Wolverhampton where the corporations concerned had signed area agreements with Midland Red in the early 'twenties.

Elsewhere, local authorities had set up joint transport undertakings, probably the earliest being the Stalybridge, Hyde, Mossley and Dukinfield Joint Board, which originated as a tramway operator in 1903. Doubtless because of local jealousies, such arrangements were never common, even in areas such as south Lancashire, where municipal tramways proliferated; an exception was the Burnley, Colne and Nelson Joint Transport Committee, formed in 1932. The rest of Lancashire remained a complexity of separate systems, within which a great deal of joint operation grew up, involving the territorial companies—Ribble, North Western and Lancashire United—as well as the local authorities. Plans for a public authority on the lines of the LPTB were canvassed during the 'thirties, but came to nothing.

By no means every urban transport undertaking in the country was established as a municipal enterprise, and the 'thirties saw a number of cases where local authorities transferred their services to the local territorial company or reached some compromise arrangement. Sir Frederick Heaton negotiated several such agreements, notably at York and Keighley early in the decade and at Brighton in 1939. At Bristol, the corporation used its powers of purchase to acquire the tramways in 1937, but arranged for a joint committee with Bristol Tramways to supervise their continued operation by the company. In Scotland, companies in the SMT group took over local services from the corporations of Ayr, Kilmarnock and Perth, while in Northern Ireland H. M. S. Catherwood Ltd took over those of Londonderry.

Part V of the Road Traffic Act gave powers to run motor buses to any local authority already providing public transport, subject to the need for a road service licence, on any road within its area. It also set up procedure for application to the traffic commissioners for consent to run on roads beyond the municipal boundary. This undoubtedly contributed to the faster replacement of tramways which took place during the 'thirties, twenty-eight systems being abandoned between 1931 and 1935, and eleven more by 1939. Several were replaced by trolleybuses, but towns as large as Preston, Rochdale and Southport turned over entirely to motor bus. The Act did not give general powers to run contract carriages (i.e., private hire coaches), and only a limited number of undertakings obtained licences for excursions.

An unexpected effect of the Road Traffic Act was the dismemberment of the system of limited-stop bus services (known as express services) which Manchester Corporation had built up. The first of these, running between Cheadle and Heywood on a thirty-minute headway, had appeared on 11 April 1927, about a year before the first Green Line type service started in London and by 1930 there was a considerable network, running as far afield as Bacup, Buxton, Congleton and Northwich. Many were run jointly with other municipal undertakings and with the territorial companies, while independents established similar services of their own. These services owed a lot to the initiative of R. Stuart Pilcher, who became general manager at Manchester in 1928. He had previously been in charge at Aberdeen and Edinburgh and later became a well-liked chairman of the West Midland traffic commissioners.

Manchester was well pleased with its express bus routes which, along with the electrification of the Manchester South Junction and Altrincham Railway, gave rise to the first tramway abandonment in the city. The police, however, believed that the express services were the main cause of congestion in the city centre and persuaded the traffic commissioners of this when the services came up for licensing. At this time the commissioner in London was encouraging the linking of express services to avoid city-centre terminals, but the Manchester ruling was exactly the reverse and the express network was broken up.

THE SETTLEMENT OF 1942

For most of the industry, the 'thirties was a decade of reasonable prosperity, marked by re-organisations flowing from the settlement with the railways and the effect of the Road Traffic Act. The combine structure was still basically that of the Tilling & British group in England and Wales, in which Thomas Tilling Ltd and BET nominated the chairman in alternate years. The partnership, however, was not always a happy one; Crosland-Taylor quotes W. S. Wreathall as saying that it 'never worked properly', and that at board level 'there was always the feeling that it was no use doing this or that because next year it might be cancelled by the next joint chairman'. In 1942, as Crosland-Taylor puts it, 'the pot boiled over'; the combine divided and the holding company, Tilling and British Automobile Traction Ltd, was wound up. There is no doubt that the partnership between J. F. Heaton and Sidney Garcke had been an uneasy one, but had it not existed it is difficult to see how the industry could have avoided falling entirely under railway control.

R. J. Howley, under whose influence the BET board agreed to the division of the combine, became a director of the company in 1923. He was deputy chairman from 1930 and occupied the chair from 1942 to 1946. His influence on the industry has been compared by E. B. Hutchinson with that of Lord Ashfield, Richard Tilling and Frank Pick. Trained as a civil engineer, he was noted for his quiet and courteous manner, as well as for the intellectual ability with which he approached the problems of the industry. C. F. Hayward, for many years editor of *Motor Transport*, recalls a rare occasion when he found Howley 'annoyed', the subject being a letter of Sir Frederick Heaton's to *The Times*, which he described as 'rot'. Howley was awarded the CBE at the end of the first world war for his work on government committees connected with transport. He died in 1955.

The settlement left the two parties free to follow their separate policies in subsequent years and, as will be seen, to differ over their attitude to nationalisation when a Labour government came to power. In the meantime, they both registered new holding companies to take over the operating companies allocated to them, BET forming BET Omnibus Services Ltd and Tilling forming Tilling Motor Services Ltd. No comment seems to have been made at the time on the geographic distribution of the subsidiaries which gave BET a preponderance of industrial territory and rural areas with relatively high density population, while Tillings received a great deal of thinly populated countryside to add to that which had been occupied by the National Omnibus & Transport Company. Table 2 indicates the distribution, from which it will be seen that the West Yorkshire Road Car Company was almost the only Tilling operator to be predominantly concerned with industrial traffic, for United Automobile and Crosville included wide areas of 'green fields', or indeed of mountain and moorland. Perhaps it was a rare failure of Heaton's foresight that permitted this, for the rural bus was of vital importance

TABLE 2. THE TILLING & BRITISH GROUP AFTER ITS DIVISION
IN SEPTEMBER 1942

1   *Companies acquired by* BET *Omnibus Services Ltd*
Aldershot & District Traction Company Ltd
East Kent Road Car Company Ltd
East Midland Motor Services Ltd
East Yorkshire Motor Services Ltd
Maidstone & District Motor Services Ltd
North Western Road Car Company Ltd
Ribble Motor Services Ltd
Southdown Motor Services Ltd
Trent Motor Traction Company Ltd
Yorkshire Traction Company Ltd

2   *Companies acquired by Tilling Motor Services Ltd*
Caledonian Omnibus Company Ltd
Crosville Motor Services Ltd
Cumberland Motor Services Ltd
Eastern Counties Omnibus Company Ltd
Hants & Dorset Motor Services Ltd
Lincolnshire Road Car Company Ltd
Southern Vectis Omnibus Company Ltd
Thames Valley Traction Company Ltd
United Automobile Services Ltd
West Yorkshire Road Car Company Ltd
Wilts & Dorset Motor Services Ltd

Companies whose names appear in italics had previously been under the
management of the other parent.

in those days, yet today it is in just these areas that the ownership
of private cars is at its highest. It is hard to see how else he
could have accepted Crosville, Cumberland Motor Services and
Lincolnshire from the BET side in exchange for East Midland
and North Western, two companies whose services lay mainly
in high-density industrial areas of the country.

The financial structure of the two combines after the settlement
of 1942 is shown in Appendix 1. The only remaining financial
link between them was the joint ownership of a handful of companies by their subsidiaries, including that of London Coastal
Coaches Ltd, owners of Victoria coach station in London. But

the territorial organisation of the industry, under the sanction of the area agreement system, remained essential to both groups, and if 88 Kingsway now became formally divorced from Crewe House, bus operation required closer relations at a lower level. This was provided for in membership of the Provincial Omnibus Owners' Association.

A CHANGING WORLD

The second world war found a motor-bus industry rendering an essential service throughout the country, instead of the scattered routes and pioneer vehicles of 1914. Bus services were kept going in spite of shortages of all kinds, and while in many places they were heavily reduced, in others the development of war industry required their extension. To a large extent the industry had to 'live on its fat', improvising wherever it could. Through the tenacity and ingenuity of the engineers, buses were kept running when spares were hard to come by, and even the shortage of fuel was overcome by the clumsy 'producer-gas' trailers, which provided some sort of alternative to petrol or fuel oil. They burned coke, were often difficult to light, and had to be stoked from time to time during the journey; they were also inadequate when the bus had a hill to climb. Most of the territorial companies, as well as London Transport, ran a number of them (it was supposed to be 15 per cent of the fleet), and they were usually concentrated on one or two garages, which had nothing else. Strange looking contraptions, they worked well enough in the situation and disproved the Ministry's contention that trailers were unsuitable on British public-service vehicles.

But while producer-gas kept the vehicles going, there were other shortages that grew more serious as the war went on. Many express and touring coaches (including all the Green Line fleet) were requisitioned early in the war, and ageing fleets were weakened by heavy losses in many blitzed cities. At first they were relieved by the transfer of buses from seaside areas and other places where there was a surplus. In this way, 422 buses from provincial areas were loaned to London Transport between

October 1940 and June 1941, while Coventry Corporation, whose tramways had to be abandoned completely after the November 1940 air raid, hired buses from seven other municipal transport departments, as well as from Trent Motor Traction and, at a later stage, London Transport itself. As the war went on, the LPTB found that it needed fewer buses, and London Transport double-deckers on long-term loan to companies such as West Yorkshire and Lincolnshire were painted in the hirer's livery.

The shortage was somewhat eased when the Ministry of Supply released a number of chassis that had been under construction when war broke out and had been put into store when manufacturers turned to more essential work. These 'un-frozen' chassis were given bodies built to a severe standard of austerity, and similar to those on the vehicles that Guys, Bristols and Daimlers were permitted to build after 1942. As many as 700 of these 'utility' buses were delivered to London Transport alone, and many remained in service throughout the country long after the war was over. The bodywork was markedly angular in design, and some were given slatted wooden seats reminiscent of tramcars.

There are many stories of the heroism of bus crews during the war. Drivers on country routes on the east coast had instructions to park under the nearest tree when an alert was heard, so as to be less conspicuous at a time when vehicles were frequently attacked by gunfire. Frequently, men drove burning buses out of garages to prevent fire spreading during the air attacks on London and other cities. At Dover, where services had to be maintained under constant risk of shellfire, conductors paid in at a temporary office consisting of a converted bus that could be driven out of range at night. After 1940, the coastal area of the East Kent company's territory became known as the 'Busman's Malta', with buses running at the driver's discretion, and it is hardly possible to give praise enough to the men and women who kept them running. One driver was killed by machine-gun fire at the wheel of his bus and the conductress of another vehicle, together with a number of passengers, was killed by an exploding bomb; in this incident and although enemy aircraft were known to be still overhead, another bus was immediately taken out to pick up the injured. In June 1942 the company's head office and works were destroyed and, throughout the years of raids and shellfire, maintenance had to be carried out with the fleet scattered in small groups on the outskirts of towns, an insurance against a complete breakdown of services.

In addition to all this the industry was faced with the prosaic, burdensome struggle of keeping vehicles roadworthy and services running in the face of shortages, overwork, and all the difficulties of life in wartime. Hours of duty for drivers and conductors do not easily fit into family life and there were many married women among the conductresses the industry enrolled, some of them working in husband-and-wife teams. Others took over as cleaners and fitters, or filled essential clerical jobs that, previously, had always been a man's preserve. In uniforms far more attractive than those issued to the 'clippies' of the 1914-18 war, they displayed the bus conductor's traditional good humour and a few even worked as drivers. In family businesses where the proprietor was called up, it was often his wife who took on the responsibility for keeping services going.

Passengers as well as staff suffered from wartime conditions. The regulations were amended to allow the seats in a saloon bus to be arranged around the sides, leaving a large space in the middle where people were permitted to stand (in ratio to the number of seats). Into this space, particularly on 'the last bus on Saturday night', passengers would be packed regardless of limitations, and no one could be said to be riding in comfort. These were officially 'perimeter seating' buses, but were usually known as 'standees'. To conserve fuel, all buses had to be in their home depot by 9 pm and no services were run on Sunday mornings. Special permits were issued to passengers whose employment required them to travel on 'ghost buses' running in prohibited hours. Many operators also introduced some form of priority for season-ticket holders on peak journeys in the evenings, which meant that shoppers and other travellers had to take their chance or travel outside the peak.

The end of the war in 1945 found the industry very little better prepared to meet changed circumstances than it had been in 1918. The material equipment of the industry was greatly reduced in effectiveness, many vehicles still in service being ones that would normally have been scrapped long since. 'Vintage' motors such as Reos and Chevrolets, as well as early models of existing manufacturers, were still in service and 'utility' or 'austerity' types represented all of the new stock—in itself a tiny proportion of the whole. Operators who had had the foresight to place substantial orders in 1939 now reaped their reward in priority for what little new construction was possible, but to make matters worse, materials (especially timber for body-building) were often of extremely poor quality.

London Transport found itself particularly hard hit by the vehicle shortage, in spite of having received a varied selection of non-standard buses, including Bristols, Guys and Daimlers, during the war. Before 1939, the LPTB had bought roughly 500 new vehicles a year, but during the following six years only some 750 were delivered. By 1947, it was said that 2,500 London buses had exceeded their normal life. It was some years before the supply of new ones became adequate, and in the meantime the passenger queues were building up as they had done after 1918. Every possible vehicle was pressed into service and twenty-seater buses ran on central London routes, but eventually it was decided to hire from other London operators. Arrangements were made with PSV Operators Ltd, the clearing house for the independents' booking agents, for the provision during peak periods of coaches to be driven by the proprietors' staff with conductors supplied by London Transport. The scheme began on 27 October 1947 and lasted until August 1949, with a maximum of 575 vehicles on hire. Some of the operators had themselves run London services before 1933, and a great variety of types, a few of them double-deckers, were to be seen on the streets. But even this was insufficient to move the traffic and at the end of 1948 it was arranged for 190 Bristols to be diverted from delivery to Tilling companies and to run for a time in London. It was not easy for passengers accustomed to the standard London Transport double-decker to adjust themselves to the 145 of these that had 'low bridge' bodies, with a side gangway on the top deck lowering the ceiling on the off side of the saloon. They remained in service until June 1950, helped out by seventeen vehicles from Leeds and three from Maidstone.

In a way, the situation was eased by the shortage of fuel, then being allocated to operators at the careful discrimination of the regional transport commissioners (who in 1946 became once again the chairmen of the traffic commissioners). Quantities were based upon the stage and express mileage licensed to each operator (including workmen's services), with a small allowance for excursions. For some time no fuel was specially allocated for private hire, which meant that some smaller operators found it difficult to undertake this work, which is generally their speciality, and the black market in fuel flourished accordingly.

The apparatus of the Road Traffic Act was progressively reinstated and holders of defence permits found themselves back in the world of road- and public-service vehicle licences. New services authorised on permits were usually allowed to continue without opposition and the main pre-occupation of the territorial companies was the restoration of their own bus services to the level they estimated the travelling public now required. This was a matter of policy on their part, chosen at the expense of the express coach field at the pressing request of the traffic commissioners. Its effect was a substantial change in the balance of power in the industry, as the independent concerns filled the vacuum and developed a whole new network of holiday express services and tours. The earliest express services to London to reappear seem to have been those of two East Anglian operators, G. F. Burgoin and B. K. Jennings, which were started in November 1945.

With certain exceptions, the territorial companies acquiesced in this course of events and the railways were unable to do more than limit it by action in the traffic courts. Passengers wanted to avoid the necessity of changing trains on their holiday journeys, burdened with luggage and often with children in tow. In case after case, the arguments that brought success in the courts turned upon difficulties of travel between London rail terminals or the demand for a direct service from suburban centres. Most established express services ran from city centres, picking up only in the suburbs en route, and an independent could thus hope to establish a series of services to seaside towns not directly served from his own suburban sector.

The outcome of many applications (where a reasonable case had been made out) was usually a licence permitting a limited vehicle allowance on a number of summer Saturdays. It was rare for single fares or bookings originating at the seaside end of the route to be allowed, but many operators did not want this anyway. Their aim was to secure balanced loads in highly profitable traffic. For most of them, Saturdays were quiet, since their concern was with five-day contract work, and excursions (which seldom attract much demand on that day), so that they were well able to cater for the peak holiday traffic. The territorial companies could not do this so easily, because of the demands of their stage carriage services. The same concentration of demand induced operators of all kinds to expand their excursion licences by adding new destinations and increasing duplication.

FORWARD TO AN UNCERTAIN FUTURE

With the return of peace, it soon became clear that the industry faced a very different world from that of 1939. Not only had the war years created a reservoir of pent-up spending power, but the years of austerity that were to follow left travel and entertainment as virtually the only outlet for it. And in the absence of television, the cinema and theatre offered entertainment that, for most people, also meant travel. Bus and coach operation thus embarked on a boom period that was largely artificial; the more so since petrol rationing continued, becoming more restrictive until, in the summer of 1947, the allowance for pleasure motoring was suspended altogether. The industry expanded from a pre-war level of about 50,000 vehicles to 62,800 in 1948, although the number of operators fell over the same period. Services were strengthened beyond their pre-war frequencies and country routes that had never justified more than one or two buses a week began to be covered on days other than market day and Saturday.

In particular, 'picture buses' were developed, bringing the cinema within reach of the villages, usually on one evening each week.

One contribution to the boom was the level of fares on both bus and coach services, which had remained virtually unchanged since the Road Traffic Act had been introduced. This gave an artificial advantage to the industry in comparison with the railway and enabled the slower coach to compete effectively with the train. The position reflected the extent to which the railways by this time were subsidising their branch lines and stopping services, for according to costs quoted in 1950 the cost per seat/mile of running an express train was then just half that of a long-distance coach.

But these spectres were of little significance in the conditions of the time. Not only was there work to do, with profits for the taking, but the future held more obvious uncertainties. The Labour party's manifesto for the 1945 election, *Let us Face the Future*, had called for the nationalisation of the railways, road haulage and civil aviation. Buses and coaches were not mentioned (which is strange, in view of the proletarian associations of the 'chara'), but it was hard to believe that they would be left out for long. What was a greater surprise was the absence of a transport nationalisation Bill in the Labour government's legislative programme for its first year of office; if this was due to the absence of a considered plan, it may well have saved the transport industry from the disastrous experience of the coal industry, of whose nationalisation Emmanuel Shinwell was moved to remark : 'I have been talking of nationalisation for forty years, but the complications of the transfer of property had never occurred to me'.

The industry waited until 1947 for the Transport Act, only to find that its uncertainties were far from being removed. The Road Traffic Act remained unaffected (save for the minor irritation of having to refer to the traffic commissioners as 'licensing authorities for public service vehicles'). The British Transport Commission was set up, with a series of executives to assist it in the discharge of its duties, and to it the railway and canal companies and the London Passenger Transport Board were immediately to be transferred. The LPTB thus became the London Transport Executive, in what was largely a financial reconstruction. The commission was given the duty of acquiring the road haulage industry, except for that part consisting of traders carrying their own goods 'on own account'. In comparison with the lengthy clauses that provided for all this, Part IV of the Act, dealing with 'Other Forms of Transport and Port Facilities' was brief, and the subject of 'Passenger Road Transport' was dismissed in three sections. Although in Part I, the BTC had been given powers to 'secure the provision' of road passenger transport services, in Part IV it was not *required* to acquire any undertaking, but merely allowed, at its discretion, to prepare and submit to the Minister 'area schemes' which would provide for the acquisition of operators within such areas, and for the organisation of suitable bodies to run the services thus obtained.

Vesting day for the railways was 1 January 1948, and in its first minutes the railwaymen were moved to scenes of apocalyptic fervour. The irrelevance of this can sadly be measured by the fact that the out-going boards of directors had exercised only the most remote power after the State had, in effect, taken control in 1939. In the road haulage industry, a multitude of small business men knew that their lives would be changed by the new Act, while a smaller number of managers in the larger firms could foresee an expansion of their role; the drivers do not seem to have shared the rosy hopes of the railwaymen. Only in the bus and coach industry was the future still unsure.

CHAPTER NINE

A PERIOD OF PROBLEMS : 1948-1967

THE Minister of Transport in the Labour government that took office in 1945 was the MP for East Ham South, Alfred Barnes, who had long been active in the Co-operative movement. He was responsible for the nationalising Act, and the fact that he held his office throughout the two Atlee administrations was something of a record in a ministry that saw many changes. He was generally regarded as a wise and able administrator.

THE PROGRESS OF NATIONALISATION

The British Transport Commission immediately came into ownership of a substantial share in the motor-bus industry for, with the vesting of the railway companies, it acquired their shareholdings in the majority of the territorial companies. In the former London Passenger Transport Board it obtained outright ownership of the buses, trams and trolleybuses that served an area far wider than that of Greater London, and became responsible for the outright monopoly of bus operation in the metropolis. In addition, it received soon after its formation a group of three companies in Nottinghamshire that had been subsidiaries of the Midland Counties Electricity Supply Company, a Balfour Beattie holding that had been vested in the Electricity Board when that industry was nationalised.

Officers of the Railway Executive duly took their seats as directors of the territorial companies, but the rule that rail nominees should not behave in a narrowly partisan fashion does not seem to have been changed. In practice, the chairmen of the companies had retained management very much in their own hands and the rail appointments had tended to become sinecures; such co-ordination as had taken place had been the responsibility of standing joint committees at a lower level of management. The BTC was also much pre-occupied throughout its existence with the growing problems of its railway undertaking, and the integration of rail and road transport was never carried beyond the stage of aspiration.

At the head of the two combines that dominated the industry after 1942 were two men of radically different temperaments. Yet the undisputed personal control that S. F. Heaton exercised over the Tilling Group was never matched in the management of BET, which was a far less centralised organisation. R. J. Howley resigned from the BET chair in 1946 and was succeeded by H. C. Drayton ('Harley' Drayton to his associates), who is best described as a financier (in contrast with Heaton, who remained rather more an accountant). Drayton, who came from a Lincolnshire farming family, joined the St David's group of companies as office boy and became the protegé of J. S. Austen, who succeeded Emile Garcke as chairman of BET in 1920. Drayton joined the company in 1933 but retained his wider responsibilities, and upon Austen's death in 1942 he succeeded to the leadership of the group of trusts controlled from 117 Old Broad Street. The close relationship between the two men was marked by Austen's bequest to Drayton of his estate at Plumpton Hall, near Bury St Edmunds. The Drayton group had investments of over £100 million, and was notable for the degree of power which Drayton was content to delegate to his colleagues and his complete confidence in them. In this he displayed a further difference from Heaton, who was a solitary man.

Drayton died in 1966 at the age of sixty-four, and he was succeeded by John Spencer Wills, whose connection with BET was at least as well-established. He was made private secretary to Emile Garcke in 1921 and joined the board of the company in 1939 at the age of thirty-five, having held various posts, including that of general manager of East Yorkshire Motor Services Ltd and managing director of British & Foreign Aviation Ltd. (He obtained a pilot's licence in 1933). During the post-war years, he was managing director, supported by men with practical experience of the industry, including pioneers such as W. T. James, who founded Lewis & James, one of the constituents of Western Welsh.

A period of uncertainty followed the creation of the BTC, which ended dramatically when, in September 1948, J. F. Heaton announced that an agreement had been reached for the sale of the transport interests of the Tilling Group to the Commission. The price, made known in November, amounted to £24,800,000 in the form of BTC 3 per cent stock, of which all but some £3,950,000 was distributed to the holding company's shareholders at the rate of £5 of BTC stock for every £1 of Tilling stock held. Thomas Tilling Ltd thus became an investment trust (which it remains to this day), but Sir Frederick Heaton retired from its management shortly after the sale of the transport side and died on 27 April of the following year at the age of sixty-eight.

In many aspects of his career, Heaton was unique among busmen. Under his guidance, the Tilling family business had been made, in the words of the *Railway Gazette*, 'into a high-powered efficient machine', and Sir John Elliot referred in an obituary notice to 'a reputation for ruthlessness in business which was not wholly undeserved'. Perhaps alone among the busmen of his generation, he was first and foremost an accountant, and while Lord Ashfield was deeply concerned with transport as a social service, Sir Frederick Heaton regarded it more strictly as a busi-ess. (The strength of BET has perhaps been due to the dispersal of power that has allowed for a working adjustment of the two attitudes). He was a member of the Inland Transport War Council from 1941 to 1944, and from 1943 to 1945 served at the government's request as unpaid chairman of Short Brothers (Rochester & Bedford) Ltd, the aircraft manufacturers.

Heaton had a reputation for cold reserve and intolerance, but those who knew him well had a different impression. W. J. Crosland-Taylor has described his ability to unbend on rare occasions, usually on tours of inspection, when the two men travelled through the Welsh hills together by car. On one such visit they stayed at the Devil's Bridge Hotel, where the sixty-three year old

Sir Frederick climbed 500 feet down to the falls and up again. He would call for the car to stop, to get a breath of fresh air, but 'when we had got back into the car he would gradually close up'. His Gloucestershire farm seems to have been his only interest outside the business, but it must be remembered that Heaton *was* Tillings in a way that no individual has ever come to dominate BET. Apart from the bus operating side, he had in 1918 formed the Road Transport & General Insurance Company, and in 1922 had added its subsidiary, Motor Credit Services Ltd, but he never diversified the group to the extent favoured by the directors of BET or the United Transport Company (Red & White). In his obituary notice, the *Railway Gazette* remarked : 'the keynote to his success was his ability to persuade others that he could make more money for them by running their businesses than they could themselves'.

In the official history of BET, Roger Fulford makes it clear that H. C. Drayton and his board felt the sale of Tillings' subsidiaries to be a betrayal of the greatest magnitude. In a public statement made when the terms of the sale were known, Drayton promised that BET would fight nationalisation 'to the last wheel', but the size of the payment was regarded in itself as a deliberate effort to tempt the directors and shareholders of the BET to reach a similar agreement. Certainly the nationalisation of public transport was not carried out with an expropriation of assets to the extent that many people had expected from a Labour government. At the same time, the BTC began shopping around; during 1948 negotiations started with Scottish Motor Traction and in January 1949 it was announced that the SMT group had passed to BTC ownership at a price of £26,800,000. The bus interests were transferred to a new parent, Scottish Omnibuses Ltd which, like its predecessor, was both an operating and a holding company, the original directors retaining Scottish Motor Traction Ltd and the motor agencies and insurance business it had built up. The fleet name 'SMT' was, however, permitted to the new group and the initials remained in the titles of the Western and Central companies. The Alexander family similarly retained in their own hands the body-building works at Falkirk. James Amos, the general manager, became chairman of the group in place of Sir William Thomson, who, like Sir Frederick Heaton, died soon after the sale was complete.

After this, although the BTC continued to negotiate, purchases of individual companies were usually made in the names of Tilling or Scottish Omnibuses subsidiaries, the principal exception being the direct acquisition of the Red & White group on 10 February 1950. Since 1939, this had been enlarged by the purchase of several companies; Newbury & District Motor Services Ltd in December 1943, Venture Ltd of Basingstoke in March 1945, and South Midland Motor Services Ltd of Oxford in October 1945. All the Red & White companies were subsequently managed as part of the Tilling Group. The parent company, Red & White United Transport, later invested in bus companies in Guernsey and went into partnership with Commander F. T. Hare in his Overseas Motor Transport Company Ltd. Commander Hare subsequently withdrew from the enterprise and an interest was obtained by BET.

BET's antipathy towards nationalisation was not only due to the directors' confidence in the group's future profitability. One of the first investment boards to embark on diversification, they had taken an interest in the laundry industry as early as 1934, when J. S. Austen remarked in his annual report that the company had 'taken in a little washing'. What always distinguished BET was a real concern for the special flair that makes a successful busman, and this has been reflected in the selection of directors since the days of Sidney Garcke. Its tradition was also influenced by the original intention of the founders to emulate the railway companies, both in the form of their organisation and in the nice balance of public responsibility and private profit. It was this that gave a special drive to the board's determination to resist nationalisation, and which was totally discounted by the financial commentators at the time; the city editor of a national newspaper called upon 'burly Mr Harold Charles Drayton, 47-year-old Investment Trust "King", to sell off the BET bus companies to the State and distribute the capital to stockholders'. BET had in its early days been accused of putting its stockholders' interests first, when it was attacked as 'the octopus', but this must surely have been due to a failure to project the image the directors of those days had of the company they served.

The BET directors thus felt quite sincerely that they could run their bus services better than the State. At the annual general meeting of July 1949, their policy was approved unanimously by the stockholders, but the extent to which the City regarded the sale as inevitable was illustrated by the increase of 180 points in the value of BET ordinary stock on the day the amount of the payment for the Tilling Group was announced. By the end of 1948, £100 of this stock was worth £2,100, and in view of the substantial interest in many BET companies that the BTC had inherited from the railways, it is not surprising that most commentators assumed the complete nationalisation of the bus industry to be only a matter of months away. They were encouraged by the sale of Transport Services Ltd, a haulage company not in the BET group but of which H. C. Drayton was chairman, apparently forgetting that it was subject to compulsory purchase under the Transport Act. What they could not know until it was revealed at the BET annual meeting, was that the company was making a bigger profit than the interest it could expect to obtain from the selling price of its bus companies.

At the same time, the BTC continued to enter into new negotiations. The West Riding Automobile Company Ltd, a prominent Yorkshire operator outside either group, was approached but did not accept the offer made. The north Lincolnshire independent, Enterprise (Scunthorpe) Passenger Services Ltd, was bought early in 1950, and though negotiations appear to have been carried on by the BTC, the actual purchase was made by the Lincolnshire Road Car Company. Enterprise became the northern area of LRCC and its founder, A. Drury, became northern area manager, a position he retained until 1965. He had already sold his business once when the company that later became East Midland Motor Services acquired it in 1925, selling it back to him three years later.

The transfer of Enterprise to LRCC was in accordance with a

policy which was followed in all subsequent purchases. The BTC also began to confine its purchases to businesses within the territories of Tilling Group companies, the obvious course of action once BET's refusal to negotiate had become clear. To have acquired a scattered empire of small businesses within 'opposition' territory would have been totally uneconomic, whereas consolidation of the Tilling companies within their agreed boundaries was in continuance of long-established policy.

For a while though, it seemed that the absorbtion of Enterprise by the Lincolnshire Road Car Company might disturb both the area agreement system and the uneasy balance of power between the BET and BTC. The agreement between LRCC and its neighbour, Yorkshire Traction, presumably required the division of the Enterprise services, to the extent that they lay outside LRCC territory. No attempt seems to have been made to do this, but neither was any overt action taken in consequence and the incident was not repeated elsewhere. Indeed, when some of the larger independents in County Durham were bought in June 1950 Darlington Triumph Services, the Express Omnibus Company and ABC Motor Services of Ferryhill were merged to form Durham District Services Ltd. This, as is shown in Map 5, had an operating area lying well inside the territory of the BET subsidiaries, Northern General and Sunderland District, but its formation as a wholly-owned subsidiary of United Automobile Services meant that no question of a division of services could arise.

The Durham District move was a further threat to BET however, and a countermove was made the following year when the small firm of Thomas Brothers (Port Talbot) Ltd was bought, along with another independent there, as well as the rather larger family business of J. James & Sons Ltd of Ammanford, and the express operator, Neath & Cardiff Luxury Coaches Ltd. Owing to the confused area boundaries of South Wales it was less obviously 'hostile' when BET retained these as direct subsidiaries, but at least it was now clear that BET was still in the market and the pace of expansion by purchase now slowed down. Developments in Scotland were of less significance, for the Scottish Bus Group had no opposition to face. Several independents were ac-

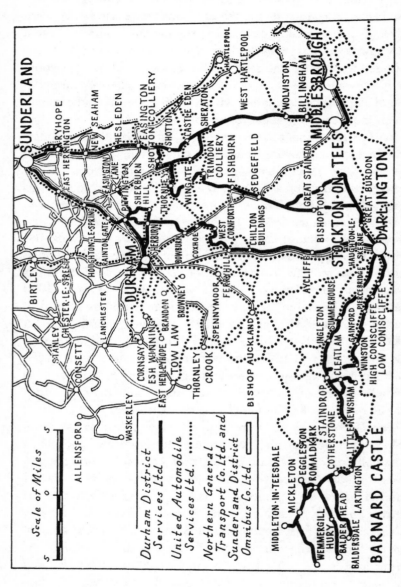

MAP 5. *The territory of Durham District Services Ltd in relation to its neighbouring area agreement companies*

quired, the largest being Young's Bus Service Ltd of Paisley and James Sutherland (Peterhead) Ltd, which were taken over on 1 March 1950 by BTC itself and transferred to the appropriate subsidiary company the following year. In 1951, BTC obtained the 50 per cent interest in the Highland Transport Company that had remained outside railway ownership, and transferred it to the Scottish group with the name of Highland Omnibuses Ltd.

The BTC placed its English and Welsh bus companies under the Tilling Group Management Board, which consisted of former directors and officers of Thomas Tilling Ltd who had been transferred to the commission's employment under the terms of sale. Although nominally part of the Road Transport Executive's responsibility, they were left from the first very much on their own, and no attempt was made to dismantle the company structure, so that many passengers could not have realised that the buses they were using had been nationalised.

Through its purchase of the Tilling Group, the BTC came into ownership of substantial manufacturing capacity. The Bristol company continued to produce bus and coach chassis, and while most of its products were fitted with Gardner diesel engines, it had its own engine available as an alternative. At Lowestoft, the body-building works of United had passed to Eastern Counties, of which it had become a wholly-owned subsidiary under the name of Eastern Coach Works Ltd. Under J. F. Heaton's management, both companies had been expanded and had sold their products to all comers, but the Transport Act prohibited the BTC from manufacturing 'anything which is not required for use for the purpose of their undertaking'. The bus and coach output of the Bristol and Lowestoft works was thus available only to the Tilling and Scottish bus groups, although spare parts might be sold to operators already running Bristol vehicles. In practice, the Scottish group was notoriously unwilling to buy Bristols and, to fill its capacity, the factory produced a number of freight chassis for British Road Services. In 1955, the manufacturing side of the company was detached to form Bristol Commercial Vehicles Ltd.

The industry watched with concern to see what the commission would do to implement Sections 63 to 65 of the Transport Act, which dealt with passenger road transport. It did not have long to wait, for at the beginning of 1948 the new London Transport Executive tested the powers of the commission in an unexpected way. W. H. Smith, a small Hertfordshire independent, ran a bus service between Buntingford and Hitchin, through the village of Weston. It was operated on Tuesdays and Saturdays, with a single journey on Thursdays, and Smith does not seem to have considered any further development of it worth while. London Transport would still have had very little chance of obtaining a road service licence to run over any part of this route but, under the Transport Act, the Executive did not need to have road service licences and had, in fact, ceased to hold any. It therefore obtained 'route approval' from the licensing authority (previously the traffic commissioner) for the Metropolitan traffic area and started a daily service between Weston and Hitchin, some of the journeys being very close to those provided by W. H. Smith.

Naturally incensed when he found what was happening and saw his passengers deserting him at Weston, Smith complained to the Passenger Vehicle Operators Association. The PVOA took advice, and while subsequent developments became known as Smith's case, it should be remembered that they were financed by the association on behalf of all its members. In April 1948, application was made to Mr Justice Vaisey in chambers for an interlocutory injunction to prevent the LTE from running the service. It was argued that such powers, if they existed, would enable the LTE to run buses between Liverpool and Manchester. The injunction was refused, although the judge expressed surprise that Smith had no claim for compensation under the Act, whereas compensation would be payable to an operator affected by an area scheme. He gave permission for an application to be made for an early hearing, but this produced the same result. In July 1949, in the Court of Appeal, the Master of the Rolls dismissed the case with costs against the appellant, but his judgment established that the LTE did not, in fact, possess powers to run outside the area defined in the London Passenger Transport Act of 1933.

The PVOA subsequently claimed that the firm action taken on behalf of Smith had prevented similar developments in other areas where the BTC was running buses, and the commission announced that it did not intend to interfere with the structure of the Tilling and Scottish bus groups until they were required to be re-organised in an area scheme. In spite of this, Smith's case was taken to its logical conclusion in March 1951, when the House of Lords rejected his prayer to declare that the London Transport Executive had acted illegally. The disputed service (which was no doubt very necessary) continued to run.

A more serious (even if slightly farcical) development co-incided with the Lords' decision on the Smith case. By this time the BTC had acquired a substantial part of the industry and the operating companies it owned had been faced with the need to increase their fares, like everyone else. Nowhere did this procedure meet with more bitterness and opposition than in South Wales, where the Labour-controlled councils were foremost in objecting to fare increases by operators of all classes. The urban district council of Ebbw Vale took their opposition a stage further than the traffic courts when they asked the High Court to rule that the licensing authority for the South Wales traffic area had no powers to deal with the application made to them by Red & White Services Ltd. The court accepted this plea, holding that the BTC, through owning 'nearly all the shares' in the company, was in effect providing a passenger road transport service which, under Section 65 (I) of the Act, was not subject to the sections of the Road Traffic Act of 1930 relating to road service licences.

This decision threw the industry into confusion. The BTC had stated that it did not intend to interfere with the company structure it had inherited, and the operating companies in the ownership of the commission were treated as if they were subsidiaries of a holding company, their relationship with other operators being governed by the Road Traffic Act as it had been before the BTC acquired them. The decision of the court meant that this state of affairs could no longer continue; the BTC companies could not voluntarily submit to the licensing system if the licensing authorities had no power to grant licences to them. At the same time, the BTC had reached a *modus vivendi* with the rest of the industry which they had no wish to disturb until the area schemes were ready. The King's Bench decision had been given on 5 March 1951; on 16 March the appeal of the BTC was upheld by Lord Justice Cohen, with costs. Such celerity had not been achieved in the case of the unfortunate Mr Smith.

The appeal decision was almost worthy of Gilbert and Sullivan. Lord Justice Cohen argued that while, colloquially, the BTC might be said to be running the bus company, the colloquial construction could not apply to the Transport Act. Legally, Red & White Services Ltd and the British Transport Commission were separate entities, and the BTC was therefore not 'providing' but 'securing the provision' of a service. If this seemed like a play upon words, as it did to many people at the time, it was no comfort to the Ebbw Vale UDC, which was returned to square one in its fight to keep fares low for its electors. On the other hand, it was no doubt extremely convenient for the commission, which was able to continue to concentrate upon the preparation of area schemes, as required under Section 63 of the Act.

On 20 June 1949, a Road Passenger Executive was set up to be responsible for this. It took over and developed the work already done by the Road Transport Executive and discharged the BTC's responsibility under Section 63 of the Transport Act to 'review the passenger road transport services operating in Great Britain with a view to determining the areas with respect to which schemes (should) be prepared and submitted'. K. M. Gwilliam has observed that the Act did not make it clear whether all undertakings in the area of a scheme were to be acquired or not, and that 'the vagueness of the Act in this respect probably represented room for manœuvre in face of any difficulties which might arise rather than any vacillation in principle'. He considers it likely, however, that the BTC envisaged itself as eventually providing all bus and coach services, including private hire, a policy which would be in line with the monopolistic trend of thought in the Tilling Group and elsewhere. The only branch of road passenger transport specifically excepted by the Transport Act was the taxi trade.

The chairman of the Road Passenger Executive was George Cardwell, who had himself been one of the pioneers of the industry. He was appointed manager of the Hartlepool Electric Tramway Ltd by BET in 1907 and was later in charge of Devonport & District Tramways and Aldershot & District Traction. On demobilisation in 1918, he was made manager of the Macclesfield branch of BAT and his genius found full expression in the creation of the later North Western Road Car Company Ltd. In 1930, he accepted from J. F. Heaton an executive appointment with Thomas Tilling Ltd, where he worked closely with Heaton and was the Tilling nominee on the boards of the Tilling & British companies administered by BAT. He moved to the service of the BTC when the Tilling companies were sold and became a full-time member of the original Road Transport Executive in 1948. Cardwell's experience at Macclesfield, where he paid particular attention to ensuring good working relationships with the municipal transport departments in his company's area, well fitted him for the task of launching the area schemes, which the change of policy after 1951 brought to an end. He retired in 1956 and died in 1961. His successor at NWRC, J. W. Womar, who began his training at Hartlepool under Cardwell, describes him as a man of strong personality, but says that 'to those who worked under him he was a real friend who considered them in every way'. Crosland-Taylor found him secretive and somewhat intolerant, although the latter he attributed to the difficulties of working with J. F. Heaton. All in all, 'Uncle' George Cardwell can be said to have left his unmistakable mark on the industry he served so well.

The first steps to extend nationalisation of the bus industry were taken in 1949 and in August of that year the BTC published a *Précis of the proposed Passenger Road Transport Scheme for the Northern Area*. Map 6 shows the boundaries of the area board which was to be set up, and of the territorial bus companies that would have been affected. Writing in *The Economic Journal* in 1951, A. M. Milne pointed out that the title was something of a misnomer, since so much of the Northern traffic area was omitted, and suggested that there had been an earlier draft which

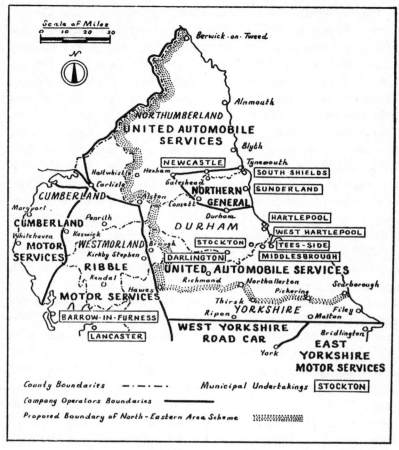

MAP 6.   *Details of the proposed North-Eastern area scheme of 1949*

had included Cumberland and Westmorland. The area of the
proposed Northern Passenger Road Transport Board was to have
been divided into three districts, each under the control of a
district manager, reporting to a general manager, who would
himself have been responsible to the board. Milne inferred that
the powers of the board would be limited by the duties of the
BTC under the Transport Act, for all the activities of the commission were to be regarded as those of one undertaking, from
a financial point of view. It seems likely that the BTC would

have retained control over charging policy and major capital developments, so that the board would have had the same relation to the Road Passenger Executive as that of the railway regions to the Railway Executive.

On the information available, Milne doubted whether the proposed board could do very much to improve co-ordination or to achieve economies in operation that had not been open to the traffic commissioners and the existing operators. He observed that there were large differences in character between different parts of the area and suggested that the likely total of 4,400 vehicles that the board would have run was 'too large a number to be controlled by one administrative unit'. The 214 operators included in the scheme consisted of eight municipal undertakings, three firms with over 100 vehicles, six with between twenty-five and ninety-nine vehicles, and 197 with under twenty-five vehicles. A further twenty-four firms with under twenty-five vehicles were excluded, but the reason for this is not clear, since according to Milne, over 40 per cent of the operators included in the scheme were primarily engaged in private-hire work.

Naturally enough, the eyes of the industry were attracted to these developments, especially as the Road Passenger Executive announced in 1951 that it had further schemes in hand for East Anglia and the South West, both areas where the BTC already had a substantial share in the industry. Indeed, it was asked why the North East had been chosen for the pilot scheme since, although the United Automobile Company was wholly owned by the BTC, the railway interest in BET's Northern General company had not even been on equal terms, BET holding one share more than the LNER. Any supposition that the Labour-controlled municipal councils in the area would support the scheme was unfounded, for municipal pride over-rode political principles and the boroughs were amongst the objectors when a public enquiry was held in 1951.

It was clear, however, that the BTC intended to forward the proposals in spite of the opposition they had met, and the scheme was, in fact, submitted to the Minister of Transport for approval, as required by the Act. It would have been implemented but for a change of government, which was followed by a standstill on acquisitions while the Transport Bill of July 1952 (the Act of 1953) took away from the commission the power of compulsory purchase. The area schemes were quickly forgotten and the Road Passenger Executive itself was wound up in October 1952. The BTC was given power to dispose of its holdings in the bus industry but did not do so to any significant extent. In the meantime, BET had taken direct action to protect its operating subsidiaries, sponsoring the formation of the Omnibus Passengers' Protection Association, which employed full-time organisers in various parts of the country to influence public opinion. When the North-Eastern scheme was announced OPPA, guided by Peter Yorke, concentrated its activities on that area, but after the passage of the 1953 Act the association was allowed to fade away.

After this, the Tilling Group management board was left even more alone to run its business, since the British Transport Commission was faced with growing difficulties on the railways. A new Road Traffic Act in 1960 did no more, so far as the industry was concerned, than gather up the various amendments made after the 1930 Act had been passed, and restate the law as it had come to stand. In December of the same year a White Paper was published which expressed the recommendations of the Select Committee on Nationalised Industries (the Low Report) and of the Special Advisory Group (the unpublished Stedeford Report). This, in turn, lead to the Transport Act of 1962, which abolished the BTC. The London Transport Executive became the London Transport Board, and the Tilling and Scottish bus groups, with the former railway shareholdings in BET companies and in David MacBrayne Ltd, passed to the Transport Holding Company set up by the Act. As a consequence, the settlement of 1928, which gave the railways such a large holding in the bus industry, was at least in form reversed, for there was no financial link between the Railways Board and the territorial operators (except for the joint committees at Sheffield, Halifax and Todmorden). In practice, the railways had never used their stake in the industry to influence its policies and co-ordination of services had rarely taken place at the level of detail. Under the new dispensation,

senior railway officers continued to sit on the boards of those
BET companies that were part-owned by the THC and on those of
certain of the THC's own subsidiaries.

THE INDUSTRY FACES NEW PROBLEMS

The period of expansion and nationalisation that ended thirty
years ago is already taking on the flavour of past history. The
problems the industry faces today are very different from those
that worried busmen in the post-war years when, in spite of
shortages and slow delivery of new vehicles, the demand for bus
and coach transport was as high as it has ever been, either before
or since. Shortage of coaches, in fact, lead many operators to use
buses for long-distance work, although this was clearly unlikely
to encourage passengers to go by coach a second time. With demand running so high, it was easy to forget that a dissatisfied
customer might not come back for more; there was always a
newcomer to take his place.

Fares generally were very low during the post-war boom,
never having been subject to a general increase since they were
fixed by the introduction of the Road Traffic Act. The war years
had seen increased costs, but the industry had made no attempt
to take advantage of the absence of strict licensing procedure.
During the boom years, operators might have been expected to
increase charges in response to increased demand, and it may
be doubted whether they were wise to have refrained from doing
so. For when in the early 'fifties the fuel tax was sharply increased
in successive budgets, both profit margins and reserves were
already under pressure, and before long it was necessary for the
additional burden to be passed on to the passenger. The Eastern
Counties Omnibus Company was the first operator to react with
an emergency application for a 'blanket' increase on all fares,
and it was followed by many others. The amount of work was
unprecedented since the introduction of licensing, for not only
did every schedule have to show the old and new fares side by
side, but the applications met with widespread objections from
local authorities. The licensing authorities also took the oppor-

tunity of probing deeply into the finances of the industry for the first time, a practice which naturally aroused a certain amount of resentment.

In 1950, the fare structure on most routes was still that of the days before 1931, when operators had allowed it to develop out of the circumstances of demand or of competition. Only where exceptionally low fares had been in force because of rate wars had there been any adjustment. The post-war years, however, were marked by the philosophy of a 'charges scheme', such as the BTC was required by the Transport Act to prepare, and the only feasible way of producing it was found to be a rate of so much per mile. In the South Wales traffic area, the chairman, H. J. Thom, was adamant in requiring the reconstruction of fare tables before he would allow any increases, and the concept of 'scientific' charging soon became accepted without question throughout the country. Pressure was brought to bear upon the smaller operators to induce them to conform. On a direct route, this philosophy was logical in an industry that had no internal competition, because it reflected the idea of averaging charges over a wide area that lies at the heart of the Road Traffic Act. In country areas, it had the disadvantage of making the passenger pay for every diversion the bus made to serve some village that he himself had no wish to visit, and this undoubtedly started the fall in rural traffic that has continued ever since.

It was unfortunate that the industry was obliged to increase its fares, and also chose to 'rationalise' them, just when its position in the inland transport market was first being challenged by the private car and motorised bicycle. For the 'rational' fare structures that came in in this way failed to allow for the fact that different people are prepared to pay different rates for what appears to be the same commodity, so that what is an acceptable level of charge in one place may be too high (or too low) in another. The art of evaluating demand is closely related to the art of survival in competition, and it was competition that was facing the industry for the first time since it had become established. Further fare increases now kept pace with inflation, and at the same time alternative outlets for spending power became

P

more and more freely available. Food rationing ended, leading to heavier demands on the housekeeping budget; consumer goods, and particularly durables like furniture and electrical equipment, returned to the shops; travel and entertainment ceased to be the only things you could buy. To some extent this meant no more than demand for transport settling at a lower level, but there were two increasingly popular articles that were far more dangerous to the economy of the public transport industry; the television set and the private car. Both took money that might have gone on travel and both kept on taking it. And while the competition of television was felt by other interests whose reaction would be to encourage people out again—the entertainment and catering industries, and the churches and clubs—the passenger who bought a motor car was a permanent loss.

It seemed to many at this time that the industry had lost ability to compete and that the readiness with which fares were increased to meet each new rise in costs might not have been quite so inescapable if fares had been allowed to rise more slowly over a longer period; in particular if they had found their own level during the boom years before 1951. It also became clear during the 'fifties that many of the rural bus services taken over in the 'thirties by the territorial operators were of marginal value. Their operation demanded either the out-stationing of vehicles, with consequent overhead costs, or heavy empty mileage (equally an overhead) at the beginning and end of the day. In his second book, *State Owned Without Tears*, W. J. Crosland-Taylor observes that some areas are so thin that 'it is far better that they should be provided for by small operators who can employ their cousins and any other relative and run very much cheaper than we do'. This situation was, in fact, faced by Crosville which, in the post-war years, transferred a number of small services in the Llandrindod Wells area to Yeomans' Motors who, in turn, transferred them to yet smaller operators during the 'fifties.

Cross-subsidisation of thin rural or suburban routes demands a monopoly, so that the 'thicker' routes can be made to subsidise the 'thinner' ones. It is, of course, inevitable that some routes will be more profitable than others; this merely reflects the relative levels of supply and demand. Cross-subsidisation only begins when money is actually being lost on the thin services—in other words, when they fail to earn enough to cover their direct costs. If it is practised on any scale, it means that charges must be raised on the better routes above the level that demand would normally justify (or services may be reduced instead). This, in a competitive world, would attract new competition and the protection of operators from competition of this kind (including the protection of the railways) was one of the most vehement arguments put forward for the Road Traffic Act.

One argument against cross-subsidisation is that is was never explicitly authorised (for the Road Traffic Act was not, in fact, canvassed in these terms), and so there is no ethical justification for a transfer payment of this kind. Neither has it ever been a very logical form of transfer, for in many places the profits from city services running through down-town areas have subsidised services in better-off residential areas with a lower density of traffic. This looks like 'robbing the poor to pay the rich', but where the opposite applies a serious weakness arises from the freedom of the 'rich' to opt out of the transaction by deciding to use private transport. This has, of course, happened on a very large scale, so that fares on some services seem to have been set too high in order to enforce the concept of average charge which is enshrined in the Road Traffic Act.

Thus the history of the industry after 1951 was one of increasing financial difficulty. On the whole, city services lost traffic less than rural ones, and inter-urban services in prosperous areas like the South East less than those in the areas of low population density. It has been observed how the settlement of 1942 left Tillings in possession of predominantly rural territory in the thinner areas. In marked contrast were the strongholds of BET, in the populous South East and the industrial Midlands and North, where travel by public transport was highest and the number of cars per household fewest.

Faced with these problems, the Tilling group set about reorganising its companies in order to increase their effective areas. With two exceptions, the former Red & White subsidiaries were

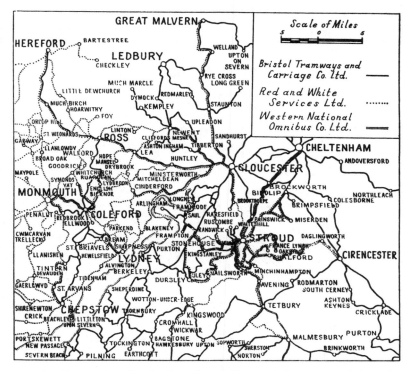

MAP 7. *Bus services in the Stroud and Forest of Dean areas before the route exchanges of 1950-51*

transferred to the appropriate Tilling company, while the Eastern National territory based on Bedford was, on 1 May 1952, handed over to United Counties. In the same year, Eastern National absorbed the Westcliff-on-Sea company and in 1950 and 1951 there was a complex exchange of routes in Gloucestershire, illustrated in Maps 7 and 8. Some of these changes were made possible by the nationalisation of the railways, after which there was no longer any reason to maintain territorial divisions that had been arranged to reflect the areas of the four main lines.

The BET group did not undergo any similar re-arrangement, apart from the winding-up of statutory companies at Chatham and Hastings with the abandonment of their trolleybuses, and a few other minor changes. In this is reflected the continued

MAP 8. *Bus services in the Stroud and Forest of Dean areas after the route exchanges of 1950-51*

existence of outside capital in many BET subsidiaries (as shown in the Appendix), but it does also seem that the board of BET paid rather more attention to the traditions of its operating companies. It would seem also that small units such as Hebble Motor Service remained in separate form partly to serve as a training field for senior managers. In later years there appeared a tendency for neighbouring BET and Tilling companies to work more closely together, especially in South Wales, while the Tilling group had pressed its rationalisation still further, grouping its subsidiaries on a broader territorial basis, with common management and financial arrangements for all the companies in each group. Here it seemed to be somewhat at odds with the policy of the Scottish Bus Group which, in 1961, took the unusual step of increasing the number of its subsidiaries by dividing the Alexander company into three.

NATIONAL DISTURBANCES AND INDUSTRIAL UNREST

Throughout most of its history, the two world wars apart, the motor-bus industry has been relatively free from industrial problems and has pursued its own course. The major interference of the Road Traffic Act in 1930 had the effect of insulating the industry still more from the wider concern of the community. After 1955 there came a series of shocks that drastically affected its prosperity and altered the pattern of its organisation and the balance of its economy.

In June 1955 the industry was faced with an emergency in the form of a widespread rail strike beginning at midnight on Whit Saturday. Bus and coach services were already filled by holiday-makers, for the weather was exceptionally fine, but those who had set out by rail seem to have had no great difficulty in returning by road. Getting to work on succeeding days was more of a problem, especially in south London, where the Southern Region electric trains were stropped (London Transport services were not affected). But the strike had been foreseen; many large firms had booked fleets of coaches in advance and the Post Office and the newspapers had made their own emergency arrangements.

London newspapers were delivered by van over short distances, by coach between 30 and 120 miles, and by air over greater distances. The northern edition of the *Daily Express* was sent from Manchester to Newcastle-upon-Tyne by coach. Because London is exceptional in its dependence upon suburban railways, provincial operators were called in to help during the week and the scale of their activities is illustrated by the hiring requirements of Barclays Bank, which needed ninety-three coaches. Generally the hirer would contract with one operator, who would then sub-contract what he could not himself provide.

Coaches were used to replace some specific rail services such as the ocean liner 'specials', but the continuing loss incurred by the railways was more serious than the short-term effects of the strike. London Coastal Coaches found that long queues were forming, not only for immediate travel but equally for advance bookings for holiday journeys. Although the buses and coaches benefited to some extent in this way, it is likely that the wider effect of the strike in encouraging the use of cars for personal travel did far more harm than good.

Towards the end of 1956 the Suez Expedition brought about cuts in the supply of fuel, perhaps not entirely unwelcome to the industry for they justified the suspension of journeys that had become uneconomic because of shrinking demand. Operators were required by the traffic commissioners to withdraw 10 per cent of their vehicle mileage during the emergency, and not all of this was subsequently re-instated. The increase in the price of fuel under the Hydrocarbons Act was more serious, although it was found possible to give a rebate to operators of rural services. On the whole, however, the industry lost quite as much as it gained out of the incident, for the uncertainty of its early days discouraged travel, while the lengthy period during which restrictions still applied after the emergency harmed the good-will of the industry.

Most service cuts had been re-instated (if at all) by the late spring of 1957, but this time of troubles had another shock in store. In July, the Transport & General Workers' Union called a strike which demonstrated how far union organisation and membership had been expanded. The dispute arose out of a claim for increased wages, but the union leaders did not seem anxious to make use of the negotiating machinery, and the subsequent arbitration gave the men an increase of 11s a week. The dispute lay between the TGWU and those companies (mainly the territorial ones) that were members of the National Council; it thus excluded London Transport busmen and the municipal undertakings as well as the independents. (The independents, to whose type of trading the national agreement is ill-suited, have usually paid wages roughly in line with the territorial companies throughout the post-war period; some slightly more and a few rather less in terms of take-home pay). With the threat of strike action spreading, many independents who had their own agreements with the union paid increased wages at once; others let it be known that they would pass on an equivalent rise when the outcome of the dispute was known. In this way they were able to continue to run their own services, although no emergency services were operated along strike-bound routes, as they had been in 1937.

The strike passed off relatively peacefully, being most serious in its social consequences in those parts of the country where the territorial companies had obtained a monopoly. What was noticeable in the rural areas was the extent to which market day produced the same crowds as if there had been no strike; country people had not allowed the absence of buses to interfere with their habits and the widespread custom of giving lifts that enables remote villages to exist with a minimum of bus services came into its own. It was, in fact, extended, for the government, to the alarm of the industry, authorised motorists to offer 'free lifts' even where they had no insurance to cover them. This was felt by operators to be unnecessary and an invitation to motorists to extend the practice of lift-giving against some form of payment which, although illegal, had spread rapidly as bus fares had risen.

There was, however, genuine hardship on account of the strike and in urban areas served exclusively by territorial companies large numbers of people were affected by it. But it proved, as the General Strike had proved in 1926, that no one means of transport is essential, and it is hard to see that it did anything but lasting harm to the industry as a source of employment. In the annual report of BET, H. C. Drayton regretted the end of an era of good relationships between staff and management in the industry, and while it is easy to scoff at such remarks, it is true that times have changed radically since the early days of the industry. It is perhaps inevitable that the rise of territorial organisation, with the complementary development of powerful but remote unions, should have destroyed the sense of partnership that was typical of the pioneer days. There have been examples of unscrupulous management in the industry, but they have always been the exception and few proprietors have succeeded in making their fortunes. That the change has been for the worse would no doubt be admitted by both sides, but it is a consequence of the increased scale of operation and not of any tendency towards exploitation. And little seems to have been done to replace the 'working agreement' between master and men that makes a personal business of stable society with something better suited to the more impersonal company structure that has everywhere taken its place. Even more serious is the apparent lack of any real wish to do so on the part of either company or union management, for the negotiating machinery that has been set up has frequently left the ordinary busman with a genuine if unrealised sense of insecurity.

The 1957 strike was followed a year later by an official strike amongst employees of London Transport, which lasted from 5 May to 20 June 1958. Here there was some operation by private firms in the early days of the strike, one operator from Berkshire running for a few days between Chiswick and Hyde Park Corner, while the People's League for the Defence of Freedom chartered a number of vehicles and obtained short-period licences for various routes at a flat fare of sixpence. The tube and suburban railways not being affected by the strike, London was far from being paralysed, although travelling in certain parts of the city became extremely difficult.

There has been increasing unrest in the industry since the 1957 and 1958 strikes and unofficial stoppages have become frequent. This is as true of the municipal undertakings as it is of the company ones and it is directed at least in part at the TGWU itself. In April 1964, Glasgow busmen struck, against the advice of local officials of the TGWU, ostensibly because of dissatisfaction with new schedules which had been agreed by the union. A staff turnover of almost 50 per cent indicates that the corporation was not a popular employer (though this reflects also the difficulty of employers in finding staff prepared to work the unattractive hours that public transport requires). But the real animus in the minds of the strikers, and the cause of their solidarity, arose from their relationship with the officials of their own union. The dispute saw a strike-breaking bus leave Parkhead Garage with a TGWU branch secretary at the wheel and ten policemen on board to protect him from his own members. The strike was effectively organised and notable for a complete absence of any violence; it was over 80 per cent complete (apart from workers who did not take part, a few buses were authorised by the strikers to run to hospitals). It was reported in the Scottish press, but hardly at all in any of the London daily papers. It was supported by the ILP and the Scottish Committee of One Hundred, and while very much a spontaneous development, genuinely popular amongst the rank and file, it carried with it a political flavour. The *Scottish Daily Express* seems to have been the only paper to detect any Communist element but, judging by the pamphlet produced afterwards by *Solidarity*, the anarchist organisation, its flavour seems to have been nearer to the syndicalism that lay behind the London strike of 1937.

Alongside the industrial unrest of recent years has been the growing shortage of staff, which has affected the territorial companies most of all. Platform work in the industry, in all its branches, implies working when others are idle and the frequent need to accept a 'split shift', with a period off duty between turns on the road. The trade unions negotiated terms of employment that provided additional pay for weekend, overtime and split-shift working, but payment may not be enough, especially in a period of full employment when jobs with more orthodox hours are easy to come by. The reduction in the number of independent operators running bus services has not helped here, for many of them made use of family or part-time labour, which has had to be replaced with staff on full union rates. The situation became so serious that the closure of the Oxford to Cambridge railway was held up for many months because the United Counties Omnibus Company was unable to find sufficient staff to work the replacement bus services.

THE AGE OF UNCERTAINTY

That all was not well with the industry quickly became apparent when the original round of fare increases in 1951 was followed by a seemingly never-ending sequence. First to feel the consequent loss of traffic were the bus services, and the 'fifties saw a growing tendency for small operators to sell their businesses. In view of the pending nationalisation, the territorial companies bought few of them at first, and when the future of the BTC became uncertain after the change of government in 1951, with denationalisation constantly expected, it was given out that the Tilling and Scottish companies would not buy at all. As the decade passed, more and more purchases were in fact made and the BET companies also returned to the market, so that bus operation came more and more into the hands of the territorial companies.

Coach work, on the other hand, remained buoyant and many new excursion licences were granted. Some of these were for extended tours at home and abroad but the notable development was the replacement of out-and-home seaside trips by new types of tour. The age of 'stately homes' was beginning, and in many places there seemed to be an insatiable demand for day tours to places of interest all over the country. Many of these demanded a second driver if the operation was to be within the limitation of working hours, but during the holiday weeks in many industrial towns passengers were content to reach home at midnight and be ready for a new tour starting next day at six or seven in the morning. Express coach services, while still retaining more trade than the buses, entered a period of decline in comparison with the post-war boom, although still well above pre-war levels of traffic.

With the building of the motorways, a further change appeared. The buses continued to lose traffic, particularly in the evenings and at weekends, and the day excursion trade shrank. Extended tours have become very much part of the travel industry, causing difficulties in recent attempts to regulate the travel agency trade, and today some of the larger agencies are operating Continental tours which compare with the practice of the travel firms rather than with the coach tours of the past; they are flying their passengers direct to the Continent instead of selling the traditional throughout journey with the same coach and driver. At the same time, the express services in the period after 1960 started to carry more passengers and more new services were opened than at any time since the ending of the postwar boom. British Rail's reaction was the untraditional one of selling faster services harder at more competitive fares, and the process has continued.

Increasing difficulties arising from the contracting demand for bus services have brought the industry before the public eye over the past thirty years to a greater degree than at any previous period of its history. The first of a series of enquiries was appointed in 1952, under the chairmanship of G. A. Thesiger, QC, (later Sir Gerald Thesiger) to report on the licensing of road passenger services. The Thesiger Report reviewed the working of the Road Traffic Act and found that it functioned extremely well; it was thus generally quoted as a justification of the system. The committee had not, however, interpreted its terms of reference as calling for a reconsideration of the aims and purposes of the Road Traffic Act, and thus failed to come to grips with the real problems of the industry. Its recommendations chiefly concerned minor matters and it has had little lasting impact on the transport problem.

The Thesiger Report was followed two years later, in 1955, by the report of the Chambers Committee on London Transport. This gave general approval of the way the London Transport Executive had carried on its business, but made it plain that certain measures were necessary if the LTE were to cease to run in deficit. Most of these were recognised to involve 'decisions and heavy capital expenditure by authorities other than the LTE', but maintenance costs were stated to be too high.

Throughout the period, however, it has been the rural transport problem that has been growing in importance. The concentration of private cars in suburban areas is offset by the lower density of population in the country, so that in some rural counties there is almost one car for every second family. Country people are also more prone to give lifts and they have never been dependent upon public transport in quite the same way as townspeople; the once weekly market bus has remained 'adequate' in many villages, while private coaches have catered for workers and schoolchildren. The early post-war years saw a general expansion of rural bus services, so that the countryside came to be better served than at any time in our history, but at the same time the nature of country life was beginning to change. Increasingly, the basic conveniences of urban life—electricity supply above all—have become available in country districts and dependable public transport is not unreasonably expected to be among them. Unfortunately, the demand for public transport has been falling at the same time and the licensing system, which was designed to put a brake upon the furious expansion of the 'twenties, hindered rather than helped the industry in adapting itself to the changes that are taking place.

The demand for rural bus services varies considerably between different areas. This, in part, reflects the pattern of settlement, as Maps 9 and 10 illustrate, but there is always a certain element of chance in the level of service that any particular village may receive. If it is the place from which a small operator works or has worked, it is likely to be far better served than otherwise might be the case. From a study of the facilities available, it would be difficult to arrive at any objective criteria as to what is an 'adequate' level of service in the countryside.

One solution that was proposed, and was expected by everyone outside the industry to deal with the rural problem, was the amendment of the regulations to permit twelve- and fourteen-seater 'minibuses' to be used as public service vehicles. The Ministry of Transport celebrated this in 1956 by publishing a piece of romantic literature called *Village Bus*, which contained a charming if idealised picture of the country cousins. (It contained a list of the traffic commissioners with their areas, of the Transport Users Consultative Committees, and of the bus companies owned by the British Transport Commission; the latter ignored more than 50 per cent of the industry).

Most busmen had serious doubts about the usefulness of the minibus, which they saw as a danger rather than an asset. In practice, their fears seemed justified, for the regular service operator found almost no use for so small a vehicle. There

MAP 9

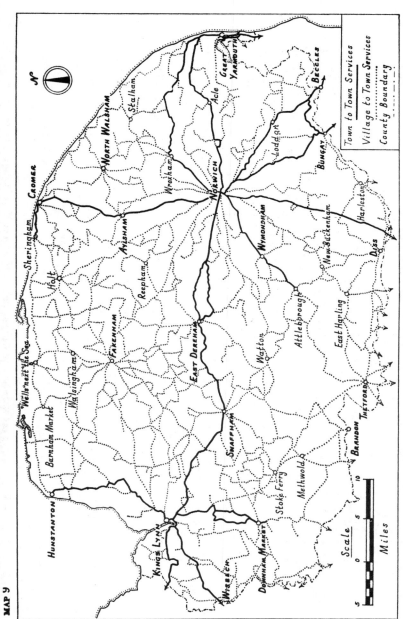

Bus services in Norfolk (above) and Kent (below), illustrating differences in development arising from different patterns of settlement.

MAP 10

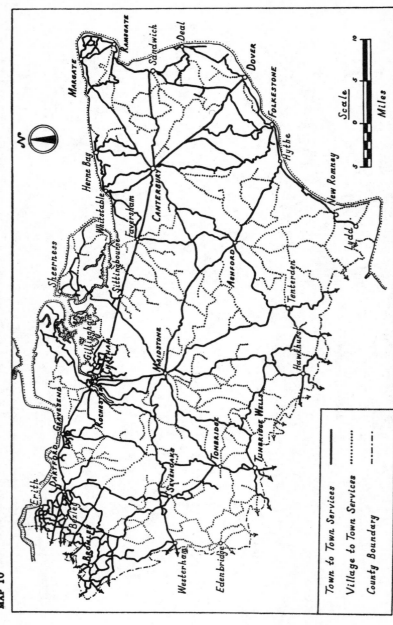

Both maps are to the same scale and show town to town and village to town services

were few routes that did not produce about thirty passengers at least once or twice a week, and at reasonable fares a service that does not is unlikely to be viable at all. A larger bus had therefore to be available, and (since the saving on the smaller one was not great) it might just as well be used all the time, especially since the traffic commissioners were usually prepared to dispense with the necessity of a conductor. The small saving reflects the high proportion of bus costs that are incurred in fuel and wage payments, and the efficiency of the diesel engine is such that it may burn little more fuel than the minibus, though the driver's wages will be the same. On the other hand, the minibuses actually lowered private-hire rates, since with their appearance the prospective customer, used to the illegal practice of a quotation expressed 'per seat', was able to drive a harder bargain for the smaller party bookings. The minibus was however taken up by private individuals, and was often used for regular journeys of very doubtful legality – indeed, it was ironic to see children being driven to private schools in vehicles that totally lacked the safety controls applied to buses taking other children to state schools, for no charge.

In 1959, the Minister of Transport instituted an enquiry into the rural problem, and the committee, chaired by Professor D. T. Jack, reported in 1961. In the same year the Highland Transport Enquiry published a report on bus services in the Highlands and Islands, and the two documents were intended to be taken together. The Jack Committee made a number of detailed recommendations for alleviating the problem, including the use of school contract buses and the carriage of a few fare-paying passengers on GPO vehicles, but both enquiries concluded that direct subsidy in individual cases, each case being considered on its merits, was the only continuing solution. A further enquiry carried out by the Council for Wales and Monmouthshire agreed with this, and the only significant difference between the three reports turned upon the method of determining and administering the subsidies.

Apart from a scheme for the remission of fuel tax in respect of bus mileage, no arrangements were made for the general provision of subsidy. In 1963 the Ministry of Transport carried out a detailed examination of the transport problem in six areas; three in England, two in Scotland and one in central Wales. A report followed, and then in 1964 a further investigation was mounted in four areas, local enquiry teams being appointed, including representatives of local authorities, bus operators, and local voluntary organisations, each with an independent chairman. These teams sponsored local adjustments and arranged for experimental services to be introduced under guarantee from the Ministry of Transport, the local authority or, in one case, from the local chamber of trade. Very few of these proved viable and, since the guarantees were for a limited period, most of the new services ceased after a few months' operation at most. They did nothing to assist the operators, large and small, in other parts of the country, who had been given to understand that the recommendations of the Jack Committee would be implemented in some form, and who have continued to run many services of very doubtful financial worth. On the other hand, the Ministry's vacillation hardly encouraged the general practice of subsidy by local chambers of trade, which in some places lead to the development of new routes rather than the adjustment of existing ones.

CHAPTER TEN

THE STATE ADVANCES –
AND RETREATS

DESPITE the various enactments of successive governments in this century, the bus industry remained largely non-political until its problems became increasingly severe in the 1960s. Managers had been subject to little interference, and the state-owned companies had been run on commercial lines, their policies inherited very often from the Tilling Group and its traditions. Councillors seldom saw their bus undertakings as being anything other than municipal trading, and while some received rate support, examples of heavy subsidy were rare. Above all, land-use and transportation planning was everywhere conducted in a separate department of the local authority, with little or no contact between planners and bus managers. After 1965, all this was to undergo a major change.

PUBLIC OWNERSHIP AND PLANNING

With the return of a Labour government in 1964 it was widely expected that state intervention would increase, but it was not until Harold Wilson had been returned with an enlarged majority that he appointed Barbara Castle as Minister of Transport, to many people's surprise. Here, it was felt, was a sign that action would begin.

The new Minister took her job far more seriously than some of her predecessors, and within two years there appeared three White Papers, setting out her conclusions and recommendations. The first of these, *Transport Policy* (1966), forecast the expected intervention, while the following year saw *Railway Policy* and—more to our concern—*Public Transport and Traffic*. Each of them showed the extent to which the Minister had studied the industry, and her willingness to consider new solutions to old problems. In particular, the railway paper embraced the principles first outlined in the Low Report of 1960, giving management the overall duty to 'be commercial', and let the elected representatives decide where subsidy should be applied. While this was abandoned under the Railways Act of 1974 (to conform with EEC rules), it was to emerge once more in the Transport Act of 1985. The public transport paper envisaged the formation of state-owned holding company structure for provincial bus operations, and before this had been enacted in 1968 the news broke (in November 1967) that the British Electric Traction Company had agreed to sell its British bus interests to the Transport Holding Company, pending the new dispensation. Though many commentators purported to be surprised at this apparent volte-face, there can be little doubt that the BET directors foresaw the economic problems that awaited the industry, from which they thus protected their shareholders.

The Transport Act 1968 set up two state-owned bodies, one for Scotland and the other for the rest of Great Britain. In Scotland the railways had considerable shipping interests, and these, along with the Scottish Omnibuses group, were transferred to the Scottish Transport Group. The buses, however, were placed in the care of an STG subsidiary, the Scottish Bus Group. Rumour had it that the second corporation was to have been called the National Bus Group, but that the initials were unfortunate, so that National Bus Company was chosen instead. Be that as it may, the NBC now came to be, through its subsidiaries, the dominant provincial operator south of the Border, outwith the activities of the municipal sector; the independent firms being predominantly engaged in the coaching trade.

Barbara Castle's White Paper also faced the issue of the division between land-use/transportation planning and the management of public transport, especially in urban conditions, and proposed the formation of Conurbation Transport Authorities to bring the two functions together. These were recognised as being *ad hoc* bodies, pending the local government reform that was then being discussed, but the Minister felt that the problem was too urgent to be left (it was to be another six years before local government changes were actually made). By the time the Transport Bill was published, these had become Passenger Transport Authorities, each of them responsible for its Passenger Transport Executive, and remarkably wide powers had been given to the PTA/PTE administrators.

The PTEs were intended to be operators, and were to acquire all the existing municipal bus undertakings within the area of the PTA. (This was defended by Richard Marsh, who succeeded Barbara Castle in 1968, on the specious argument that the multitude of small municipal undertakings in, for exampe, Greater Manchester, meant that passengers had to change buses at their boundaries; whereas in fact these operators all worked joint cross-boundary services, many shared with local NBC companies.) The PTAs were to have in effect the powers of the Traffic Commissioners to licence services in their areas, thereby acting as 'judge and jury in their own case' should the PTE object; but these clauses were never activated. They were however enabled to enter into agreements with other operators, including British Rail, for the provision of services. The PTEs were given singularly wide trading powers, ranging as far as the sale of ice-cream.

The idea of these new authorities had not been welcomed by the industry. In August 1967 the trade paper *Motor Transport* recorded the development of opposition orchestrated through a campaign called VOICE, promoted by the Passenger Vehicle Operators' Independent's Committee, which seems to have extended its activities beyond the members of the Passenger Vehicle Operators' Association (PVOA). Its regional co-ordinating committees certainly included directors of BET companies (this was prior to the agreement of BET to sell its bus undertakings to the state), as well as owners of substantial coaching businesses. It is understandable that committees should have been set up for Liverpool and Manchester, but more interesting perhaps that there should have been a meeting of 60 operator's representatives held at Canterbury that month, which was addressed by Denis Quin, then national secretary of the PVOA, and later to become Director-General of the Bus and Coach Council. But VOICE must have lost its impetus with the decision of the BET board to sell its bus subsidiaries, so that there is in hindsight an irony in *Motor Transport's* headline: 'VOICE gets louder'. No attempt to recruit support from the general public, as in the case of the Omnibus Passengers' Protection Association fifteen years before, seems to have been made, and all that remains is a pervading odour of cynicism.

The first PTAs to be set up under the Act covered Merseyside, South-East Lancashire & North-East Cheshire (SELNEC), Tyneside and the West Midlands. Their boundaries conformed generally to those of the conurbations, whether or not these co-incided with local government boundaries, and the members of the PTA were persons nominated by the local authorities concerned, together with others appointed by the Ministers. They had power to precept upon these authorities for funds beyond their direct revenue. Each PTE was the responsibility of a Director General appointed by the PTA.

Amongst other things, the Act also provided for subsidy to bus operators, directly from central and local government; by way of a rebate on fuel tax; and through the New Bus Grant. The latter was used to achieve a truly substantial change in the marketing of bus services: by specifying the type of bus that could attract a grant, and making this—among other things—a front entrance vehicle, the Ministry triggered off the conversion of most bus operation to driver-only, making the traditional bus conductor (or, in the north-west, guard) an endangered species. (There were 42,000 in 1972, and just under 11,000 ten years later.) The new buses had to have the engine removed from its traditional place (where the horse would have been) and this usually meant it was at the rear, leading to maintenance problems until bus engineers came to terms with the new arrangement.

But the Act had yet another change for the industry to live with. A combination of dissatisfaction with the provisions of the 1930 licensing system and the requirements of EEC law brought about the introduction of an Operator's Licence, for both freight and passenger road transport. The need for it was demonstrated by the falling standards that became apparent in the 1960s and 1970s, which the vehicle licensing system of 1930 was inadequate to handle. Serious weaknesses in maintenance were not limited to the private sector; Midland Red and Cardiff Corporation were among the public sector operators to fall from grace during these years. In subsequent years the O-Licence was to be developed as an effective means of securing improved standards, as will be seen.

THE PATTERNS CHANGE

With vesting days for the NBC, the SBG and the Passenger Transport Executives, the British bus map started a process of change that was to continue longer than many people might expect. The NBC was set up on 1 January 1969, but the process of integration of BET and Tilling Group interests had already begun, so that it was on 5 January that the United Automobile services in Carlisle were taken over by Ribble. There followed a period in which companies with long-established territories were merged, or just disappeared, little attention being paid to the customer loyalty that they should have built up. Old-established liveries went, along with distinctive styles of fleet name, and many commentators suggested that rationalisation was being pursued at the cost of other values that the industry could ill afford to lose. It was as if tidy-mindedness had come to be the supreme good.

Change was less rapid in Scotland, though in July 1969 the STG acquired the boats, lorries and buses of MacBraynes; the buses passing to the Bus Group, where the services went to its operating companies. But in the south the NBC continued the policy of purchase that had marked its predecessors ever since 1931, and several of the more substantial independents bowed out at this time—notably Birch Brothers, who withdrew their bus services in the autumn of 1969, and 'King Alfred' of Winchester, who sold to the Hants & Dorset company in April 1973. NBC rationalisation included the final re-organisation of South Wales, to leave only South Wales Transport and a merger of Red & White and Western Welsh, renamed National Welsh; a consummation finally achieved on 26 April 1978. Here an attempt was made to build upon nationalist sentiment, with a Welsh language fleet name on the offside of the buses – De Cymru for SWT and Cymru Cenedlaethol for National Welsh.

The need for some companies to exist now disappeared, because no longer were Tilling and BET subsidiaries in separate camps. It was because of this that the complex pattern of ownership in south Wales could be tidied up, and Durham District Services, whose genesis we saw in Chapter 9, was wound up as part of the same process.

Not all of the rationalisation at this time proved successful. As early as 1967 the West Yorkshire company had acquired the business of Ledgards with whom they had operated many joint services; much of the demand seemed to disappear with the departure of Ledgard's buses from the scene. BET had bought Neath & Cardiff Luxury Coaches in 1953, with a long-established limited stop service between Cardiff and Swansea, and had kept the 'Brown Bombers' in separate management; on 1 January 1971 it was merged, along with United Welsh and Thomas Bros., into South Wales Transport, and local opinion was highly critical of the change. In the West Midlands, National Travel acquired two substantial coach operators, Everalls of Wolverhampton and Worthingtons of Birmingham, each of which had a high reputation for customer care, and local newspapers came to carry stories that described a sad falling-off in standards, so that the payment for the goodwill in the two firms seemed to have been squandered.

Re-organisations following from the establishment of the PTEs on 1 April 1969 were no less momentous. Tyneside was formed out of only two undertakings, Newcastle and South Shields, but its area was served by NBC companies, none of which it eventually acquired. Instead, it entered into agreements whereby they operated in accordance with PTE policy, and repainted their vehicles in PTE livery, while retaining their own fleet names. On Merseyside the new executive acquired the Liverpool, Birkenhead and Wallasey fleets, and, perhaps because of a long tradition of agreement with the NBC companies, Crosville and Ribble integrated their services while leaving their livery and management unaffected. Initially the same policy was followed in the West Midlands, where the NBC subsidiary Midland Red had a dense network of services in the Black Country as well as providing for the needs of Solihull and Sutton Coldfield. The West Midlands PTE also ran into a certain amount of difficulty in seeking to integrate the management of its acquired undertakings, at Birmingham, Walsall, West Bromwich and Wolverhampton; its choice of a livery remarkably similar to that of Birmingham City Transport may not have helped matters.

The SELNEC PTE had the biggest problem of integration, for it came into being with no less than eleven contributory fleets—those of Bolton, Bury, Manchester, Oldham, Rochdale, Salford, Stockport, Ashton-under-Lyne, Leigh, Ramsbottom and the Stalybridge, Hyde, Mossley & Dukinfield joint board. In addition, its area included services of three NBC companies, Crosville, North Western and Ribble; one large independent, Lancashire United; and a long-established family business with a busy stage service into central Manchester. The PTE began by setting up three operating subsidiaries (in company form), and it then negotiated the takeover of the NBC services (this lead to North Western giving up stage service operation in January 1972, its remaining routes being transferred to Crosville and Trent). In due course Lancashire United lost its independence, but Maynes, the smaller firm, held out with a co-ordinating agreement.

The benefits of such mergers had been discussed earlier, when in 1967 the councils of Leigh, Preston, St Helens, Warrington, Widnes and Wigan had discussed the possibility of some form of link between themselves (all bus operators) and with Crosville, Ribble, North Western and Lancashire United. The *Omnibus Magazine,* commenting on this, observed that the smaller municipal fleets tended to have lower costs—working expenses per bus mile (in old pence) were 38.85d at Ramsbottom, with twelve vehicles, compared with 42.247d in the case of mighty Manchester. In 1974 the chairman of the West Midland traffic commissioners went on record to question whether the public had benefited by the formation of the local PTE. Yet as early as 1962 research was questioning the assumption that there are unending benefits of larger scale in bus transport, suggesting that the Act of 1986 had lead to an attack of giantism.

The Transport Act of 1968 had the further effect of ending the direct connection between the railways and the major bus operators. The great promise of co-ordination that was seen to follow from the bus operating powers gained by the four main lines in 1929, and by the settlement with Tilling & British, had produced little more than a flow of cash into railway accounts. The link was finally broken when the joint omnibus committees at Halifax, Huddersfield, Sheffield and Todmorden ceased to exist on 1 January 1969, just forty years after the first JOC had been set up at Sheffield.

But the process of change from above was far from ended. Now, after much debate, the promised reform of local government took shape, and in 1972 the Local Government Act redrew boundaries (interfering with ancient institutions), and created a set of Metropolitan Counties, whose councils, it declared, were to be Passenger Transport Authorities for the purposes of the Transport Act 1968. In the 'shire counties' the Act required the appointment of a co-ordinating officer, and obliged bus operators and British Rail to co-operate with each other and with him in achieving the mystical goal of co-ordination; each type of council was to administer public funds by way of subsidy to operators. For the future, county councils were to prepare for the Minister 'Transport Policies and Programmes', containing a five-year forward plan for their overall transport responsibilities and a submission for the funding necessary for one year.

In this the government was acting within a broad (if temporary) consensus, which assumed that intervention in public transport, and the use of subsidy, could offset the ever-increasing demands of highway engineering for both capital and maintenance expenditure. The so-called 'balanced approach' to the growth of car traffic and the burden it placed on public finance had been examined by the House of Commons Expenditure Committee in a Report, *Urban Transport Planning*, that appeared in 1972 and was partially accepted by the government (by now Conservative again). Its principal exponent was to be the new South Yorkshire

County Council.

The Local Government Act came into force on 1 April 1974, with a series of consequences for public transport that do not seem to have been seriously considered. Six years previously the Teesside Council had been formed, bringing together in the process the bus undertakings of Middlesbrough, Stockton and the Teesside Railless Transport Board (initially a trolleybus operator). Such adventitious groups were extended by the formation of the metropolitan counties, whose boundaries were drawn for political purposes, with little if any thought of their transport implications. Thus the West Midlands PTE acquired Coventry Corporation Transport, and Merseyside gained Southport, even though there was little logic in these developments from the operators' point of view. SELNEC changed little, save for becoming Greater Manchester PTE, and winding up its wholly-owned subsidiaries, but Tyne and Wear meant that a great stretch of green fields was added to the PTE along with the municipal undertaking at Sunderland.

Two entirely new PTAS were created by the Act, with the formation of metropolitan counties in south and west Yorkshire. Each duly acquired the municipal undertakings to form its PTE; in South Yorkshire they were Sheffield, Rotherham and Doncaster, while West Yorkshire absorbed the fleets of Leeds, Bradford, Halifax, Huddersfield and Todmorden. The new PTEs made no move to acquire NBC operations in their areas (although they both took over some local independent firms). SYPTE was to develop the most radical charging policy of any local authority undertaking, at very considerable cost in subsidy, but WYPTE did not at first reach the headlines. Later its METRO logo and style, and its co-ordination agreement with British Rail, showed that it was developing a recognisable identity of its own.

In 1972, acting under the 1968 Transport Act, the government set up a PTA/PTE for Greater Glasgow, which acquired the Corporation's transport undertaking along with powers of co-ordination over a wider area. This was followed by the Local Government (Scotland) Act, 1973, which produced a more radical (and longer-lasting) revision of the Scottish system than was to come from its English equivalent. The new Regional councils were given the bus operating powers of the cities that had previously possessed them (namely Edinburgh, Dundee and Aberdeen), but only within the former municipal boundaries; again it is possible to speculate how far the Act was drafted with transport issues in mind. (In due course a further tidying-up converted the Greater Glasgow PTE into the Strathclyde PTE, in December 1980.)

Welsh local government reform had fewer dramatic effects, there being no metropolitan county in South Wales, as had been expected. Some local authorities changed their names; Aberdare became Cynon Valley, a new authority called Rhymney Valley absorbed the fleets of Caerphilly, Gelligaer and the Bedwas & Machen UDC, and Pontypridd became Taff-Ely, while the two councils that had formed the West Monmouthshire joint board became one, with the name of Islwyn. In the north, Colwyn Bay, the smallest municipal operator of all, with only a seasonal activity, became plain Colwyn, while Llandudno became Aberconwy.

Before the re-organisation of local government, one further change took place when the West Midlands PTE acquired, by negotiation, the Midland Red services lying in its area, together with several depots and a number of vehicles. Thus there ended an area agreement of some 60 years standing, but it was not without problems, for there were repercussions within the work force, which lead to a strike over conditions and pay. Midland Red in turn acquired two quite substantial independents to the north of the Black Country, Harper Brothers of Heath Hayes and the Green Bus Service of Rugeley, not without public discontent in each case.

It is doubtful how far the intentions of the White Paper *Public Transport and Traffic* concerning the co-ordination of public transport with land-use and transportation planning were ever seriously pursued. Barbara Castle's conurbation transport authorities became in effect the transport committees of the new metropolitan county councils, insulated from the planners by the structure of local government. Here and there, though, attempts were made to bring bus operation into the broader process, starting as early as 1967, when, almost adventitiously, Reading Corporation discovered the advantages of the contra-flow bus lane. More notable examples were the 'zone and collar' scheme that was never seriously developed at Nottingham, due to changes in political control of the council—it was meant to be an example of the balanced approach, discouraging car use and providing a public transport alternative. Only in the New Town of Runcorn has there been a large-scale development of bus-only roads (although they exist elsewhere, in Redditch for example). But the decision to make Milton Keynes a car-based city, when a high-tech system was found too expensive, proved to be as problematic for the local bus operator, United Counties, as had been foreseen at the time.

THE POLITICS OF LONDON'S TRANSPORT

While Paris and Buenos Aires play a bigger part in the political life of France and Argentina than London does in that of the United Kingdom, successive governments throughout the twentieth century have paid particular attention to the transport problems of the metropolis. One has only to think of the length of time taken by the joint select committee of both Houses in considering the London Transport Bill introduced by Herbert Morrison, but only enacted—some three years later—in 1933.

Under the Transport Act of 1962, which abolished the British Transport Commission and transferred the Tilling and Scottish bus groups to the new Transport Holding Company, the erstwhile London Transport Executive became the London Transport Board; an ownership and managerial entity in its own right. Alec Valentine (later Sir Alec) was chairman at this time, a former protegé of Frank Pick, but in 1965 he was succeeded by Maurice Holmes (later Sir Maurice). Holmes was a barrister, who had been chairman of the Tilling group, and had earlier in his career been associated with the management of Hicks Bros. Ltd., a sizeable Essex independent bus firm, sold to the BTC in 1950. Two years later, Barbara Castle persuaded a slightly reluctant Greater

London Council, at that time controlled by the Conservatives, led by Sir Desmond Plummer, to accept responsibility for the London board, subject to the government writing off a significant element of debt. Thus the London Transport Board became once again the London Transport Executive, though this time with a management board of its own.

The transfer was effected by the Transport (London) Act of 1969, carried through by Richard Marsh, who was later to become chairman of the British Railways Board, and it became effective on 1 January 1970. Holmes, his period of office expired, was not renewed as chairman and the GLC appointed Sir Richard Way, whose background was in the Civil Service. Though personally successful, his period of office (which ended in 1974) was marked by troubles on the bus operating side, with growing congestion due to increased car usage. The LTE approach to driver-only operation produced a pained amusement among provincial operators, whose automatic ticket equipment was generally simple and robust, making boarding times as short as possible: the board equipped its vehicles with turnstiles more reminiscent of the entrance to an underground station, which presented severe problems to passengers joining the bus with shopping bags, push-chairs and toddlers in tow.

Neither could the GLC refrain from meddling with the finances of the board, whether under Plummer's control or under that of the Labour administration which took office in 1973. At the same time the board experienced a severe shortage of buses and spares, and found it necessary to dispose of large numbers of single-deck buses, bought for one-man operation, since it concluded that they were not suited to the conditions of metropolitan traffic—a conclusion that again caused some raised eyebrows among provincial operators. Price freezes and subsequent sharp increases, and a growing deficit (to which a free off-peak travel scheme for pensioners contributed) marked the three years in office of the chairman, Sir Kenneth Robinson, who had been a Minister in Harold Wilson's government, and subsequently a staff manager in the British Steel Corporation. It will be noted that the period of office of the chairmen was reducing with each new appointment.

The Conservatives returned to power at the County Hall in 1977, led now by Horace Cutler. In the same year the Select Committee on Nationalised Industries recommended the government (now Labour once more) to confer upon the GLC the powers and duties of a Passenger Transport Authority under the 1968 Act, and to make London Transport its Passenger Transport Executive, thereby gaining the machinery for co-ordinating LT and BR railway services in the county. But this the government refused to do. Robinson and Cutler could not see eye to eye, and the chairman was replaced in 1978 by Ralph Bennett, who had been appointed deputy chairman in 1971, after a successful career running buses in Manchester.

Bennett's period of office was to be even shorter—only two years—and it was marked by the onset of an extraordinary episode, that did a great deal to undermine the standing of the board and the morale of its managers and staff. Those (of whom the present author is one) who have experienced the hospitality of the board at 55 Broadway will have realised that Lord Ashfield set out to emulate the standards of the most opulent companies of the day—and they will do well to recall that, in doing so, Ashfield was acting as the chairman of a commercial undertaking.

Leslie Chapman, a 'rebel civil servant', had published a book called *Your Disobedient Servant*, which attracted Horace Cutler's attention. Cutler sent Chapman a telegram—itself an action properly described as melodramatic, not least in that it was sent to Chapman's publishers—and this said, in faintly Churchillian terms, 'Must see you urgently about matter of great importance'. Chapman, after some doubts, accepted Cutler's offer of a part-time appointment to the board, for two years beginning early in 1979.

Chapman proceeded to allege that the board permitted 'massive waste', and to attack the scale of management perks as well as the areas in which he discerned possible improvements in productivity that were not being actively pursued. As to the latter, it seems that trade union restrictions had grown over the years to an extent that the provincial public transport industry would not have tolerated. Certainly the National Bus Company had refused to allow London Transport's "country bus services" to be transferred to its appropriate operating subsidiaries in 1979, because of the levels of pay and conditions of service enjoyed by London Transport busmen operating services essentially similar to those employed by companies like Eastern National; the result was the formation of a new NBC subsidiary called London Country Bus Services, and quickly nicknamed 'the mint with the hole in the middle'. The fear was that the transfer of LCBS garages to companies like Eastern National would lead to inflated wage claims throughout the NBC subsidiaries in the Home Counties.

As to the issue of perks, there is reason to suppose that the board had indulged itself, in the tradition of its predecessors. In a recent book, Sir John Colville's 'Downing Street diaries', *The Fringes of Power,* there is mention of Churchill being wined and dined by the LPTB, in the company of Sir Ralph Wedgwood (at that time—19 November 1940—the chairman of the Railway Executive), in their air raid shelter converted from the closed underground station at Down Street, Piccadilly. Caviar featured on the menu, with an expensive wine and 1865 brandy, not to mention the excellent cigars. One can but marvel at such extravagance in times of national emergency, and ask whether Chapman may have had something to complain about.

The press made a feature of Chapman, 'the axeman', as might be expected, and in December 1979 the board's own auditors were asked to investigate. Some two months later they reported that, while some economies and cost-cutting were possible, the management perks were comparable with those in other nationalised industries (thereby perhaps begging the question as to how public bodies may be expected to behave). But a more critical report followed in April 1980 from an independent firm of management consultants, which questioned the managerial ability of the board's executive management. Under pressure from Cutler, Bennett released this report in June 1980 for publication.

Not surprisingly, the press had a further field-day, and on 24 July Cutler informed Bennett that his contract was terminated, with two and a half years still to go; it must be recorded at once that Bennett later obtained substantial compensation for this action. But once more the board was without anyone at the helm, and Cutler had to admit on television that he had no-one in mind. In the event, he appointed as 'caretaker' a most distinguished transportant, Sir Peter Masefield, who remained in post for a further two years, and did a great deal to restore the shattered morale to London Transport staff at all levels. During this period, Masefield and several colleages threatened to resign if Chapman's appointment was extended, and so in due course the axeman left 55 Broadway, ending what can only be described as a bizarre episode in the history of transport administration.

This, though, was as nothing compared to what followed when Labour regained control of the GLC in May 1981, and Ken Livingstone took over from the party leader, Andrew McIntosh, who had been in charge both in opposition and during the election. Livingstone appointed Dave Wetzel, once a London Transport bus inspector, to chair the GLC transport committee, and the stage was set for a further period of political controversy.

It had been said that Labour won the 1981 GLC elections because of its transport policy, which included a 25 per cent cut in fares and other travel concessions. On 4 October 1981, Wetzel's committee instructed the board to reduce fares by an average of 32 per cent, increasing the subsidy from the rates to £125 million for a full year. This was followed by legal action on the part of Bromley London borough council, which had a Conservative administration, challenging the right of the GLC under the 1969 Act to require its London Transport Executive to cut fares to such an extent.

The issue turned upon the clause in the Act laying a duty on the Executive to provide an 'efficient' and 'economical' service. In the Divisional Court judgement was given for the GLC, but this was overturned by Lord Denning on appeal, whereupon the GLC took the case to the House of Lords. There—despite some uncertainty in their Lordships' minds as to what 'economical' meant—the Law Lords upheld Lord Denning's decision, and the GLC 'Fares Fair' policy was ruled ultra vires. The decision was given on 17 December 1981, and on 21 March 1982, the LTE increased fares, at the GLC's instruction, by 96 per cent. In the ensueing public debate, Professor Ezra Mishan suggested that London should be regarded as a special case, and that the LTE subsidy should come from national taxation instead of local rates, thereby causing still more raised eyebrows in the provinces.

Next, after what amounted to a nudge from David Howell, by then the Conservative Secretary of State for Transport, the GLC began to look for acceptable ways of increasing the subsidy, and produced what it called the Balanced Plan, incorporating a reduction of 25 per cent in the average level of fares. The board, doubtful about the legality of this, and concerned to keep within the requirements of statute, went to the length of challenging the policy of the Balanced Plan, and at the end of January, 1983, the High Court ruled in favour of the GLC, awarding £14,000 costs against the LTE! But in the meantime there had been passed the Transport Act of 1983, which was intended to give the Secretary of State powers to control subsidies to public transport in London and the metropolitan counties, so the GLC itself sought counsel's advice as to the legality of the Plan. Only then was it formally approved and the reduction in fares took place on 22 May 1983, along with a second simplification that produced three fare zones for the whole of London. The final outcome of the extended and expensive affair was that fares were brought back to where they had been when Livingstone had taken power at the County Hall, two years earlier.

Meanwhile Sir Peter Masefield had played a far more constructive role than his 'temporary' appointment as chairman might have lead one to expect. A re-organisation planned before his term of office began was put into effect, which among other things provided for a 'Bus Board', responsible to the Executive, and having eight Bus Districts, each with a General Manager, answerable to the LT board. Masefield's active involvement in all the affairs of the LTE did a great deal to restore morale, and his successor was to pay tribute to his 'steadying hand and influence' at a very serious juncture in the history of London Transport.

There was general surprise when the GLC advertised the vacancy, after twice extending Sir Peter's supposedly caretaker appointment. Far from the political appointment that some expected, the new chairman, who took office in September 1982 for a five year term, was Dr Keith Bright, previously manager of Huntley & Palmers, whose policy rapidly showed itself to be heavily concerned with the promotion of efficiency and productivity. Yet Bright had been some six months only in office when Leslie Chapman returned to the attack on the Executive, for its supposed extravagance. When this had died away—and the report of the Monopolies & Mergers Commission in no way supported Chapman's criticism—the stage was set for another political storm, which must have left LTE managers wondering when they would be allowed to get on with their not undemanding jobs.

By 1983 the government was committed to a further reform of local authorities, including the abolition of the Greater London Council. But in a White Paper that appeared on 26 July, not long after the general election that renewed the Conservative's majority at Westminster, it was announced that responsibility for London Transport was to be transferred from the GLC to a new authority, London Regional Transport, operating through wholly owned subsidiary companies, but not having any planning or highway responsibilities such as those given in 1968 to the Passenger Transport Authorities. The ultimate control over LRT was to be with the Secretary of State for Transport, thus retaining the element of politics at the highest level that had been successively increased ever since 1947.

As was to be expected, Livingstone and the GLC resisted the new legislation, while at the same time becoming embroiled once again with the board over two contentious issues. The first of these was the future of the LTE workshops, and the proposal to close the Aldenham Bus Overhaul Works, with substantial redundancies. (The Metropolies and Mergers report had been critical of the Executive in this area.) But the summer of 1983 had seen the LTE achieving substantial cost savings, greatly improved performance, with 'lost mileage' on the bus services down to less than six per cent, and an overall increase in carrying of twelve per cent in the five months after Travelcards had been introduced, in May of that year. (Much, but not all of this being on the railways.) What really made the headlines was the appointment of new board members, which was seen to be overtly political.

There followed a most unpleasant episode, in which Dr Bright was accused of racial prejudice, which he vigorously resisted, recalling that the Executive had 'on its own initiative called in the Commission for Racial Equality to make sure there was no unintentional discrimination'. The appointments were confirmed in November 1983, and in the subsequent debate on the London Regional Transport Bill, the Secretary of State, Nicholas Ridley, attacked the GLC for politicising the Executive. This did not prevent the GLC from nominating, in February 1984, a 'well-known Marxist' as a further part-time member of the board. But with the enactment of the Bill later in the year, the confrontation between the GLC and those responsible for managing its public transport executive came to an end; the GLC nominees were replaced by a non-political group of eight part-time members, and Dr Bright and his colleagues were appointed to full-time posts with the new London Regional Transport. Thus ended one of the most remarkable episodes of transport history, with the London undertaking still far from being the autonomous agency that Lord Ashfield and his associates had intended it to be.

CHANGING THE STRUCTURE

There is a very important difference between politicising an industry and the enactment of statutes and regulations designed to ensure its safe and reliable function. Since 1970 these 'quality controls' have been changed and developed so as to invalidate much of the description given in chapter five. The process began with the Road Traffic Act 1972, itself largely a consolidating statute, and has continued ever since.

One aspect of quality control that has still to work its way through the bus industry arose from the Health & Safety at Work Act of 1974, which greatly extended the scope of the former factory inspectorate. By stating that the cab of a vehicle was a workplace within the meaning of the Act, the conditions of all drivers were brought into the new system of control, and if this has been felt mainly so far in the road haulage industry, it may be expected to affect bus and coach operators in the future.

But the reform of quality control really started with the Transport Act of 1968, which as we have seen introduced the requirement for road transport operators to hold an Operator's Licence, partly to conform (at least in the letter) with the requirements of EEC law. The Transport Act 1980 brought about substantial changes in the system, ending the need to hold several of the quality licences established in 1930; the PSV licence, the Certificate of Fitness, and the PSV conductor's (but not the driver's) licence. Vehicle authorisations were now attached to the O-licence, and made subject to stringent annual inspection and spot checks at any time.

Three requirements were set up for the holding of an O-licence: to be of good repute, to be of appropriate financial standing, and to be professionally competent. Adequate facilities for maintenance also had to be available, either on the operator's premises or by contract with a suitable garage. The requirement of professional competence was to be discharged by holding or employing as manager the holder of a certificate of professional competence. Initially some were able to obtain this through 'grandfather rights', but for most it is given after successfully passing a multiple-choice examination, conducted by the Royal Society of Arts (in the Irish Republic, the similar examination was entrusted to the Chartered Institute of Transport).

The syllabus for the CPC examination covers road safety, technical standards and aspects of operation, regulation of road passenger services, business and financial management and law, and there is a supplementary syllabus for those wishing to obtain the CPC (International). From its inception the examination proved popular, and numerous courses were set up to prepare candidates, either on a residential basis, or by part-time study or distance learning. There can be little doubt as to the value of the new requirement in raising the general standard of bus and coach operation, not least because the professional bodies accepted the CPC for admission to their qualifying examinations.

In the meantime the EEC regulations about drivers' hours of work were introduced, step by step, over a period of just two years beginning on 1 January 1978. The industry resented their complexity from the first, and it was generally felt that they were unsuited to British conditions, but it would appear that their acceptance was a *quid pro quo* for the abandonment of plans for strict quantity control, on the continental pattern, to be made part of the Common Transport Policy. A further consequence of EEC membership came when the fitting of tachographs on vehicles used for certain purposes became compulsory, in January 1980, a move which was probably less widely resented among busmen than it had been in the road haulage trade, where the tachograph had been resisted as a 'spy in the cab'. This may well have been due to the fact that vehicles operating regular services of a route length under fifty kilometres were exempted from the need for a tachograph, thus causing the great majority of the drivers who belonged to trade unions to escape their threat.

Quality control, though, is largely about technical matters, and since 1974 there has been a more substantial shift in the structure of control. To begin with, the Labour government took a further look at transport policy, and in 1976 published a Green Paper (confusingly, it had orange covers) which, while less incisive than the Barbara Castle studies of ten years before, lead to a White Paper, which appeared in April 1977. In this the objective of transport policy was stated as the maximisation of 'social mobility and access', a concept that, however worthy, failed somehow to catch the public imagination. To achieve it, the White Paper took up the proposals of the Expenditure Committee report, *Urban Transport Planning*, of five years earlier, proposing the diversion of funds from the roads programme to provide local bus subsidies.

The logical development of subsidy is the notion of 'fares free' public transport, an idea that had been around for some years. Those who advocated it were by no means always political extremists, for there were councillors of all parties who were coming to see public transport as a service comparable to that of the public library. But when newly elected labour majorities in London and the West Midlands looked at the cost in public funds diverted from other uses, and the unpredictable consequences for land use and settlement, they backed away, preferring policies of limited subsidy, such as the GLC's balanced plan. Only in the self-styled 'socialist republic of South Yorkshire' did the county council in 1976 decide to hold fares constant until inflation made them too small to be worth collecting.

But changes do not always come from policy decisions, and the previous twenty years had seen the spread of minibus ownership and use, largely, as we have seen, on the fringes of legality. These vehicles, while used to a limited extent by commercial firms, proved valuable for numerous activities, in both town and country, that became known as 'community transport', and thus what was in itself a technical development came to influence policy, leading to two statutes of 1977 that began to nibble at the structure of quantity control.

The first of these, the Minibus Act, sought to extend quality control of vehicles used for community transport, without imposing the full weight of the licensing system. It was an oddly conceived act, permitting among other things the operation of full-size buses by community associations, despite its name. Because of the difficulties of definition, it created a 'grey area' of many complexities in seeking to encourage non-profit-making users while maintaining the full rigour of the licensing system for others. Even greater were the complexities of the Passenger Vehicles (Experimental Areas) Act, of the same year, which sought to encourage various ways of providing services in 'deep rural' areas, without affecting the finances of commercial or semi-subsidised services, or the employment of those who worked on them.

The combined policies of these Acts were taken further by the Transport Act 1978, which made it easier to use volunteer drivers (paid expenses only, where need be) on community bus services, and facilitated car-sharing. It also provided for non-metropolitan counties to submit passenger transport plans, so extending still further the interest of government in the actual provision of bus services, and reducing by another step the autonomy of managers.

In May 1979 the return of a Conservative government committed to the reduction of the role of the state was seen to have portentous significance for the bus industry. Legislation followed without the interim phase of a Green or White Paper, in the form of the Transport Act 1980, which became law on 30 June of that year, while Norman Fowler was Minister of Transport. This was the first measure of deregulation, and it was to have unexpected results—which will be described later in this chapter. The relevant changes were as follows—

★ All long-distance services were exempted from the need for a road service licence (the definction of an express service, which had turned upon the minimum fare, was changed to be one on which no passenger travelled less than thirty miles, measured in a straight line)

★ All remaining services were also exempted (subject to a few residual powers, never used) from price control (previously, and probably without authority, fare tables had been enforced as a condition of the road service licence)

★ The 'burden of proof' was shifted from the applicant to the objector, the traffic commissioners being required to grant a road service licence unless they were satisfied that to do so would be 'against the interests of the public'

★ County Councils were enabled to ask the Secretary of State to set up 'trial areas' (not to be confused with the 'experimental areas' of the 1977 Act), within which no road service licence was required at all

—and, as we have seen, the Act provided for Operator Licensing in place of the 1930 system that had been based on the public service vehicle.

The Act was introduced in stages, the principal deregulation aspects on 6 October 1980, and the O-Licence system on 1 April 1981 (it is remarkable how often the civil service chooses all-fools day for major changes in the administration). Its consequences will be described in the next and final section of this chapter, but many felt that it had gone quite far enough in the reduction of state power over the bus and coach industry.

The following year saw a consolidating measure, the Public Passenger Vehicles Act 1981, which was generally welcomed on account of the complicated state that bus licensing had got into. But the Local Government Finance Act of 1982 was to have consequences that few foresaw, and seems to have been yet another example of legislation with implications for transport that have not been appreciated by the sponsoring department. In brief, and among other things that need not concern us, it brought the management of the Passenger Transport Executives within the control of local government audit, and thereby significantly reduced their freedom to take commercial decisions involving risk. Its effects were to be short-lived, since three years later the PTEs were to lose their operating powers, replaced by companies subject to normal commercial audit, but it was to be followed by yet another inter-departmental measure.

First, though, the government's pre-occupation with public spending, and the subsidising policies of the metropolitan councils, produced in 1982 a White Paper, *Public Transport Subsidy in Cities*, to be followed in 1983 by an inquiry into bus subsidy policies by the House of Commons Transport Committee. Out of all this came the Transport Act 1983, which gave the Secretary of State power to make 'guidelines' for the size of public transport subsidies in the metropolitan counties and (as we have seen) Greater London. Detailed financial three-year plans were also required of the councils, and they were given powers, along with their transport executives, to put ancillary activities and actual services out for competitive tender.

In June 1983 the Conservatives were returned to power for a second term, and in October Nicholas Ridley became Secretary of State for Transport. It was soon clear that further deregulation was to be expected, but first there came a local government White Paper, *Steamlining the Cities*. As things were to turn out, its policies, largely enacted in the Local Government Act of the following year, confused much of the argument over deregulation—with accompanying privatisation—that followed from the publication of Ridley's White Paper, *Buses*, in 1984, and the subsequent Transport Act of 1985; the last in this series of government measures at the time this book was revised.

Looking back, it is surprising how long it took for the economic significance of regulation to be recognised. In 1953, it seemed that the government thought that road haulage could be returned to market competition by de-nationalising it, without recognising the constraints of the quantity licence introduced in 1933. Indeed, the Transport Act of 1953, by seeking to shift the burden of proof from the applicant for an A-licence to the objector, actually tightened quantity control, and it was only abandoned by Barbara Castle in the Transport Act of 1968, following the recommendations of the Geddes Committee. In the bus industry, the tendency of quantity control to set up state-protected monopolies had been recognised by Chester in 1935, with the fear that they would lead to uncontrolled inefficiency.

The 1985 legislation started from the premise that the public would be better served if operators, existing and potential, had unrestricted access to the market, and therefore swept away the whole system of road service licensing. Price control had gone in 1980: now quantity control was to go too. At the same time, operators were no longer to receive 'network subsidy', which was seen to have lead to inefficiency; services considered necessary by local authorities were to be put out to competitive tender. To allow this to work, and to provide a limit to the possible speed of change, any O-licence holder was given the right to register the intention to provide a 'local bus service'; a new category introduced by the Act, covering services where no passenger travelled for more than fifteen miles, measured in a straight line (thus reducing the minimum distance for an express service from thirty miles to fifteen). The Act also ended the duties of co-ordination introduced by the 1972 Local Government Act.

The Secretary of State had said that he felt stricter penalties to be necessary against what he called 'foolish practices', and the Act tightened quality control still more, by first reducing and then removing the rebate of fuel duty for offending operators; then prohibiting them from registering local services; and, for further offences, rescinding their Operator's Licence. The information to be given when registering was limited to the outline of the route and a broad indication of frequency, with a few minor matters, no mention of fares to be required. Commencement of the service was to be not less than 42 days after registration, and a similar period of notice was required if it was to be varied or discontinued.

An extension of the system gave the right to register a service to taxi proprietors and holder of minibus permits; taxis were also freed from local authority quantity control, and given limited rights to charge separate fares. Certain local authorities were enabled to ask for traffic regulation conditions to be attached to O-licences, where they feared congestion or similar problems, but the traffic commissioners were not to grant these so as to restrict competition. In a move whose consequences were hard to assess, the bus and coach industry was brought within the scope of the anti-monopoly legislation (from which it had been exempt), and thus introduced to the control of the Office of Fair Trading.

But deregulation was not expected to be enough to ensure the working of a free market, so long as there existed the dominant position of the National Bus Company and the long-established traditions of municipal transport. The Act therefore included provisions for winding up the NBC and transferring its subsidiaries to private ownership, though for reasons unexplained this was not to extend to the Scottish Bus Group. (London was also exempt from privatisation, and from deregulation as well, on the argument that enough change had already taken place, and that LTR needed time to settle down.) Local authorities owning bus undertakings were required to transfer beneficial ownership to companies, whose shares for the time being they were to continue to own. The procedure here was hedged about with provisions to make these 'initial companies' genuinely commercial, though in the case of the erstwhile metropolitan counties, they would remain very large. Perhaps the chief difference was to arise from the application of company audit, meaning that these businesses would be permitted to take a greater element of risk in their policies, and could also face liquidation if they failed to succeed.

Significantly the Secretary of State resisted pressure to place the National Bus Company on the market as an entity, which might have produced more income for the Treasury; perhaps one of the few examples of principle overcoming Treasury precedent. While the whole package was welcomed by apologists for the free market, politicians of all parties feared that it would decimate rural public transport, and the provision of off-peak services in towns. Much of the resistance to the measure in its passage through parliament was confused with the impact of 'rate-capping', though, and the real question was how far local authorities would be able to accept tenders for operations abandoned as the Act came into force. A transitional grant for rural services was provided to ease the problems, but by the middle of 1986 the future of the industry looked to many people as unsure as it must have done in the middle of 1931.

Changing the organisational structure of the bus industry, by merger and division of companies, has been the happy pastime of holding companies, whether private or state-owned, since the formation of the East Kent Road company in 1916, at least. In 1981 the NBC took an unusual step, after more than a decade of mergers, when it broke up Midland Red, once the largest of the provincial companies, into units capable of a more 'hands-on' style of management. The Scottish Bus Group, too, broke up some of its subsidiaries, and likewise started to promote customer and staff loyalty as part of a marketing drive. Midland Red (North), based at Cannock, introduced brand management, with four brand names; once again, customers seemed pleased with what they took to be a change of ownership, and a new start became possible in public relations. The impact of the 1985 Act in breaking up the NBC before privatisation, with still more new titles appearing on the sides of buses (and new liveries too), is thus part of a much longer process than it might seem.

THE PROGRESS OF THE INDUSTRY

Too much attention to the statutory framework of the industry may blind us to the way it has developed of itself. While it is true that the legislation gave managers more freedom to take their own decisions, it was apparent from the 1970s that a new, younger, more entrepreneurial generation was taking over from the orthodoxy of the past. This was specially true in the NBC and SBG companies, but it was not unknown in the municipal sector, and it was paralleled by a growing professionalism among the independent firms.

The new atmosphere made itself felt with the systematic review of local bus services pioneered by Midland Red in 1976, which came to be called a Market Analysis Project. Although MAP exercises were less than true market research, they lead to more productive use of resources, and were followed by some of the first attempts to create a brand image since the early days of the bus industry. It came as something of a shock for managers to find how low the reputation of their company was, when they re-christened it and passengers expressed pleasure at the idea of a new operator taking over!

The later 1970s also saw the introduction of pre-payment, with plastic cards for pensioners and the disabled, and also for normal commercial traffic. Travel cards quickly proved popular, and encouraged greater use of the buses at a time of generally falling demand, as well as improving boarding times on conductorless vehicles. They were not always rewarding in revenue terms, as we saw in the case of London Transport, and they had the further drawback of virtually ending the flow of information for management, other than by sample checks made on the buses. This problem though was overcome by the alternative of the fully computerised ticket machine, appearing in the 1980s, which threatened to overwhelm managers with the volume of financial and statistical data produced.

So the changes in the licensing system must be seen to some extent as freeing progressive managers from constraints that were already seen to be restrictive, and if the industry did not entirely welcome the changes that were enacted, there was a growing feeling that some relaxation of licensing control was desirable. The most spectacular developments were expected from the appearance, on 6 October 1980, the day the Transport Act came into force, of a consortium of coach operators challenging the National Express network of services.

British Coachways, launched by the Minister of Transport, Norman Fowler, at a ceremony at their 'coach station' (a disused railway goods yard at Kings Cross), was designed to be the Trailways to National Express's Greyhound Corporation, but its promoters seem to have missed the point that the two-operator equilibrium in the USA was a produce of a licensing system far more restrictive than that which, anyway, had just been dismantled in Britain. The consortium adopted a marketing stratgy of undercutting National Express fares, but NE matched this pound for pound, and then, finding that there was a considerable untapped demand at lower prices, greatly increased its frequencies on the main intercity routes—Birmingham–London was served half-hourly in the summer of 1981.

National Express thereby attracted a good deal of traffic from the trains, which lead to British Rail adopting a more aggressive marketing policy as well, but British Coachways benefitted little, since most of the first-time coach passengers booked at their High Street travel agency, which usually had the NBC franchise. With the withdrawal of Grey Green and Wallace Arnold from the consortium its days were clearly numbered, and it collapsed with a minimum of publicity just two years and twelve days after its launch. Its effect had been to trigger off a general reduction in fares on principal routes, and a great increase in frequency; although there was some loss of mileage and increase of fares on cross-country services, the general outcome seemed to have been a benefit to the public (including those using the train). NBC was accused of unfair advantage in its back-up of subsidy and tax rebare, though it was noticeable that many independent services also came to be licensed as stage carriage (divided into sections of less than 30 miles) so as to gain the same benefits.

While a few independents tried their hand at express operation, the lack of an established network of booking agents hampered them, and in any case there were few at first who sought to compete head on with National Express, no doubt learning from the experience of the consortium. But in Scotland there appeared a series of true express coach services, and as in due course the new generation of super-luxury coaches became available (from continental manufacturers at first), there was a move up market. A new quality service began to appear, pioneered by independent firms, but soon emulated by NBC operators and by Passenger Transport Executives too. A west of England firm adopted the brand name *Rapide*, and when they were joined by National Express on their Plymouth–London service, with full joint service, National took the same title for all of their up-market operations, where films were screened and hostesses served refreshments at every reclining seat. The remarkable progress in coach design that marked the early 1980s saw also the expansion of shuttle services to continental destinations, some firms committing large sums to the development of this traffic, or working on hire to package holiday operators.

Nothing so extensive was expected of the provision for 'trial areas', where road service licensing could be suspended, though for a time the main focus of contention lay in an Order declaring a trial area obtained by Hereford and Worcester County Council. This came into force on 27 July 1982, covering the whole of the former county of Hereford, including the city itself. In the rural parts of the area there was some loss of service mileage, but the council's subsidy policy was used to adapt operations in such a way as to make it hard to draw any conclusions. In the cathedral city, however, there was almost an atavistic re-enactment of the competition remembered from the era before licensing was introduced.

The next two years saw the appearance of various private operators on city services in Hereford, previously the monopoly of Midland Red. There was fierce competition, rate wars leading to free services at times, and not a little danger to the public, as well as congestion on the streets. It has been said that Midland Red made use of resources from outside the city, and from NBC itself, in its successful campaign that in due course left it once more the sole urban operator in Hereford; be that as it may, the episode was used to demonstrate the disastrous consequences of deregulation of local bus services. It seems unlikely that so sweeping a conclusion could be sustained, since on the one hand it was a unique event, and on the other it has to be admitted that the traffic commissioners' control over the safety of vehicles left something to be desired. However, the council was about to designate a further trial area, in rural Worcestershire, when the procedure lapsed with full deregulation under the Act of 1985.

The only other trial areas were those in mid-Devon and central Norfolk, and in neither case was there much of consequence to report, save for the fact that the mere absence of change indicated that road service licensing had become meaningless in rural areas. Somewhat more came from the shift in the burden of proof, which was expected to make it easier for newcomers to enter the market, but here again the consequences were both limited and varied.

Taking the industry as a whole, there must have been many small changes and extra services put on that had little individual significance but may well have added up to considerable public advantage. There were also several applications that still failed, doubtless due to the difficulty of deciding in advance what 'the interests of the public' really are. Apart from a small suburban service on the eastern fringe of Nottingham, the two cases that made news were the successful applications for town services in Whitehaven and Cardiff, where private operators, with difficulty, obtained licences to challenge the NBC in the former town, and the city transport department in the latter. At Whitehaven the local operator lost his licence again on appeal, after an acrimonious battle through the courts; in Cardiff the operator's business collapsed, but this did not appear to have anything to do with the viability of the services he offered. In both cases there was evidence of resentment on the part of the 'established' operator that a small competitor should be successful, and popular with the public; an attitude of mind illustrated by the frequent attempt to brand the independent operators as 'cowboys'.

In some ways the most lasting consequences of the Transport Act 1980 were felt in the new air of innovation that was most marked in the southern half of England. One aspect was the development of commuter coach services into London, notably from Kent and Essex, and from the west. To many people's surprise, two municipal operators—Reading and Southend-on-Sea

—joined in this activity, along with NBC companies and independents. But less visible was the consequence of removing price control, which freed bus managers to experiment with all sorts of promotional fares, with success comparable to that obtained by British Rail after 1965.

There is thus a very real sense in which the Transport Act of 1980 paved the way for the developments that followed from the 1985 Act. This was not so readily visibile in the course of the legislation, when opposition to Mr Ridley's reforms was both fierce and, too often, factitious. There is space here for no more than an outline of the course of events since 1985, but it is already plain that the story has been complicated by the inter-action of several factors, so that it would be a gross mistake to refer to the years since then as an age of deregulation.

First, there has been a shift in fiscal policy that has had far-reaching consequences. It has taken the combined effect of the Transport Act 1983, of the government's policy of 'rate-capping', and of the prohibition of 'network subsidy' by the Act of 1985, not to mention the transfer of the PTE and municipal fleets to the ownership of 'arms-length' companies, to reverse the dependence of the industry upon public funds, and to cause an 'agonising reappraisal' of its costing practices. (The technique developed by the Chartered Institute of Public Finance and Accountancy—CIPFA—for allocating subsidy was of little value as a decision-making tool for managers.) Power has been returned to management, for power flows where money flows, and the industry has shown that its managers are well able to use it. Not since 1930 has there been such freedom of action, but the removal of price control in 1980 gave the first taste of freedom to a new generation that was ready to use it.

Second, there has been what is best called the restructuring of the industry (which, as this chapter is being written, is to be extended to Scotland and the London region). 'Privatisation' is altogether too simplistic a word to describe what is going on. By choosing to sell the NBC subsidiaries individually, Mr Ridley started a process whose ending we shall not see for many years, for ownership can now change as readily as it does in the retail and catering trades, and it probably will. The really significant consequence here is the re-commercialisation of bus businesses, now that they are no longer either publicly owned nor the channel for social support to the needy. There has been a startling change in the attitude of managers themselves, as well as in the attitude of financiers and journalists; it might be said that bus operation has 'come out of the closet'. Managers are using the language of business and marketing; the financial world is realising that these businesses, though not showing high profit performance, nevertheless have a very healthy cash flow, with much of it 'up front'. A bus company must now look like a very sensible investment for the portfolio manager of a conglomerate, which wants to balance the delayed payment that other subsidiaries suffer from.

But of course the third factor, deregulation, remains the central and necessary change, to which the others relate. It is already clear that it has been ambiguous, and it is far too soon to try to evaluate its consequences; in some ways, the bus industry today has more regulation, not less to put up with. One thing seems plain, which is that the forecasts of the prophets of doom, from the period of opposition to Mr Ridley's Bill, have not been justified by the event, and perhaps a fair assessment is that there has been a net gain, taking the country as a whole. Yet in some places, this has been offset by confusion and loss of traffic.

Nowhere has this been more true than in the former metropolitan counties. The deregulation clauses of the Act came into force on Sunday 26 October 1986, and on the same day the PTE and municipal fleets were transferred to new companies, whose shares are owned by the councils involved. Too little time seems to have been available to the managers of the new companies to prepare for 'D-day', and on the Monday morning there was chaos on the streets of some of the towns and cities concerned. (This was notably absent where NBC companies provided urban services, many of whom had put the revised operations into effect weeks or even months before.) This, rather than competition (which was chiefly to be found in Manchester and Glasgow), was the cause of a significant loss of traffic in the areas concerned, and to an increase in the use of railway services; a totally unexpected outcome, since the future of urban railways had been seen to be threatened by the Act.

One of the consequences of this period of radical change has been the retirement of many of the older generation of managers, for whom the new dispensation was simply unattractive. Their early retirement made way for the younger generation, for whom the freedom to manage was a real challenge and an attraction, and while they have made their mistakes, they have shown that they do not need the leading strings of quantity control to keep the industry on course for survival. New services have been developed; competition has broken out in various places, with rare examples of its less attractive side. The provision of socially necessary services has been adequate, within the financial limits imposed by government. A period that began with the apothesis of state intervention in the British bus industry has ended with its almost complete removal; of this it may be said that the consumer has in consequence become a much more important individual than he has been these fifty years and more.

CHAPTER ELEVEN

A MISCELLANY

IN his book, *The Railway Age*, Michael Robbins quotes *The Times* of 1850 as observing : 'There are thousands of our readers, we are sure, who in the last three years of their lives, have travelled more and seen more than in all their previous life taken together'. In 1930 this could have been said of millions, most of whom would never have read *The Times*, and it is arguable that the development of bus and coach services caused a greater change in society than the building of the railways themselves. The spread of towns that took place in the 'thirties could hardly have occurred at such a low density of population if the electric tram had remained the prevailing form of transport, for tramways need a concentrated population to justify the heavy capital outlay involved in their establishment. Even the trolleybus has this drawback, and only the flexible motor bus could ever have served the housing estates that have been built around the fringes of our cities. In the countryside, the bus has been chiefly responsible for the social revolution that has ended the isolation of the village and broken the sharp division between town and country life. Cheap travel by coach has opened new horizons, at home and abroad and, more recently, the alternative of fast travel by air has combined with the economy of the slower coach to lead to the rejuvenation of the express train. Yet today, with the wider ownership of private cars, there must be many who never use a bus or coach at all, any more than they do the railway.

But buses and coaches are still a common sight and many people must wonder how the industry works, who owns it and how it has come to be as it is. The earlier chapters have set out to answer some of these questions, but it is not only the broader aspects of the story that can bring the whole thing to life. There are the smaller things, with which we are more familiar, about which the unanswered questions often turn, and this chapter is, therefore, more of a passenger's-eye view of the industry and its history.

NUMBERS AND NAMES

Over most of the country we take the numbering of bus routes for granted, although there are many exceptions. These route numbers certainly mean less to country people and, where rural buses are still run by small firms, it is often the driver who is looked for to identify the right bus to go home on. The author recalls an elderly lady with a shopping basket who once addressed him rather sharply, saying: 'Conductor, is this my bus?' This informality looks back to the days of the carrier and his cart and, like their predecessor, the country bus crew will often know every passenger and stop at the gate of any cottage. Destination blinds do not matter a great deal on such routes. Although the coach may well be a modern one (small country businesses do not usually specialise to the extent of running buses, but make coaches do all sorts of work), the methods of operation in the country have not changed a great deal since the early days of the industry.

Some of the territorial companies themselves have only taken to numbering their routes in quite recent years and the use of roller blinds has become general only since the second world war. Certain companies used a form of flapped board for many years, but the advantages of the transparent blind that can be illuminated from within are obvious. The difficulties of ensuring that correct destinations are shown have lead recently to a reduction in the number of blinds (frequently to a single one at the front), but even here standards vary throughout the industry and some companies leave a lot to be desired in their provision of adequate information to the public.

The stage coaches had been known by their fleet names and the horse buses carried numerous details of the neighbourhoods they served, generally painted on the vehicle and invariably placed at the sides, where they shared the available space with advertisements of all kinds. The advent of the motor bus made two changes; it was a faster vehicle and thus had to be more easily identified by prospective passengers and its greater cost meant that it could not economically be limited to a single route with the relevant details painted permanently on the coach-work. Tillings reflected these changed conditions as early as 1904, when they began to introduce destination boards on the front of their buses, while in 1905 G. S. Dicks initiated another big change by painting the title 'Vanguard' in large letters on the sides of the London Motor Omnibus Company's vehicles. The 'fleet name' immediately became popular, with the LGOC using 'General' and the Road Car Company adopting 'Union Jack'. The older operators, such as Tillings and Birch, continued to show geographical titles for some years, but by 1911 fleet names had become general in London and were widely used elsewhere.

Dicks was also responsible for the introduction of route or service numbers, which the Vanguard buses began to use on 30 April 1906. They were copied elsewhere in London and when the merger of 1908 took place they became standard throughout the enlarged LGOC. In 1909, the Metropolitan police issued regu-lations governing the use of destination indicators and also con-trolled advertisements to prevent confusion. Many of the London bus routes have continued to carry basically the same route numbers from that day to this for, as the LGOC increased its hege-mony in London, it was able to impose a logical practice of its own. When the 'pirates' appeared after 1922, many went to work on existing routes and adopted their numbers as the easiest means of obtaining traffic, but at about this time Chief Constable Bassom, who as we have seen played an important part in the working of the London Traffic Act of 1924, extended the General's numbering system and imposed it upon all the oper-ators in the Metropolitan police district.

The Bassom numbering system was highly logical, which was the main reason for its failure. It was based on that of the LGOC but it allocated the route number to the extreme extent of the service, which in most cases was only reached on a few occasions, while short workings and deviations were given letter suffixes. Thus the majority of buses on route 11 during the Bassom era carried the indication '11E' and the number '11' itself applied only to an infrequent extension of the route at one terminal, operating on Sundays only. The purpose of service numbers being to help the passenger to find the bus he wants, the Bassom system had little to commend it and was abandoned by the LPTB.

Elsewhere in the country, even stranger systems were to be found. In Birmingham, the corporation transport department as a general rule had the outer terminal of the route displayed on its buses, irrespective of the direction they were going, which meant that bus stops had to indicate whether they were 'To City' or 'From City'. Most Birmingham routes had quite simple numbers, but to add a complication there were one or two which broke the rule and had a different number according to direction (these being cross-city services), while there were in addition three circular routes which at times used the same roads as the radial services. Add to this the Birmingham practice of running buses with the blind reading 'SERVICE EXTRA', and it will be appreciated that citizens of the second city must have highly developed instincts for use when travelling. A certain novelist who made his hero catch a bus in Birmingham labelled 'STATION' must have raised an ironic smile from anyone who read his book after visiting the city unprepared. That is one destination which has never been shown.

But if numbers offer a field for ingenuity in assisting or misleading the traveller, fleet names have always tempted operators to use their imagination to the full. The territorial companies have usually chosen territorial names, although National and United are exceptions, and so is Crosville, which is based on a family name. J. B. Walford's Ortona company at Cambridge is said to have been named after a ship which, in turn, took the name from a town on the Adriatic coast of Italy. The London pirates produced some memorable titles and though the early days before 1914 saw the 'Olympic', the appropriately named 'Pioneer' and the even more appropriate 'Nil Desperandum', it was the competition of the 'twenties that saw the full flowering of high-sounding names. The LGOC obtained an injunction against the user of the title London Genial Omnibus Company, but similar ingenuity produced the 'Pro Bono Publico' and the 'Uneedus', while C. H. Pickup was blessed with a singularly fortunate surname which he used to good purpose. 'Eclipse', 'Matchless' and 'Supreme' were obvious choices, but there is little to indicate why titles such as 'Poppy' or 'Shanghai' should have appeared. 'Fieldmarshal' and 'Admiral' were clearly competitive with 'General', while 'Waverley' and 'Claremont' had an air of nobility; 'Overground' was another obvious choice. Finally, amongst them all ran the buses that carried proudly the names of the men who owned them, disdaining any disguise—perhaps the most intriguing (for the sake of the Shakespearian association) were those called simply 'Henslowe'.

In the provinces there were oddities as well, including the naming of individual buses. MacBraynes named their earliest buses after animals and some of them seem oddly chosen, like *The Rabbit* and *The Weasel*. South Shields Corporation was probably unique among municipal operators in naming both buses and tramcars, choosing titles such as *North Star, Rob Roy, High Flyer, Commerce* and *Industry*. A small firm at Wirksworth in Derbyshire gave its three buses the names *Adam Bede, Seth Bede* and *Dinah Morris*. Elsewhere, buses were given nicknames, such as the four red and cream Albions that appeared in Wolverhampton in 1914, and were known as 'scarlet runners', and the 'red lettuce' of a certain northern town.

Amongst smaller operators outside London a certain group of fleet names has been popular since the 'twenties and shows no sign of dying away. An early concern with what we now call the 'public image' produced titles like 'Reliance', 'Progressive', 'Economic' and 'Select', or (more boldly) 'Favourite' and 'Supreme'. Later, in this class we had 'Airborne' and 'Pathfinder' and even 'Have-Coach-Will-Travel'. Colours have always been popular, matching (usually) with the chosen livery. Exotic names like 'Gipsy Queen' are to be found, while the North East had a series of romantic titles such as 'Moorland Heather'. Names are generally lettered more or less flamboyantly on the coachwork, but MacBraynes became known by their 'Highlander', which is perhaps the most striking device to have been used in this form of publicity.

SOME FINER POINTS OF DETAIL

The passenger on a bus or coach must sometimes wonder about the details of the organisation and equipment that makes the journey possible. Perhaps the first object of his interest will be his ticket, which will be manifestly different from the one he has for a train journey and, if he is on unfamiliar ground, may be quite unlike the ticket he is used to getting at home.

A railway ticket is evidence of a contract entered into between the passenger and the railway authority, but there is doubt as to the legal significance of a bus ticket. Some say it is no more than a receipt, and the requirement of the Road Traffic Act that a ticket must be issued is frequently ignored by small operators in the country, whose revenue is often too small to justify the cost of having a ticket system at all. Tickets were by no means general in the horse-bus age and the attempts to introduce them made by the LGOC have been described in Chapter 2. Originally, a numbered ticket was issued from a roll (the practice is still found occasionally today), but in 1878 the Bell Punch Company was formed to acquire the patents of a punch that had been invented in the U.S.A. and used on certain London tramways. Its advantage was that it registered each ticket punched and at the same time rang a bell which the passenger could hear. This meant that, provided the passenger insisted upon receiving a ticket, the conductor's way-bill record of tickets issued could be checked to see that it tallied with the number of tickets punched.

All systems of ticket issue that have since been developed turn upon the same principle of using the co-operation of the passenger to check the honesty of the conductor. This, in turn, rests upon the assumption that no passenger will want to see others making illicit gains in which he has no share, and the fact that little mutual gain can be achieved by the conductor and the passenger in collusion. Thus the purpose of the travelling inspector in checking tickets on a bus is not so much to exercise control over the conductor as to see that no passenger is 'over-riding', or travelling beyond the point he has booked to; a practice which a busy driver cannot always prevent.

Figures 7 and 8 illustrate the development of the ticket from its primitive state. The bell-punched ticket was used for many years and reached a high level of sophistication, so that an experienced eye could read from the waybill virtually a complete record of the passengers carried on each journey. This depended upon the ability and willingness of the conductor to conform to the system, issuing the right tickets and 'booking up' on his waybill at the correct points, and perhaps a system of this kind was only feasible at a time of relatively high unemployment when some degree of enforcement could be employed. But the system had its disadvantages and these gave rise in the course of the 'thirties to a demand for greater mechanisation, re-inforced since the war by the rising cost of labour and increasing scarcity of platform staff.

Mechanisation offers two attractions which have influenced its course. The first is the saving in clerical labour; the second the reduced risk of fraud, combined with the parallel reduction in the cost of preventing it. It has developed so far that today there is no business of any size that still uses the original bell-punch system. As for the element of fraud, the various mechanised systems offer the advantage of dispensing with a stock of tickets which, because they bear a value, represent an asset that is vulnerable and so must be subject to audit. A few (such as No. 21 in Figure 8) involve nothing more valuable than paper rolls, which have no cash value until printed with the appropriate data by the machine. Others use a partially pre-printed roll on which the data is either printed or written by hand (in the latter case a carbon copy is kept). In many types of mechanised system the correlation between ticket issue and punch register, which has been seen to be vital to the bell-punch method, is replaced by a series of counters on the machine. In others, a record is kept within the sealed container itself. One of these has now been developed which issues tickets in such a way as to enable the record to be read electronically, thus doing away with the need for a waybill and consequent clerical analysis. This is the final stage of detail in the development of the completely mechanised system of ticket issue and accounting that computer science has made possible.

The law that requires the passenger to be issued with a ticket also states that a timetable must be carried by the conductor and be available for consultation on request. Here again, the small country operator frequently avoids the expense, for if you run a bus twice a week to the nearest market town and have done so for fifty years, you may assume that anyone who wants to use it knows when it goes. Strangers from outside will not be welcome, and anyway the bus will be of little use to them. But the larger companies, as well as many of the smaller ones, issue timetables that vary even today in their content and usefulness, and they have developed a long way from the simple lists of departure

---

A SELECTION OF BUS TICKETS (see pages 284 and 286)

Tickets have their own history, and the selection on these pages shows their development from the simplest original through various degrees of complexity to a renewed simplicity. (Selection prepared from the Omnibus Society and Transport Ticket Society Collections by R. J. Durrant.)

1 *Simple form of bell-punched ticket showing only the fare paid.*

2 *Early motor-bus ticket with list of stage points. Overprint shows the direction of travel and the fare.*

3 *Stages indicated by numbers, with direction of travel according to the side of ticket which is punched.*

4 *Type of ticket indicating the full permissible journey. The punch hole indicates the boarding point, with the alighting point immediately opposite.*

5 *Full availability of journey shown in both directions.*

6 *Early form of mechanised ticket issue. Punch holes indicate fare, class and stage boarded.*

7 *Ticket torn from a paper roll. Issued prior to the general use of a punch.*

8 *Fare stages shown both by name and by number.*

9 *Details of fare, etc., printed by machine, with month and date and special details added by punching. An exceptionally complex ticket.*

10 *Stages indicated only by numbers. One ticket can be used for all services.*

11 *Early motor-bus ticket with full availability of journey shown for each stage.*

12 *Multi-value ticket. The fare is shown by cutting off the portion of the ticket below the fare paid. The cut off portion is retained for accounting.*

FIG. 7

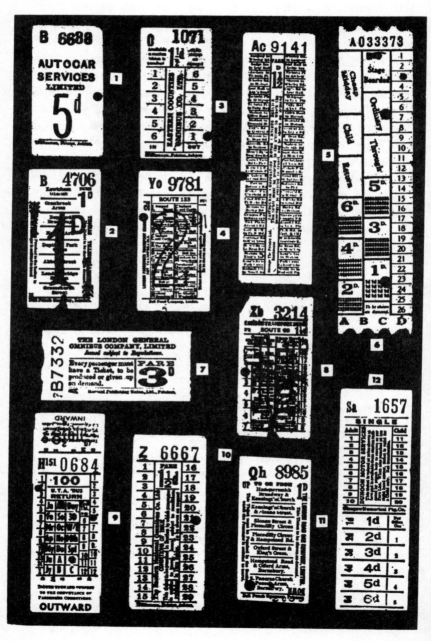

times that first appeared. Over the last few years there has been a wide measure of standardisation, with the use of 24-hour timings, but today considerable differences remain in the publications even of the territorial companies.

Amongst other things, timetables usually carry the conditions of carriage of the operator and occasionally this rather dull legal wording may be of interest. In its early days, Southdown Motor Services laid down that 'Ladies are not allowed to travel on the front seat unless accompanied by a gentleman', and (more understandably) that 'Under no circumstances will passengers' dogs be allowed to run with the bus'. Clearly the company expected both species to be kept under control.

Some countries produce comprehensive timetables of all bus services, but no such publication has ever appeared in Great Britain. During the 'twenties some attempts were made, but the multiplicity of routes and operators made the project impossible as a commercial proposition. The *Roadway* timetable was at least as thick as *Bradshaw*, with a larger page, and never achieved more than partial cover. The *Travel by Road* guide attempted to overcome the size problem by listing departure times with a

---

13 *Multi-value ticket. The fare paid is indicated by the amount shown after all higher prices have been cut off.*

14 *Composite form of ticket to indicate class of passenger as well as class of fare paid.*

15 *Ticket for use as single or return with punching to indicate day of issue.*

16 *Multi-journey ticket allowing for punching on each journey taken.*

17 *Ticket issued in exchange for a return or similar ticket. The value of that surrendered is shown by the punch hole.*

18 *Simple form of return ticket available between the two specified points.*

19 *Composite form of ticket for use as single or return. Fare stage number and date can be indicated by punching.*

20 *Fully pre-printed ticket validated by printing stage number. For city routes with short stages; the machine holds a selection of values.*

21 *Fare details printed by machine on a roll of paper pre-printed only with the company's title.*

22 *Details of fare, etc., printed by machine on a pre-printed ticket..*

23 *Details entered in manuscript on a pre-printed ticket. A carbon duplicate is retained in the machine for accounting.*

24 *Complete ticket printed by machine on a roll of blank paper.*

FIG. 8

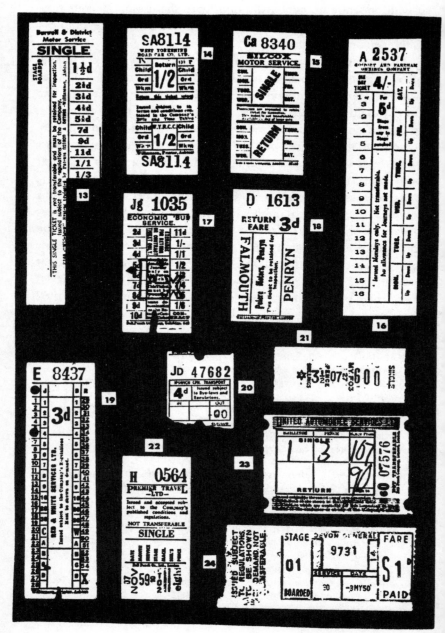

note of journey durations, but this lead to such complexities that it is hard to see how anyone but an expert could have used the guide with any success. Instead, there grew up a custom whereby in many (though by no means all) provincial towns a local printer would compile and issue a rail and road timetable which would be more or less inclusive of the services available. These local books have been a casualty of the rising cost of printing since the war, combined with the shrinking demand for public transport, and few now remain.

The publicity issued by the British Railways Press Bureau in 1930 to 'sell' the idea of the railways' interest in the bus combine claimed that one form of co-ordination would be 'Combination of railway and omnibus timetable matter . . .' This turned out to be no more than a pious hope, except insofar as a list of train departure times appeared at the back of some of the companies' timetables. The railways continued to treat the bus industry as if it did not exist, apart from a handful of bus services in Scotland which appeared in the LNER timetable book, with no apparent reason for their choice. Indeed, in one case there was a worsening, for the GWR had always included in its rail timetables the bus service it had opened in October 1928 between Oxford and Cheltenham. In 1932 this was transferred to Bristol Tramways, whose publicity never included the connecting train times although the service was intended as a feeder to rail; the GWR continued to include it, but after nationalisation it disappeared from the railway timetable as well.

More recently a serious attempt was made to remedy the situation, arising out of public antipathy towards British Rail's withdrawal of train services. Regional rail timetables included lists of places not served by train, with the name of the bus operator offering connections, while a later development was the issue of comprehensive rail and road timetable books for certain areas. The first of these was issued for Wales in 1966 and consists of a series of tables showing rail and road connections arising from the replacement programme; it also included a table of connections to places not previously served by train, many of them being quite small villages. The list of oper-

25A—25F] NOTE—LIGHT FIGURES FROM 1201 A.M. TO 1200 NOON / HEAVY DARK FIGURES FROM 1201 P.M. TO 1200 MIDNIGHT **[25A—25F**

GENERAL TABLES

EAST KENT ROAD CAR CO., LTD.

25A — CANTERBURY, STODMARSH, PRESTON & MINSTER — 25A

DAILY

	N												SS			
CANTERBURY (ST. PETERS)	810	930	955	1100	100	155	230	350	455	535	655	765	835	..	..
LITTLEBOURNE (ANCHOR)	824	944	1009	1114	114	209	244	404	509	545	709	809	849	..	..
ICKHAM	829	949	1014	1119	119	214	249	409	514	554	714	814	854	..	..
WICKHAMBREUX	834	954	1019	1124	124	219	254	414	519	559	718	819	859	..	..
STODMARSH	846	1004	..	..	135	..	..	424	..	..	..	..	909	..	..
GROVE	..	..	1029	1134	..	229	..	432	529	..	729	829	..	..	..
PRESTON (MOON & STARS)	..	..	1035	1139	..	235	..	..	535	..	734	835	..	..	..
STOURMOUTH (RISING SUN)	..	..	1040	..	..	240	..	..	540	..	..	840	..	..	..
STOURHAVEN	..	..	1048	..	..	243	..	..	543	..	..	843	..	..	..
MONKTON (NEW INN)	..	..	1053	..	..	255	..	..	553	..	..	853	..	..	..
MINSTER (BELL INN)	..	..	1100	..	..	300	..	..	600	..	..	900	..	..	..

		N											SS			
MINSTER (BELL INN)	..	..	..	1145	..	315	..	620	..	915	..	..
MONKTON (NEW INN)	..	..	..	1152	..	322	..	627	..	922	..	..
STOURHAVEN	..	..	..	1202	..	332	..	637	..	932	..	..
STOURMOUTH	..	..	..	1205	..	335	..	640	..	935	..	..
PRESTON (MOON & STARS)	..	..	1145	1210	..	340	..	645	740	940	..	..
GROVE	..	..	1149	1216	..	346	440	651	744	946	..	..
STODMARSH	850	1005	..	..	145	..	448	..	..	915	..	..
WICKHAMBREUX	900	1015	1159	1226	155	300	356	458	610	701	754	956	..
ICKHAM	905	1020	1204	1231	200	305	401	502	615	706	759	930	1001
LITTLEBOURNE (ANCHOR)	910	1025	1209	1236	205	310	406	507	620	711	804	935	1006
CANTERBURY (ST. PETERS)	924	1039	1223	1250	219	324	420	522	634	725	818	949	1020

N NOT SUNS.   SS SATS. AND SUNS. ONLY.

25C — CANTERBURY, PETHAM AND WALTHAM — 25C

DOWN				UP	
N	DAILY			N	
750	CANTERBURY (ST. PETERS)	..		855	DOWN BUSES LEAVE CANTERBURY 750N : 900 : 1015 : 1150 :
804	GRANVILLE INN	..		841	200 : 330 : 450 : 645 : 810 : 930 SS (NOT BEYOND
811	PETHAM	..		834	PETHAM)
820	WALTHAM	..		825	UP BUSES LEAVE WALTHAM 825N : 935 : 1105 : 1230 : 240 :

400 : 530 : 725 : 850 : 956 SS (FROM PETHAM)

N NOT SUNS.   SS SATS. AND SUNS. ONLY.

25D — CANTERBURY, CHILHAM AND CHARING — 25D

DOWN							DAILY		UP						
820	905	1105	205	405	605	805	CANTERBURY (ST. PETERS)	1013	1053	1253	353	553	753	953
827	912	1112	212	412	612	812	THANINGTON (CHURCH)	1006	1046	1246	346	546	746	946
833	918	1118	218	418	618	818	CHARTHAM (STN.)	1000	1040	1240	340	540	740	940
845	930	1130	230	430	630	830	CHILHAM (WOOLPACK)	948	1028	1228	328	528	728	928
856	941	1141	241	441	641	841	MOLASH (GEORGE INN)	937	1017	1217	317	517	717	917
900	945	1145	246	445	646	845	CHALLOCK LEES (HALF WAY HOUSE)	925	1015	1215	315	515	715	915
913	958	1158	258	458	658	858	CHARING (QUEENS HEAD)	920	1010	1200	300	500	700	900

FOR ADDITIONAL BUSES CANTERBURY AND CHILHAM SEE 25E

25E — CANTERBURY AND ASHFORD — 25E

DOWN				UP	
750	CANTERBURY (ST. PETERS.)	..		860	DOWN BUSES LEAVE CANTERBURY 740N (FROM WYE) : 750
758	THANINGTON (CHURCH)	..		842	900 : 1020 : 1200 : 150 : 305 : 427N (FROM WYE) : 450 :
804	CHARTHAM (STN.)	..		856	855 : 715 : 830 : 1005
814	CHILHAM (WOOLPACK)	..		828	UP BUSES LEAVE ASHFORD 750 : D 830N : 910 :
823	GODMERSHAM (P.O.)	..		817	1020 : 1220 : D 110N : 150 : 320 : D 410N : 450 : 855 :
832	WYE (CHURCH)	..		808	710 : D 780 : 900 : 1010
840	KENNINGTON (GOLDEN BALL)	..		800	
850	ASHFORD (HIGH STREET)	..		750	

D NOT BEYOND WYE.   N NOT SUNS.   FOR ADDITIONAL BUSES CANTERBURY AND CHILHAM SEE 25D
EXPRESS BUSES CANTERBURY AND ASHFORD SEE TABLE 25C

25F — WYE AND ASHFORD VIA BROOK — 25F

DOWN				UP	
N	DAILY			N	
915	WYE (CHURCH)	..		1155	DOWN BUSES LEAVE WYE 915N : 1000Sa : 1220N : 200 :
928	BROOK	..		1142	350 : 500 : 635 : 755 : 920
956	HINXHILL	..		1134	UP BUSES LEAVE ASHFORD 1130 : 246 : 415 : 545 : 840 :
942	WILLESBORO	..		1128	1005
950	ASHFORD (HIGH STREET)	..		1120	

N NOT SUNS.   Sa SUNS. ONLY.

FIG. 9   *Page from 'Roadway' Timetable of 1930*

ators at the end indicated clearly the dependence of the area upon small independent undertakings. Quite different was the booklet issued in 1967 showing bus and rail services from Newcastle and Gateshead; this had every bus service concerned shown in full, along with coach, air and shipping services, but its rail cover was much smaller. Only twenty-six of its 388 pages were devoted to rail times, and for the East Coast main line these revert to the practice of listing arrivals and departures only. A third was based upon Carlisle.

In the United States and Canada, the post-war years have seen the railways lose their passenger traffic to the airways, which are faster, and the coaches, which are cheaper. The Greyhound and Trailways organisations, with their associates and a multitude of smaller coach lines, provide a national network on a far more comprehensive scale than that of the British long-distance coaches and the outcome has been the publication of a monthly basis of *Russell's Official National Motor Coach Guide*. Today, this consists of around 1,000 pages of timetables and editorial matter, including long-distance services throughout the United States as well as some in Canada and Mexico. In comparison, the British *ABC Coach Guide*, which first appeared in 1951, was about half as thick, although it included far more advertising matter. But the *ABC* appeared only twice a year and the comparison between the two publications indicates the higher level of trading to which the industry in North America is geared. Transcontinental travel by coach is now unknown (over a dozen services leave New York for the West Coast every twenty-four hours) and the coach is far more widely accepted as an alternative to the railway than it is in Great Britain.

The commonplace features of travel by bus and coach also have histories which are important to those who use them all the time. Communication between conductor and driver is something that has changed and yet remained the same, for the primitive methods have never been entirely superseded by technical change. At first the conductor used a whistle, and the code of signals (one bell to stop, two to start, three meaning 'I am full, don't stop to pick up', and four or more for emergency) probably goes back to the earliest days. The bell worked by a string slung along the ceiling of the saloon is also an early device and one that is still used; it has the advantage of being cheap to install and easy to maintain. But the post-war double-decker which might have a string bell for the lower saloon, would have an electric one for the top deck, whereas its forerunner often depended upon some mechanical ingenuity, like the brass plunger at the head of the stairs that worked the string bell by means of a trip placed on the platform.

With the electric bell came the problem of where to put the press-button, and it is not always in the ideal place for the conductor, who may have to be something of a contortionist to reach it. The most recent development has been a strip fastened to the ceiling, which can be pressed anywhere along its length. But just as the string bell remains effective, so the whistle has returned to favour, being standard issue in some companies as a means by which the conductor can assist the driver in reversing. There is a story of a bus in South Wales which was being reversed in a railway station yard; when the conductor blew his whistle the train drew out, leaving the guard standing on the platform.

The provision of uniform for road staff has always had two aspects; the need for industrial clothing to allow for the wear and tear the job incurs, and the commercial advantage of a 'well turned out' crew that is in the tradition of the liveried servants of the horse and carriage days. Amongst the smaller firms the provision of uniform is rare, although not unknown, but this does not seem to handicap such firms in recruiting staff or seriously affect their commercial success. Indeed, one aspect of the history of the industry has been the growing industrial unrest that seems to have occurred as family businesses have been swallowed up by territorial companies. Whatever it is that attracts men to the small employer, it is not fringe benefits of this kind, although it may have something to do with the ability to identify with the firm of limited size and the need to be treated as an individual by the 'real boss'. On the other hand, the standard of maintenance of buses and coaches is appreciated by those who work on them, and this may be good or bad in firms of all different sizes. A

R

Suffolk coach driver praised a rival employer to the author by likening him to 'a farmer that always kept good horses', and there is no doubt that turnout and smartness have always mattered in the trade.

Fashions have changed in the livery of buses and coaches and the traditional red double-deckers of London have never been representative of the industry The territorial companies, searching for economies, achieved the greatest standardisation, and Tilling Group companies, with few exceptions, used either green or red. Perhaps for some reason connected with paint technology the bigger firms, which are probably more cost-conscious, have rarely used blue or yellow. But it is amongst coach fleets that the greatest variations are to be found, for in this competitive world the public image matters far more than it does amongst the buses. Even so, small firms do not always maintain consistency and the habit of buying second-hand, which recent economic pressures has increased, has led to fleets of mixed livery in many places.

For a time the National Bus Company extended the Tilling practice of standardised liveries, and, presumably for reasons of economy, it chose overall painting in a single colour, with no variation or relief. Lettering too was standardised, with a simple upper case fleet name, and a logo consisting of two Ns, which George Behrend christened 'Nasty National'. As a public relations exercise, the whole thing appears disastrous, for a single house style in so individualistic an industry is a lowest common denominator of dullness. Subsequently, though, brighter and more imaginative liveries have returned, though there has been a general tendency among all kinds of operator to adopt an angular style in place of the sweeping lines of the 1960s. The tendency to break up large territorial companies has also meant that new fleet names, often with new marketing impact, have appeared, and the industry seems to have passed out of a period of depressing respectability, doubtless to the regrets of the traditionalists.

The motor-bus industry has not so far undertaken much in the way of market research, and little is known about the attitudes and motives of those who use the buses and coaches. It is only quite recently that the study of transport has begun to acquire a certain intellectual status, and such is the remaining glamour of the railways that there is still a tendency to regard road transport as a poor relation. In cities that have run their own passenger transport systems since the start of the century, it has not been unknown for the transport department to be ignored in the preparation of plans for future growth. It would be dangerous for the planners to think that bus operation is a mere servant of their own disciplines, and it is largely up to the industry to see that this does not happen. The value of tradition is now becoming appreciated, and it is the need to retain the loyalty of both staff and passengers that lay behind the retention of the company structure in the organisation of the NBC and SBG. The 1968 Act meant that numerous municipal undertakings disappeared, though, and for a time it seemed that large operating units were to be favoured. This was perhaps to do with the statement in the 1967 White Paper, calling for transport to be 'the servant of the planners, not their master'; a phrase that we are less likely to hear today.

It was for the passenger that the industry came into existence, and it will be the passenger who will have the last word; it is he to whom transport should be the servant. In 1937 there took place what was perhaps the only strike on the part of passengers, when about 200 GWR workers at Swindon walked to work rather than pay increased fares on the corporation buses. Within a few days the weather made them change their minds, but since then the spread of private cars and motor-cycles has offered the consumer a substitute. The future health of the motor-bus industry must still depend above all upon its ability to face the most serious competition it has ever known.

FINANCIAL STRUCTURE OF THE COMBINES, 1942

Based upon Chart in *Modern Transport*, 5th September, 1942

A. *BRITISH ELECTRIC TRACTION GROUP (BET)*

Ordinary Shares

Company	Total Capital	Capital in direct or indirect ownership of BET		Railway Capital				'Outside' Capital
		Owner	£	LMSR	LNER	GWR	SR	
	£			£	£	£	£	£
Birmingham & District Investment Trust Ltd (B&D)	1,119,560	BET BETO	870,274 111,400 }	—	—	—	—	137,886
Birmingham & Midland Motor Omnibus Co Ltd (BMMO) (1)	1,440,000	B&D	720,000	432,000	—	288,000	—	Nil
National Electric Construction Co Ltd (NEC)	185,000	BET	184,603	—	—	—	—	397
Devon General Omnibus & Touring Co Ltd	200,000	NEC	68,196	—	—	40,917	27,279	63,708
Mexborough & Swinton Traction Company	105,480	NEC	68,142	—	—	—	—	37,338
Oxford Transport Trust Ltd (OTT) (2)	122,515	NEC	40,425	—	—	—	—	82,090
City of Oxford Motor Services Ltd	226,000	OTT	113,000	—	—	113,000	—	Nil
Rhondda Transport Co Ltd	261,242	NEC BET	16,078 116,416 }	—	—	—	—	128,748
Western Welsh Omnibus Co Ltd	507,500	NEC BET	101,250 152,500 }	—	—	253,750	—	Nil
British Electric Traction Omnibus Services Ltd (BETO)	2,000,000	BET	1,933,141	—	—	—	—	66,859
Aldershot & District Traction Co Ltd	250,000	BETO	82,721	—	—	—	82,721	84,558

For Notes see page 297

A. BRITISH ELECTRIC TRACTION GROUP (BET)

Company	Total Capital £	Owner	Capital in direct or indirect ownership £	LMSR £	LNER £	GWR £	SR £	'Outside' Capital £
East Kent Road Car Co Ltd	450,000	BETO	151,356	—	—	—	151,356	147,288
East Midland Motor Services Ltd	250,000	BETO	125,000	41,667	83,333	—	—	Nil
East Yorkshire Motor Services Ltd	300,000	BETO	149,362	—	149,362	—	—	1,276
Maidstone & District Motor Services Ltd (3)	750,000	BETO	263,492	—	—	—	263,492	223,016
North Western Road Car Co Ltd	750,000	BETO	373,337	248,888	124,444	—	—	3,331
Ribble Motor Services Ltd (4)	1,200,000	BETO	530,445	530,445	—	—	—	139,110
Southdown Motor Services Ltd	750,000	BETO	249,793	—	—	—	249,793	250,414
Trent Motor Traction Co Ltd	540,288	BETO	225,440	150,293	75,147	—	—	89,408
Yorkshire Traction Co Ltd	437,500	BETO	214,478	107,289	107,289	—	—	8,344
Hebble Motor Services Ltd	120,000	BET	60,000	45,000	15,000	—	—	Nil
Northern General Transport Co Ltd (5)	831,081	BET	365,768	—	365,767	—	—	99,546
Potteries Motor Traction Co Ltd	541,250	BET	376,375	—	—	—	—	164,875
South Wales Transport Co Ltd (SWT)	400,000	BET	387,899	—	—	—	—	12,101
Swansea Improvements & Tramways Company	130,000	SWT	129,090	—	—	—	—	910
Yorkshire Woollen District Transport Co Ltd	528,000	BET	264,000	176,000	88,000	—	—	Nil

B. THOMAS TILLING LTD GROUP (TT)

Ordinary Shares

Company	Total Capital £	Owner	Capital in direct or indirect ownership of Tillings £	Railway Capital — LMSR £	LNER £	GWR £	SR £	'Outside' Capital £
National Omnibus & Transport Co Ltd (NO&T)	1,250,000	TT	1,176,720	—	—	—	—	73,280
Eastern National Omnibus Co Ltd	900,000	NO&T	450,000	225,000	225,000	—	—	Nil
Southern National Omnibus Co Ltd	542,200	NO&T	271,000	—	—	—	271,000	Nil

For Notes see page 297

Company	Total Capital £	Owner	Capital in direct or indirect ownership of Tillings £	Railway Capital				'Outside' Capital £
				LMSR £	LNER £	GWR £	SR £	
Western National Omnibus Co Ltd (WNOC)	2,000,000	NO&T	1,000,000	—	—	1,000,000	—	Nil
Bristol Tramways & Carriage Co Ltd (BT&C) (6)	1,550,308	WNOC	1,042,005	—	—	—	—	508,303
Bath Electric Tramways Ltd (BEL.T)	165,000	BT&C	149,897	—	—	—	—	15,103
Bath Tramways Motor Co Ltd	60,000	BT&C / BEL.T	30,150 } 29,850	—	—	—	—	Nil
Tilling Motor Services Ltd (TMS)	2,000,000	TT	1,933,142	—	—	—	—	66,858
Caledonian Omnibus Co Ltd	125,000	TMS	118,494	—	—	—	—	6,506
Crosville Motor Services Ltd	1,100,000	TMS	549,428	412,071	—	137,357	—	1,144
Cumberland Motor Services Ltd	150,000	TMS	49,999	49,999	—	—	—	50,002
Eastern Counties Omnibus Co Ltd (ECOC) (7)	756,000	TMS / UAS	209,372 } 326,263	25,282	184,089	—	—	10,994
Hants & Dorset Motor Services Ltd	550,000	TMS	213,556	—	—	—	213,556	122,888
Lincolnshire Road Car Co Ltd	200,000	TMS	79,914	15,985	63,929	—	—	40,172
Southern Vectis Omnibus Co Ltd	115,000	TMS	57,500	—	—	—	57,500	Nil
Thames Valley Traction Co Ltd (8)	250,000	TMS	121,701	—	—	85,191	36,510	6,598
United Automobile Services Ltd (UAS) (9)	1,627,233	TMS	798,412	—	798,412	—	—	30,409
West Yorkshire Road Car Co Ltd (10)	787,500	TMS	391,686	195,843	195,843	—	—	4,128
Wilts & Dorset Motor Services Ltd	120,000	TMS	30,724	—	—	—	30,724	58,552
Brighton, Hove & District Omnibus Co Ltd	400,000	TT	400,000	—	—	—	—	Nil
United Counties Omnibus Co Ltd	390,000	TT	379,386	—	—	—	—	20,614
Westcliff-on-Sea Motor Services Ltd	250,000	TT	227,076	—	—	—	—	22,924

For Notes see page 297

C. JOINTLY OWNED COMPANIES

Company	Ownership	Combine
Black & White Motorways Ltd	Birmingham & Midland Motor Omnibus Co Ltd Bristol Tramways & Carriage Co Ltd City of Oxford Motor Services Ltd	BET Tilling BET
Blackpool Omnibus Stations Ltd	Ribble Motor Services Ltd East Yorkshire Motor Services Ltd North Western Road Car Co Ltd Yorkshire Traction Co Ltd Yorkshire Woollen District Transport Co Ltd Hebble Motor Services Ltd West Yorkshire Road Car Co Ltd	BET BET BET BET BET BET Tilling
County Motors (Lepton) Ltd	Yorkshire Traction Co Ltd Yorkshire Woollen District Transport Co Ltd West Riding Automobile Co Ltd	BET BET Independent
Fawdon Bus Co Ltd	Northern General Transport Co Ltd Yorkshire Traction Co Ltd Yorkshire Woollen District Transport Co Ltd West Yorkshire Road Car Co Ltd	BET BET BET Tilling
Majestic Express Motors Ltd	Birmingham & Midland Motor Omnibus Co Ltd North Western Road Car Co Ltd	BET BET
Omnibus Stations Ltd	North Western Road Car Co Ltd Ribble Motor Services Ltd	BET BET
Otley Omnibus Stations Ltd	West Yorkshire Road Car Co Ltd Samuel Ledgard	Tilling Independent
Sheffield United Tours Ltd	East Midland Motor Services Ltd North Western Road Car Co Ltd Yorkshire Traction Co Ltd	BET BET BET

1. Also owning : North Warwickshire Motor Omnibus & Traction Co Ltd* and Worcestershire Motor Transport Co Ltd*

2. Also owning : City of Oxford & District Tramways Co Ltd*

3. Also owning : Hastings Tramway Company, and Chatham & District Traction Company

4. Also owning : W. C. Standerwick Ltd and Wright Bros (Burnley) Ltd

5. Also owning : Gateshead & District Tramway Company, Sunderland & District Omnibus Co Ltd, Tynemouth & District Transport Co Ltd, Tyneside Tramways & Tramroads Company, and Wakefield's Motors Ltd

6. Also operating: Bristol Joint Services

7. Also owning : Eastern Coach Works Ltd and Norwich Omnibus Company Ltd

8. Also owning : Ledbury Transport Co Ltd*

9. Also owning : Orange Bros Ltd and Bell's Services Ltd

10. Also operating: Keighley—West Yorkshire Services Ltd and services of the York-West Yorkshire Joint Committee

* Non-operative companies.

SELECTIVE BIBLIOGRAPHY

Contributions to bus history have multiplied remarkably since the first edition of this book appeared in 1968, and it would be impossible to do justice to them all here. The following titles have been of particular value in its preparation and revision.

Books

Aldcroft, D. H. *British Transport since 1914* (David & Charles, 1975). Several of the essays in this text throw valuable light upon the economic history of the industry.

Anderson, R. G. and Frankis, G. C. A. *History of Royal Blue Express Services* (David & Charles, 2nd. edn., 1985). A major contribution to our knowledge of the way express coach services developed.

Barker, T. C. and Robbins, M. *A History of London Transport* (George Allen & Unwin, Vol. 1 1963; Vol. 2 1974). A truly magisterial and scholarly history, the similar treatment of the provincial bus industry is still awaited.

Barker, T. C. and Savage, C. I. *An Economic History of Transport in Britain* (Hutchinson, 3rd. edn., 1974). Still indispensible for the broader background.

Bird, A. *Roads and Vehicles* (Longman, 1969). Useful supplement to the present book, which has insufficient space to do justice to Bird's subject matter.

Bonavia, M. R. *Railway Policy between the Wars* (Manchester University Press, 1981). A very interesting section on the sadly neglected subject of the railway companies' policy towards the road transport industry.

Caunt, P. *North Western Road Car Company Limited – A Driver's Reminiscences* (Oxford Publishing Company, 1984). Anecdotal, but an invaluable impressionistic contribution to the understanding of the bus industry. The publishers are to be criticised, as in so many examples of 'enthusiast' literature, for the lack of an index.

Chester, D. N. *Public Control of Road Passenger Transport* (Manchester University Press, 1937). Still essential for understanding the 1930 licensing system.

Clegg, H. A. *Labour Relations in London Transport* (Blackwell, 1950). Important for the inter-war period—here again there is a need for a more general study.

Copeland, J. *Roads and their Traffic* (David & Charles, 1968). Much useful material for the 18th and 19th centuries.

Crawley, R. J., MacGregor, D. R. and Simpson, F. D. *The National Way:*

The Years Between 1909 and 1969 (Vol. 1, *The National Story*, Mac-Gregor, Sible Hedingham, Essex, 1979; Vol. 2, *The Eastern National Story from 1930*, Oxford Publishing Company, 1984; Vol. 3 awaited). Despite the vast quantity of detail, there emerges a real sense of what it was like to be running buses over a long period of history. A source book and also a more general study.

Crosland Taylor, W. J. *Crosville: The Sowing and the Harvest* (Littlebury Bros., Liverpool, 1948) and *Crosville: State Owned without Tears* (Littlebury Bros., 1954). The memoirs of one of the great men of the industry, full of insights and full of true humanity. Both have been re-issued by the Transport Publishing Company.

Cummings, J. *Railway Motor Buses and Bus Services in the British Isles, 1902–1933* (Oxford Publishing Company, two volumes available as one, Vol. 1, 1978; Vol. 2, 1980). A fine and scholarly treatment, full of fascinating detail and broad principle too.

Dunbar, C. S. *Buses. Trolleys and Trams* (Paul Hamlyn, 1967). Because the author wears both his scholarship and his enthusiasm lightly, yet excels in both, this is a most valuable source book, with a fine selection of illustrations.

Dyos, H. J. and Aldcroft, D. H. *British Transport. An economic survey from the seventeenth century to the twentieth* (Leicester University Press, 1969). Commissioned by the Chartered Institute of Transport, the bus chapters suffer from reflecting the orthodoxy of the 1960s to the exclusion of the independent tradition.

Garbutt, P. E. *London Transport and the Politicians* (Ian Allan, 1985). Slightly breathless but invaluable record and commentary concerning the latest ten years of the government of London's transport.

Glaister, S. & Mulley, C. *Public Control of the British Bus Industry* (Gower, 1983). Successor to Chester's critique of the licensing system, and essential background to the reforms of 1980 and 1985.

Hibbs, J. (Editor). *The Omnibus. Readings in the History of Road Passenger Transport* (David & Charles, 1971). An annotated collection of Omnibus Society papers used in the preparation of the present book, and intended as a supplement to it.

Hibbs, J. *The Bus and Coach Industry, its Economics and Organisation* (J M Dent & Sons, 1975). Amplifies some of the points in the present book, and develops the importance of Sir Henry Maybury in understanding inter-war policy for the bus industry.

Holding, D. *History of British Bus Services: The North East* (David & Charles, 1979). Detailed and thorough study of the regional background.

Holding, D. and Moyes, T. *History of British Bus Services: South Wales* (Ian Allan, 1986). Does us a similar service for the region.

Jones, D. *Urban Transit Policy: an Economic and Political History* (Prentice-Hall, 1985). A classic study of the industry in the U.S.A.

Klapper, C. F. *The Golden Age of Tramways* (David & Charles, 1974).

Masterly and encyclopaedic survey of its subject.

Klapper, C. F. *Golden Age of Buses* (Routledge & Kegan Paul, 1978). A mine of detailed information rather than a continuous history; invaluable none the less.

Morris, C. *History of the Hants & Dorset Motor Services Ltd.* (David & Chakles, 1973). Thorough and many-sided study of a not untypical territorial company.

Morris, C. *History of British Bus Services: South-East England* (Transport Publishing Company, 1980). Excellent study of the region, marred by the inexcusable lack of an index.

Mulley, C. "The Background to Bus Regulation in the 1930 Road Traffic Act", *Journal of Transport History*, Third Series, Vol. 2, No. 4. Gives added depth and information, and should be read by all serious students of the industry.

Preece, C. *Wheels to the West* (Travel & Transport Ltd., 1974). Ranks with Crosland Taylor's books as that rare contribution, the manager's story.

Savage, I. *The Deregulation of Bus Services* (Gower, 1985). Contains a useful history of regulation (but the publishers must be censured for omitting an index).

Starkie, D. N. M. *The Motorway Age: Road and Traffic Policies in Post-war Britain* (Pergamon, 1982). Fills the gaps about the roads, which the present book has not had space to cover.

Strong, L. A. G. *The Rolling Road. The Story of Travel on the Roads of Britain and the Development of Public Passenger Transport* (Hutchinson, 1956). The present book was written not least to offset the bias and correct the factual errors in what is really a superb piece of professional authorship. The novelist was commissioned to write the book and provided with data by the establishment of the bus industry of the day, and should therefore not be held responsible for its shortcomings.

Turns, K. *The Independent Bus* (David & Charles, 1974). A splendid series of case studies (or vignettes) of a good cross-section of private firms.

Other sources

Apart from the Omnibus Society papers included in *The Omnibus* (see above), there have been numerous others published, as well as the many historical articles that have appeared in *The Omnibus Magazine*. To these all historians of the industry must be indebted, as they must to various articles in *The Journal of Transport History* and *Transport History*. There are also several entries concerning the bus industry in the *Dictionary of Business Biography*. All this material is too voluminous to catalogue here, as indeed are the many monographs that have appeared, of which the following have been of special value in the preparation and revision of the present book. Priority must be given to the contributions by that most scholarly of bus enthusiasts – Lee, C. E., *The Horse Bus as a Vehicle* and *The*

Early Motor Bus (both issued by the British Transport Commission), his Newcomen Society paper *The Rise and Decline of the Steam-Driven Omnibus*, and his Institute of Transport Silver Medal paper *Voluntary Organisation*. The latter has never been published, although excerpts appeared in the trade press, and it would be a most valuable contribution if it could now be made more widely available; it was an indispensible source for much of the present book. Other monographs that have been used, in alphabetical order of author, are: Brearley, H., *The Development of the Trolley Bus* (along with Kidner's two contributions and that of Dr Whitcombe, listed below, a text in the invaluable series of Locomotive Papers from the Oakwood Press); Brewster. D. E., *Motor Buses in East Anglia 1901–1931* and *Motor Buses in Wales;* Kidner, R. W., *The London Motor Bus* and *The London Tramcar*; Lingard, P., *First Bus in Yorkshire,* the story of Laycock's business; and Whitcombe, H. A., *History of the Steam Tram.*

Readers who wish to keep their understanding of the industry's story up to date should take up membership of the Omnibus Society – Honorary Secretary, 6 Ardentinny, Grosvenor Road, St Albans, Hertfs. AL1 3BZ.

ACKNOWLEDGEMENTS

Before attempting the impossible task of identifying those who have helped me in preparing and revising this book, it is proper to pay a debt of gratitude to the Omnibus Society, of which any serious historian of the industry should be a member. In particular, it has been through membership of the Society that I have made many of the friends whose names will follow, with more than the conventional expression of thanks. I hope that anyone whose name is omitted through my oversight will accept this general acknowledgement.

First, then, must be the late Charles E. Lee, of whom I can only say that if he had chosen to write this book I would most certainly never have tried. His and my friend Charles F. Klapper read and commented on the original outline of the book, and I owe much to his friendship over many years and to his encyclopaedic knowledge of the industry; with his death, the industry lost a doughty friend and commentator, and historians a source of information only partly filled by his 'Golden Age' books. With their names must go that of Charles S. Dunbar, who first encouraged me to write bus history, and whose friendship has never altered despite our divergent views on bus regulation.

David St John Thomas suggested that I should write the book as we walked along Dartmoor lanes discussing railway policy, and contributed much to the shape it took. Eric Axten contributed not only the maps, but also did the research upon which they were based (in this edition there are included some of the maps he drew for another book of mine, *The Bus and Coach Industry* – see bibliography). Others whose names appeared in the first edition must be recorded again here: J. G. T. Anderson, late of the Ulster Transport Authority; A. F. R. Carling of British Electric Traction, who also made the company's printed history available to me; W. Coombs; A. J. Corfield, for material concerning the Transport & General Workers Union; R. J. Durrant; Commander & Mrs F. T. Hare (with gratitude for their hospitality); E. Halfpenny, who provided me with a copy of his paper on Pickfords, printed in *Business History*; E. B. Hutchinson; John Loft; G. J. Ponsonby; Commander F. B. Proudfoot; and Mrs J. Southgate, of the Institute of Transport Library.

The initial impetus to write this book arose out of curiosity about the industry in which I found myself when I started work. This led me to prepare a paper for the erstwhile Beds., Cambs. and Hunts. Section of the Institute of Transport at Luton in 1955, which in turn formed the basis for a contribution to the postgraduate seminar on transport at the London School of Economics in 1960. Alongside these papers I was at the time conducting extra mural classes on transport history for the WEA and the Universities of London and Cambridge. My purpose in recording these things is to pay tribute to the help I had from so many people at the formative stage of the book's preparation, and it is to all of them that it is dedicated now.

John Hibbs
Birmingham,
1986

INDEX